Northern Illinois
University

Center for
Southeast Asian
Studies

Monograph Series
on Southeast Asia

An Introduction to the Thai Poem
"Lilit Phra Law"
(The Story of King Law)

Robert J. Bickner

Special Report No. 25, 1991

This manuscript represents the result of working with several printers and Thai fonts. In order to present this material in its most readable and accessible form, certain conventions have occasionally been overridden. It is our sincere hope that the utility of this work will justify a few departures with convention.

Series Editor: Grant A. Olson

Copy Editor: David A. Mullikin

© 1991 Northern Illinois University
   Center for Southeast Asian Studies

Center Director: Michael Aung-Thwin

ISBN# 1-877979-75-9

An Introduction to the Thai Poem
"Lilit Phra Law"
(The Story of King Law)

Robert J. Bickner

TABLE OF CONTENTS

Chapter 6

Chapter 7

Chapter 8

Appendix 1

Appendix 2

Appendix 3

ACKNOWLEDGEMENTS

A number of people have helped me prepare this monograph, which is a complete revision and expansion of my Ph.D. dissertation. I thank them all, and hope that anyone whom I have failed to mention, knowing of my gratitude, will not feel slighted.

Professor William J. Gedney, who was my teacher at the University of Michigan, introduced me to the beauty of Thai poetry, and has always been supportive and encouraging of my work. I thank him once again for the richness of the gifts he has given me.

At various times the Graduate School and the Research-Service Grant Committee of the University of Wisconsin provided salary and other financial assistance. This support speeded my work and, I am confident, contributed greatly to its quality.

The director and staff of the National Library in Bangkok prepared microfilm copies of all of the *samùt khɔ̀y* copies of *Lilit Phra Law* in the Library collection. The reader will see how significant these copies have been for my work.

The Department of Thai Language of the Faculty of Humanities of Chiang Mai University graciously provided me with office space during two summers that I spent in Chiang Mai, and members of the department were personally supportive of my work. Also, nine students from the Thai department (Phaisan Sangiam, Orasa Wattana, Siriporn Wattanathum, Orachorn Ruankham, Jantana Khadfa, Supit Pholklang, Wiyada Kheowan, Kullaya Keawragmuk, and Sirilak Yottpanya) worked cheerfully and carefully for six weeks at the essential but very tedious job of collating and cutting and pasting copies of each line of the text of *Lilit Phra Law* as it appears in the many *samùt khɔ̀y* manuscript copies. Their help in dealing

ix

with the more than 50,000 very small pieces of paper involved was invaluable. In the United States, Ms. Patchanee Sutthanuson and Mr. Tongchai Peyasantiwong also contributed to this work.

The Department of South Asian Studies of the University of Wisconsin-Madison has also been most supportive. A computer system was put at my disposal, and it proved to be indispensable as I worked through many versions of the text. Ms. Sharon Dickson helped facilitate a number of complicated arrangements, all the while laughing at my jokes. Ms. Brenda Slaney and Ms. Chris Schoepp cheerfully typed the original draft, working from an uneven assortment of typed and handwritten pages.

Professor Jack Street of the University of Wisconsin Department of Linguistics gave me both his knowledge and his time as I labored to create an appropriate phonetic character set for the computer. The Center for Southeast Asian Studies provided funds to purchase software to produce the necessary Thai characters.

Because of a number of factors, not the least of which was my absence from the United States for an extended period of research in Thailand, more than a year elapsed between the time I submitted a completed draft of this manuscript and the time at which I was able to begin work on the final stylistic revisions. For technical reasons, it became necessary to convert the text to a more recent version of the word processing program that I had originally used, and to a different set of page dimensions. This proved to be an extremely complex and frustrating task that stretched out for an additional twelve months, and required a great deal of help from people who are far more experienced with computers than I am. Dr. Bruno Browning of the Learning Support Services, College of Letters and

Sciences, University of Wisconsin, was particularly helpful, and I thank him once again.

A host of individuals helped me learn to work one day at a time, and I thank them, according to custom, anonymously.

Finally, I thank my wife, Dr. Patcharin Peyasantiwong, who has listened to me, advised me, and assisted me in every step of my work on *Lilit Phra Law*. If anything has been accomplished with the present study, she deserves a great share of the credit. In this work, as in many other things, she has helped me more than she will ever know.

Robert J. Bickner
October 23, 1990
Madison, Wisconsin

Chapter 1

THE STORY OF PHRA LAW

The Story as an Object of Study

The poetic tradition of Thailand is a rich and complex one, woven deeply into the fabric of Thai life, and the finest examples of Thai poetry rank on a par with the best that Western traditions have to offer.[1] A European observer noted during the middle of the last century that every Thai village had its own orchestra (Vella 1957: 43), and we have an account from as recently as the early part of this century of a vigorous tradition of singing competitions conducted by rival teams from neighboring villages competing in extemporaneous poetic composition (Bidyalankarana 1926: 101-127). Poetic art remains a vital part of everyday Thai life, as well. Every educated Thai is able to recite from memory at least some lines from the recognized body of literature that is taught in the schools, and classical themes and allusions are common in art, from its purest to its most commercial forms. Many public messages, from billboard entreaties to avoid littering, to reminders to library patrons to guard their personal belongings, are done in couplets composed in modern *klɔɔn* poetry forms. Even much of the graffiti that one finds in Thailand is composed in verse form.[2]

The ancient Thai poem entitled *Lilit Phra Law* (*lílít phrâ? lɔɔ*) holds a position of great importance in the literary heritage of Thailand. It is acknowledged by all who know Thai literature as one of the oldest, if not the oldest, and most significant examples of Thai poetic art. Officially recognized as a literary masterpiece by the Wannakhadi Samoson (literally "literature association") of Thailand, founded in 1914, the poem was made part of the official school and university curricu-

1

la in 1934 (Wibha 1982: 1-4). Since that time countless students have read the poem and memorized passages from it, and most educated Thai can recite from memory at least a few lines of the poem, even long after they have left school.

Opinions frequently differ regarding the propriety of parts of the poem, some of which are quite erotic, but there is general agreement that it is unparalleled among ancient works for its beauty and for its ability to evoke a deep emotional response from its audience. The introduction of the edition of the poem produced by the Ministry of Education of Thailand praises the poem for "its great beauty, eloquence of expression, and poetic phrasing that so deeply matches nature, love, grief, and courage that latter-day intellectuals have taken the plot" as the basis for their own work (1984: iv). Among these works are dance dramas, renditions of the poem done in modern poetic forms, a children's book, and a prose version that appeared in serial form in *Satri Sarn*, a popular Thai woman's magazine, before being published in book form in 1973 (Wibha 1982: 119-124).

For much of this century the story of Phra Law found great favor with audiences in Thailand,[3] and at one time the story also reached Western audiences in the form of an English language drama entitled *Magic Lotus*. This was an adaptation of the Phra Law story by Prem Chaya (Prince Prem Purachatra), which was broadcast by the BBC in 1938 and later appeared in published form under the title *Magic Lotus: A Romantic Fantasy*.

And yet, despite the enduring popularity of the story, and the high regard in which the original poetic version is generally held, those who composed the poem are frequently, if politely, criticized. They, and the composers of other ancient poetic works, are taken to task for certain supposed lapses, seeming

2

flaws in the use of the poetic forms, and even
for what are interpreted as willful distor-
tions of words said to be the result of their
attempts to obey the constraints of the forms
known as *khloong* and *râay*. They are compared
unfavorably with modern writers who, it is
said, follow poetic rules with more care and
precision, and allegedly follow a higher
standard, which is attributed to the benefits
of modern education.

The modern attitude toward the ancient
poets and their work can best be illustrated
in the form of a quotation. In a paper presented to the Siam Society in 1925, Prince
Bidyalankarana, himself a man of letters and
an extremely skilled poet, discussed the topic
"The Pastime of Rhyme-Making and Singing in
Rural Siam." The paper is a delight to read,
and it gives a fascinating description of part
of the once flourishing oral folk art of the
central plain of Thailand. In his talk, the
Prince observed that the elders of his time
must have been shocked at the attitude of his
generation who, he said, freely criticized
previous generations of scholars and poets.
The Prince explained the attitude of his
generation in this way.

> Modern students and minor poets
> (and I speak as one of them) have no
> desire to dethrone our old famous
> writers, many of whom deserve their
> places of honor in the literature of
> the Country. We respect them: we
> admire their fine qualities. Find-
> ing faults in them even if the
> faults are real enough, does them no
> harm. They are too big to be seri-
> ously damaged. But we have become
> fastidious, and feel aggrieved when
> we find a flaw in a good poetical
> passage which would, without it, be
> a brilliant piece of work. Imagine
> yourself lost in the enjoyment of an
> exquisite poem, sailing serenely

3

through the air, so to speak: and then receiving a sudden jar which flings you back to earth - you probably know the feeling. One may also liken it to the discovery of a bitter pill concealed in a delicious morsel of food. (1926: 101)

There is, then, a curious dichotomy of opinion among modern scholars who have studied the classics. The ancient poets are appreciated for their skill, but also criticized for the imagined limits of that skill. The implication is that those poets were capable of creating poetic forms, but not of using them well. It is even suggested that the oldest of the Thai forms of poetry were actually borrowed from other languages, as though the poets of long ago could not create forms suited to their own tongue.

The critical attitude is basically the result of comparisons inadvertently made between two different kinds of poetic work: collaborative compositions created for oral performance; and written pieces created by individual authors, intended, at least in part, for silent reading. The fact that these inappropriate comparisons have been made is, I believe, part of the great, although as yet largely unrecognized, changes in attitude toward language that resulted from the spread of literacy and the introduction of print technology in modern Thailand.[4]

The present study addresses this curious dichotomy in modern treatments of ancient work by examining the text of *Lilit Phra Law* and the verse forms used to create it, as well as the criticisms made of it by contemporary scholars from the point of view of modern linguistic analysis. The study uses the insights of linguistics to demonstrate that many of the supposed flaws in the text are simply the result of errors, or ill-advised "corrections" made by misguided editors, during the process of copying and printing.

More importantly, many of the apparent errors can be shown to be the result of fundamental changes in the structure of the language itself and consequent changes in the nature of the *khloog* and *râay* verse forms in which *Lilit Phra Law* is composed. Most of those who have written about the poem have been unaware of these changes, which have rendered the language of the poem distant and remote from modern speech and, in previously unrecognized ways, have forever altered the poetic arts. A detailed study of the text helps to clarify the fundamental nature of the *khloog* and *râay* verse forms and provides a demonstration of the fact that the verse forms were not borrowed from any other language, but sprang from the rhythms of the everyday speech of the time.

Any study of *Lilit Phra Law* must address some of the material that Prince Bidyalankarana was alluding to in the passage quoted above, and some may see in it an attempt to "dethrone" those who have gone before. Such an attempt is in no way the purpose of the present study. It is undertaken as an attempt to bring new light to a subject that has been of interest to many scholars, some of preceding generations and some working today, and it is clear that Prince Bidyalankarana would not have been offended by this effort. The intention of the study is not to criticize, but to eliminate a few of the "jars" and "bitter pills" of which the prince spoke. No matter how successful the attempt, it is undertaken with the utmost respect for the artists and scholars who have studied the poem previously. The observations made in this study will not lessen their stature, but may help modern readers to appreciate more fully the work of the poets of long ago.

A detailed examination of the text, one that takes into account all information pro-

vided by modern linguistic studies of the Tai
language family, leads to the inescapable
conclusion that the ancient poets were every
bit as skillful and disciplined as their
modern counterparts. Our written records,
however, are at best an imperfect and mislead-
ing representation of the ancient work, and
they must be interpreted with great care if
errors are to be avoided, or at least mini-
mized. This study discusses these points in
hopes that a better understanding of how the
present situation has come about will enable
modern readers of this poem, and other poems
composed in the *khlooŋ* and *râay* verse forms,
to come to a deeper appreciation of the poets
of long ago, and to a clearer understanding of
the history of the Thai poetic arts.

Lilit Phra Law in Summary Form

No attempt has yet been made to translate
the oldest extant version of the story, and so
the text is virtually inaccessible to those
who do not speak Thai well. Even for those
who have attained some mastery of the language, the situation is not much better.
There are handbooks to the text written in
Thai, but they are of only limited use to
foreign students of the language. The interpretation offered for obscure passages is
often rendered in a highly poetic style that
is only somewhat less obscure for non-native
speakers, and many passages for which there is
no attempt at clarification are badly in need
of it. An amalgam of versions of the text as
it appears in manuscript copies made during
the last century, with all of their now
archaic language and obscurity, is the only
version that is continually kept in print and,
therefore, readily available. Advanced students of Thai language in the United States
are sometimes introduced to the work in their
classes, and the reaction is generally one of
appreciation of the beauty of the sections
covered, along with relief that no more than

introductory work is required. In the end,
the difficulty of translating the text pre-
vents even ambitious students from attempting
to go much further with the poem.

It is no wonder, then, that this important work, quite possibly the oldest extant
poetic work produced by Thai speakers, remains
little known outside of Thailand, even among
specialists in Thai studies. For those not
yet familiar with the poem, a summary of the
text is given below. Passages have been
selected for translation that illustrate the
different verse forms used in the poem. There
is much that cannot be included in a summary,
of course, and that will have to wait for a
full translation to be completed, but the
major events of the tale are covered. The
interested reader should find that the material included is sufficiently detailed for those
who wish to follow the analysis given in the
rest of this study and, it is hoped, for those
who wish to read portions of the text on their
own.

The story as presented in the texts of
Lilit Phra Law available to us today, begins
with two stanzas of praise for the city and
the king and two more stanzas of introductory
matter written in the poetic form known as
khloong 4, as given below. Stanza numbers are
those assigned in the text produced by the
Thai Ministry of Education.

Stanzas 3-4 (*khloong 4*)

#3

เ ๓ รู้มลักสรบศาสตร์ถ้วน   หญิงชาย

จักกล่าวกลอนพระลอ   เลิศผู้

ไพเราะเรียบบรรยาย   เพราะยิ่ง เพราะนา

สมบี้ลู้เสียงลู้   ล่อเล้าโลมใจ

7

Being fully versed, oh men and
women,
I will recite for you the poem of
Phra Law, surpassing man,
A euphonious and well-arranged tale
of great beauty,
Fit to be played on the pipe, and
beguiling to the heart.

#4   ๔ สรวลเสียงขับอ่านอ้าง   ใดปาน

ฟังเสนาะใดปูน   เปรียบได้

เกลากลอนกล่าวกลการ   กลกล่อม ใจนา

ถวายบำเรอ ท้าวไท้   ธิราชผู้มีบุญ

Happy sound, what could equal it?
Hear the rhythm, what could compare
to it?
A polished poem, told with artistry,
soothes the heart.
I present it to the royal meritori-
ous one.

The story itself then begins as the
narrator gives a brief summary of the background to the main events related in the poem,
starting with a stanza composed in the poetic
form known as *râay*. The stanza introduces the
parents of Phra Law, King Mansuang (*mɛɛnsŭaŋ*),
the ruler of the city named Suang (*sŭaŋ*), and
his queen, Lady Bunlua (*bunlŭa*). The stanza
is number 5 according to the numbering system
of the Ministry of Education text of the poem.

Stanza 5 (*râay*)

#5   ๕ กล่าวถึงขุนผู้ห้าว   นามท่านท้าวแมนสรวง   เป็นพญาหลวง

ผ่านเผ้า เจ้าเมืองสรวงมีศักดิ์ ธมีอัครเทพพิลาส ชื่อนางนาฏ

บุญเหลือ ล้วนเครือท้าวเครือพญา สาวโสภาพระสนม ถ้วนทุก

8

กรมกำนัล มนตรีคั่ลคับคั่ง ช้องม้ามั่ง มหิมา โยธาเคียรคาษ
หล้า หมู่ทกล้าทหาร เผ้าภูบาลนองเนือง เมืองออกมากมียศ
ท้าวธมีเอารสราชโปดก ชื่อพระลอดิลกล่มฟ้า ทิศตะวันตกหล้า
แหล่งไล้ สีมา ท่านา

       I speak of a bold king, with
the noble name Mansuang, a sovereign
of vast power who ruled the great
city of Suang. He had a beautiful
queen, herself of royal blood, known
as Lady Bunlua, and consorts and
attendants, each of radiant beauty.
Ministers attended him in throngs,
and he possessed elephants and horses in vast numbers. His troops over-
flowed the earth, and bold warriors
flooded about him. His many vassals
themselves possessed high rank. The
noble king had a young son, named
Phra Law, of such refinement as to
have descended from the heavens. The
city lay to the west, set off by
royal boundary markers.[5]

There was also another great king whose
treasures equaled that of the first. He was
known as Phimphisakhonrat (*phimphísǎakhɔɔn-
râat*), and he ruled the city of Song (*sɔɔŋ*).
His son, named Phichayphisanukon (*phíchay-
phítsanúkɔɔn*), was married to a lady of royal
birth named Darawadi (*daaraawadii*). They had
children whom they loved, two daughters said
to be as beautiful as the moon, named Phra
Phuan (*phǔan*) and Phra Phaeng (*phɛɛŋ*), who
were known to all for their loveliness.

At one point King Mansuang decided to
overpower the city of Song and take it for a
vassal state. To this end he raised a great
army to carry out his attack, which was quickly met by his rival, as is described in stanza
8, below.

#8

๘ ส่วนนรินทรราชา   พิมพิสาครราชา   พระบาทครั้นได้ยิน
ว่าภูมินทร์แมนสรวง   ยกพลหลวงมากระทั่ง   ท้าวธก็สั่งพล
ออกรับ   ตับตามกันเดียรดาษ   พระบาทเสด็จบมิช้า   พล
หัวหน้าพะกัน   แกว่งตาวฟันฉฉาด   แกว่งดาบฟาดฉฉัด   ซ้อง
หอกซัดยะยุ่ง   ซ้องหอกพุ่งยะย้าย   ข้างซ้ายรบบมิคลา   ข้างขวา
รบบมิแคล้ว   แกล้วแลแกล้วชิงข้า   กล้าแลกล้าชิงขัน   รุมกันพุ่ง
กันแทง   เข้าต่อแย้งต่อยุทธ์   โห่อึงอุด เอาชัย   เสียงปืนไฟกึกก้อง
สะเทือนท้องพสุธา   หน้าไม้ดาบืนดาษ   ธนูสาดศรแผลง   แข็ง
ต่อแข็งง่าง้าง   ช้างพะช้างชนกัน   ม้าผกผันคลุกเคล้า   เข้ารุก
รวนทวนแทง   ระแรงเร่งมาหนา   ถึงพิมพิสาครราชา   พระบาท
ขาดคอช้าง   ขุนพลคว้างขวางรบ   กันพระศพกษัตรีย์   หนีเมื้อ
เมืองท่านไท้   ครั้นพระศพเข้าได้   ลั่นเขื่อนให้หับทวาร   ท่านนา

    King Phimphisakhonrat, learning
that King Mansuang had raised a
royal army to attack, ordered a
counterattack. His troops went out
in abundant ranks, and he, too, came
without hesitation. The forward
troops clashed, brandishing their
swords, cutting, clanging; brandishing their swords, slashing, ringing.
Javelins were hurled in profusion,
thrown from each side. On the left,
they fought but could not advance.
On the right, they fought but could
not break through. Brave against
brave, they grasped and killed. Bold
against bold, they grappled and
twisted. They gathered, thrusting
and stabbing. Joined together, con-
testing and making war, they called

out after victory. The echoes of
cannon fire vibrated the battle
field. A multitude of crossbows and
longbows sprayed arrows with force.
Strong against the strong, they
reared back to strike. Elephants
crashed into elephants. Horses
reared up, mixing in the fray. En-
tering the mob, opposing, stabbing,
urged on they reached Phimphisakhonrat, who perished, still mounted on
his elephant. His officers fought to
interpose themselves, and protect
the body of their king. They fled to
the city and, the royal corpse safely inside, they threw the bolt,
locking the gate behind them.

The duties of leadership fell to Phichayphisanukon who held funeral rites for his
father. He then sent his daughters, along
with their ladies-in-waiting, to live with
their grandmother in her palace.

At the same time King Mansuang arranged
for his son, Phra Law, to marry the beautiful
Lady Laksanawadi (*láksanawadii*). In due
course the king died, and Phra Law ascended
the throne. His fame was spread far and wide
by roving balladeers who sang in praise of his
perfection. Young women everywhere were
driven to distraction by these ballads of
praise, even in the city of Song, where the
royal sisters Phra Phuan and Phra Phaeng fell
under the spell. Seeing the sisters sick at
heart with longing, their ladies-in-waiting,
named Run (*râun*) and Roy (*rooy*), were amazed
and asked what was wrong. The reply is given
in the often quoted 30th stanza of the poem.

Stanza 30 (*khlooŋ 4*)

#30   ๓๐ เสียงฦาเสียงเล่าอ้าง   อันใด พี่เอย

          เสียงย่อมยอยศใคร   ทั่วหล้า

สองเขือพี่หลับใหล   ลืมตื่น ฤๅพี่
สองพี่คิดเองอ้า   อย่าได้ถามเผือ

What are all these tales and rumors
    about?
Who do they praise to the ends of
    the earth?
Have you two slept so deeply that
    you've forgotten to awake?
Figure out for yourselves (what's
    bothering us). Don't ask.

Run and Roy promised to find a way to
attract Phra Law to the two sisters and decided to send trusted retainers into the city of
Suang, there to pretend to be wandering mer-
chants and to gather information while spread-
ing a tale of their own. While in the city
the retainers sang the praises of Phra Phuan
and Phra Phaeng. They were overheard by Phra
Law who was, in turn, mesmerized by the descriptions of the beauty of the two sisters,
so much that he composed verses of praise for
them.

Word of this development was brought back
to Run and Roy, who then went to a sorceress
for help in enticing Phra Law from his home.
She was reluctant to try to help, saying that
her skill was no match for the power of such a
monarch. Instead, she lead them to another
practitioner, who was similarly reluctant but
in response to their pleas told them that only
one individual had the power to help the
revered Lord Samingphray (*samĭŋphraay*).

Stanza 54 (*rǎay*)

#54 ๕๔ หมอว่าในใต้ฟ้า   ทั่วแหล่งหล้าผู้ใด   ใครจักเทียมจักคู่

ปู่เจ้าปู่สมิงพราย   ธว่าให้ตายก็ตายทันเห็น   ธว่าให้เป็นก็เป็น

ทันใจ จะลองใครใครก็มา   จะหาใครใครก็บอยู่   จะไปสู่ท่านไซร้

ไว้ตูจะนำไป   เท่าว่า ทางไกลจรล่ำ   วันนี้ค่ำสองนางเมือ

12

พรุ่งเช้าเขือเขียว มา   สองนางลาหมอเถ้า   ไปบอกแก่สองเจ้า
สองอ่อนท้าวยินดี ยิ่งนา

The magician said, "Beneath the heavens, and in all the earth what person can hope to compare, to equal, Puu Caw Samingphray? He says, 'Die,' and it dies, instantly. He says, 'Live,' and it lives, immediately. If he calls anyone, they come. If he calls anyone, they cannot resist. If you wish to go to him, I will lead you there. But the way is long, and slow. Tonight you two return home, and in the morning hurry back." The two women took leave of the magician and went to tell the two princesses, who were both well pleased.

Run and Roy returned to the palace where they gave the good news to Phra Phuan and Phra Phaeng. They also won permission for their trip from the king by claiming that the distress of the royal sisters could only be cured by a healing ceremony known as *rápkhwăn*, which would have to be performed in the mountains. At cock's crow they left the palace and made directly for the practitioner's home. In something of a preview of the elaborate display of skill that will be performed later on in the story by Samingphray, the magician first appears to the ladies as a comely youth, and then reverts to his normal appearance before mounting his elephant for the trip into the forest.

Run and Roy admired their surroundings as they moved through the flat lands, but as they reached the foothills the surroundings took on a frightening aspect. As they moved on, the ladies-in-waiting became terrified by the increasingly threatening scene, but the practitioner only laughed, saying that it was all just the work of Samingphray.

13

Eventually they reached the foot of the mountain and were brought in to see Samingphray. As they entered they saw him attended on either side by tigers. These frightening beasts, however, were magically transformed before their eyes into beautiful felines.[6] Samingphray also transformed himself magically before them, appearing first old and gray, then young and virile, and finally middle aged and handsome. Run and Roy, deeply impressed by all they had seen, presented offerings from Phra Phuan and Phra Phaeng and in their name begged Samingphray for his help.

Stanzas 79-82 (*khlooŋ 2*)

#79   ๗๙ ทุกข์ธิดาเท่าฟ้า   เห็นแต่พระเจ้าข้า

       พระปู่เจ้าองค์เดียว

> The suffering of the royal daughters [that is, Phra Phuan and Phra Phaeng] is as great as the sky.
> They look to you alone, Phra Puu Caw.

#80   ๘๐ ขับเขียว มาแต่เช้า   สองให้เชิญพระเจ้า

       โปรดเปลื้องทุกข์หลาน   ท่านเทอญ

> We have hastened here, traveling since morning,
> And they bid us to entreat you to relieve their suffering.

#81   ๘๑ เชิญช่วยภารลุแล้ว   เงินแลทองกองแก้ว

       อเนกข้าขอถวาย

> Please, help relieve them,
> And we will present you with gold

14

and silver and countless
varieties of precious stones.

#82   ๘๒ กามกรรหาย เหิมไหม้   พระช่วยพระชักให้

ราชพ้นความตาย

> The fires of desire are consuming
>   them.
> Please, Lord, help the royal sisters
>   escape death.

Samingphray thereupon went into a meditative trance in which he saw that the three
royals were destined by fate to come together,
but that they would also soon thereafter die
due to the weight of their karma. But recall-
ing that Phra Phuan and Phra Phaeng had been
faithful in seeking his protection, he decided
to help them nonetheless. Gratefully, Run and
Roy prepared to leave, asking only one additional favor, that they not face as frightening a trip on the way home. Samingphray only
laughed, but the trip out of the forest was an
easy and comfortable experience, with all of
nature turned beautiful and benign.

In due time Samingphray plaited a magic
device and on it affixed an image of Phra Law
with Phra Phuan and Phra Phaeng at his sides.
He then caused the device to spin in the
breeze at the top of a tall tree. Carried on
the wind, the spell reached Phra Law, who fell
into a state of discomfort so obvious that it
caused distress throughout the city. Lady
Bunlua, anguished at her son's condition, sent
Kaew (*kêɛw*) and Khwan (*khwǎn*), personal attendants to Phra Law, to summon practitioners of
her own who sought with all their skill for a
remedy.

#122   ๑๒๒ ยอกท้าวพึ่งลูกไท้   ทูลสาร

ถนัดดั่งใจจักลาญ   สวาทไหม้

น้ำตาท่านคือธาร   แถวถั่ง ลงนา

ไห้บ่รู้กี่ไห้   สระอื้นอาดูร

The queen listened as her son
    explained,
Her heart consumed by the fire of
    her love.
Her tears were a stream, cascading
    down.
Sobbing out countless sobs, and
    sighing in pain.

#123   ๑๒๓ ตีอกโอ้ลูกแก้ว   กลอยใจ แม่เอย

เจ้าแม่มาเป็นใด   ดั่งนี้

สมบัติแต่ มีใน   ภพแผ่น เรานา

อเนกบรู้กี้   โกฏิไว้จักยา พ่อนา

She beat her breast saying, "Oh son,
    oh my beloved son,
How did you come to this?
All the riches that are in this land
    of ours,
The countless varieties and sums, I
    will use to care for you.

#124   ๑๒๔ นายแก้วอย่าอยู่เร้ง   ไปหา

เร็วเร่งพระโหรมา   อย่าช้า

หาหมู่หมื่นแพทยา   หมอภูต มานา

หาแม่มดถ้วนหน้า   หมู่แก้กฤติยา

Kaew! Waste no time. Go!
Hurry to bring the royal astrolo-
      gers.
Bring the court physicians, and
      sorcerers.
Bring sorceresses, and everyone
      skilled in breaking spells.

#125   ๑๒๕ นายขวัญหาจุ่งถ้วน   ทั้งหลาย

         ทุกหมื่นขุนมุลนาย   ช่วยไสร้

         เถมินไพร เร่งขวนขวาย   ยาป่า มานา

         ยาเทศ ทั้งปวงไว้   ฝ่ายข้างชาวคลัง

Khawn! Go get everyone,
Get officials of every rank to help.
Get groups of hunters to search for
      herbs,
And let palace officials bring every
      type of foreign medicine.

#126   ๑๒๖ คลังกูคลังลูกแก้ว   กูนา

         จักจ่อมจ่าย เยียวยา   หน่อเหน้า

         สิ้นทั้งแผ่นดินรา   แม่ลูก ก็ดี

         สิ้นแต่สินจงเจ้า   แม่ได้แรงคืน

My fortune, and your future my be-
      loved son,
I will pay it all to care for you.
Even if I should use up everything
      of ours,
They are only things. Please, my
      son, recover!"

17

#127　　๑๒๗ ขวนขวายถึงขนาคพร้อม　เพรียงกัน

หมอว่าใดทำสรรพ์　　สิ่งนั้น

บนานพระลอพลัน　　สรว่าง เสบยนา

ถ้วนหมู่หมอมาหั้น　　ท่านให้เหลือเพื่อ

They searched until everything was
　　brought together.
The practitioners said, "Whatever
　　can be done, is done."
Before long Phra Law recovered, and
　　again felt well.
To each group of practitioners, Lady
　　Bunlua gave great rewards.

#128　　๑๒๘ ออกท้าวธิราชได้　　แรงรมย์

นางพระยาพระสนม　　ชื่นหน้า

มนตรีไพร่เมืองชม　　สดชื่น เสบยนา

ลอบพิตรเจ้าหล้า　　สว่างคลุ้มหายมัว

The Queen recovered her good
　　spirits.
Lady Laksanawadi and the royal
　　consorts and attenants were
　　pleased.
The officials and the citizenry felt
　　restored and happy,
As Phra Law was relieved of his
　　confusion.

Another exchange ensued with more powerful spells and countermeasures used on each
side, but again Phra Law was cured of his
affliction. Samingphray then raised up an
army of spirits to attack the city of Suang,
and in a tremendous battle he vanquished the
defending spirit forces and overcame Phra
Law's resistance with a charmed potion of

18

betel nut. In the end, after much debate, and to the dismay of the entire city, Phra Law determined that he must go to the city of Song to see Phra Phuan and Phra Phaeng, and he ordered an army raised to accompany him. After completing extensive preparation, Phra Law dressed in his royal finery and left his palace to take up his position in the great military procession.

Stanza 224 (*râay*)

#224 ๒๒๔ โศกเสื่อมคลายใจราช เสร็จสั่งนาฏสั่งสนม ถ้วนทุก กรมกำนัล ท้าวธบทันไสยา แสงจันทราโอภาส ดาราดาษ ดารก ตกต่ำคล้อยเจียน รุ่ง ผกาย พรึกพุ่งอัมพรา ไก่ ตื่นตาปรบปรือ ปีกกระพือขันเรา เสียงดุเหว่าเกรีนร้อง เสด็จ สู่ห้องบังคน นางถวายชลเอางาน ภูบาลสู่ที่สรง ชำระ พระองค์บนาน ทรงสุคนธ์ธารกลิ่น ละลุง ปรุงปนทองธารทรง ผจงสนับเพลาบวร ภูษาภรณ์เลื่อมลาย รัดพัสตร์ พรายไพจิตร พิศชายไหวยะยาบ ชายแครงคาบเครือวัลย์ พิพิธพรรณเสื้อ สนอบ รัดอุระรอบเรื่องรอง สังวาลตรอง ตามประดับ ทับทรวง แสงร่วงรุ้ง พลอยเพชรพุ่งยรรยง ทรงทองกรจำรัส พาหุรัด รูปมังกรกลาย ธำมรงค์พรายเพริศแพร้ว มกุฎแก้วแสงใส ทรงพิชัยอาวุธเสร็จ บพิตรเสด็จนวยนาด ดั่งพระยาราชไกรสร จากศิขรคูหารัตน์ บัดถึงเกยบมินาน ขุนช้างชาญความขับ ประทับเทียบเกยแก้ว ทรงคอคชสารแล้ว เคลื่อนแคล้วพลพฤนท์

The great sadness slowly faded from his heart. He instructed his queen and his attendants, but before he was finished and went to his rest, the multitude of stars faded, and the moon with her brilliance sank low before the encroaching dawn, and the rising morning star.

The rooster stirred and beat its
wings, crying out, and the koel
sounded its cry. Phra Law went to
his toilette while the water ladies
performed their tasks. The king went
to his bath and quickly cleansed
himself. He put on fragrances, mixed
with gold. He put on his undergar-
ment, finely made, and his outer
garments, beautifully decorated. He
fastened his shimmering belt, ob-
serving the delicate grace of its
decoration. His scarf hung, a cascading vine, over garments of di-
verse colors. He fastened his breast
cloth, glowing intensely, and
strands of chains over his golden
collar. His breast plate shimmered
with the light of the dawn, encrust-
ed with magnificent diamonds and
jewels. He put on shining bracelets,
arm bands in the shape of the
maŋkɔɔn, dazzling finger rings and a
jeweled diadem, shining with pure
light. Having put on the royal victory weapons he went forth with the
grace of the lion king from the
pinnacle of his gem dwelling, and
soon arrived at the royal elephant
platform. The master of the elephants expertly brought his mount to
the gem platform. Having mounted the
neck of the great beast, he caused
the multitude of his troops to em-
bark.

Despite his determination to go to the
city of Song, Phra Law was himself in great
turmoil.

Stanzas 231-233 (*khlooŋ 4*)

#231   ๒๓๑ พระองค์โอภาสเพี้ยง   ศศิธร
              เสด็จดุจเดือนเขจร   แจ่มฟ้า

ดวงดาวดาษอัมพร เรียงเรียบ

ดูดุจพลเจ้าหล้า รอบล้อมเสด็จโดย

His royal majesty was as lustrous as
the moon.
And he moved as does the moon,
lighting the heavens as it
passes.
The heavenly stars, arrayed across
the skies,
Resembled his troops, surrounding
him as he went.

#232 ๒๓๒ พระเล็งแลราษฎร์รั้ว เรือนสวน เรือกนา

พิศไร่นานึกอวล อ่อนไท้

ปานนี้รูปรอย ครวญ ถึงพี่

อกอ่อนระทวยไหม้ คร่ำแค้นใครโลม

He cast his gaze upon his people,
their homes, gardens, fences.
As he looked his thoughts turned to
his loved one.
By now that beautiful one must be
weeping over me,
Lovely lady, consumed by fire, who
will comfort you?

#233 ๒๓๓ จักไปปใคร่แคล้ว เทพี พี่เอย

จักใคร่คืนคิดศรี ฝ่ายหน้า

ไปดีอย่าไปดี ใดดั่ง นี้นา

คิดเร่งอ้างว้างว้า ห่วงหน้าคิดหลัง

Going, I do not wish to leave my
consort.

21

Wishing to return, I think of the
     ladies ahead.
It is good to go; it is not good to
     go. Which then of these?
Thinking only speeds me to loneli-
     ness. I worry over what lies
     ahead, yet yearn for what is
     behind.

The doubts and anguish continued throughout the trip. Even as he prepared to cross
the river Kalong (*kaalŏŋ*) into unfamiliar
territory, Phra Law was torn between the
desires that called him forward and the duties
that called on him to return. In a famous
passage he looked to the water of the river
for a sign, only to see a clear omen of im-
pending disaster.

Stanzas 296-297 (*khlooŋ 4*)

#296   ๒๙๖ มากูจะเสี่ยงน้ำ   น้องไป ปรี่นา

        น้ำชื่อกาหลงไหล   เชี่ยวแท้

        ผิวกูจะคลาไคล   บรอด คืนนา

        น้ำจุ่งเวียนวนแม้   รอดไส้ร้จงไหล

Come, I will seek an omen in there
     rushing waters.
This river named Kalong flows most
     swiftly.
If I should proceed further, not to
     return in safety,
Let the waters circle about me. If I
     am to be safe, let them flow.

#297   ๒๙๗ ครั้นวางพระโอษฐ์น้ำ   เวียนวน อยู่นา

        เห็นแก่ตาแดงกล   เลือดย้อม

        หฤทัยระทดทน   ทุกข์ใหญ่ หลวงนา

        ถนัดดั่งไม้ร้อยอ้อม   ท่าวท้าว ทับทรวง

22

As soon as his words had passed from
        his lips, the waters circled,
And turned deep red, as though mixed
        with blood.
His heart was beset with a terrible
        suffering,
As though crushed by a tree a hun-
        dred spans in girth.

Phra Law decided that he must proceed,
despite the danger, but he took with him only
a small portion of his forces and his two
faithful attendants, Kaew and Khwan.   But as
he was waiting for an auspicious day to go
further, the two royal sisters were anxiously
pleading with Samingphray to speed matters
along.   Samingphray responded by selecting a
forest cock of unusual perfection to lure Phra
Law toward the city.   The lure was successful,
and Samingphray thus completed his role in the
story, all the rest of the activity motivated
by normal forces.

Phra Law and his attendants decided to
disguise themselves and assume false names in
order to inspect the area without giving away
their   presence.   By   the   judicious   use   of
bribes they arranged to see the royal pleasure
garden of Phra Phuan and Phra Phaeng.   That
evening Phra Law and Phra Phuan and Phra
Phaeng, as well as their four attendants, all
had   dreams   filled   with   symbols   that   they
interpreted as omens portending the imminent
joining of the lovers.

In the morning the four attendants, Run
and Roy, and Kaew and Khwan, all met in the
garden pool.   In a light and humorous scene
described with elaborate nature images they
shared amorous pleasures and fell in Love.
After close questioning, Kaew and Khwan admit-
ted that they had hidden their true identities
and were traveling with Phra Law, who had come
to see the royal sisters.

23

#431 ๔๓๑ มาจะหัว ให้หายหิวอยากเข้า   เชิญบอกอันจริงเจ้า

แก่น้องอย่าอำ   หนึ่งรา

Come, let us satisfy our hunger with
    laughter,
And tell us the truth, with no
    deceptions.

#432 ๔๓๒ สองสนองคำอ่อนพร้อง จะบอกจริงแก่น้อง

อย่าเย้ยหยันตู

They replied to the ladies' request,
"We will tell you truly, don't be
    harsh with us."

#433 ๔๓๓ พระภูธรอยู่เกล้า   ลอราชพระเสด็จเต้า

เผือพี่เลี้ยงมาตาม

The exalted ruler of the earth,
King Law has made his way here and
    we,   his   attendants,   have
    followed.

#434 ๔๓๔ ขุนงามบอกข่าวไท้   เสมอดั่งสองนางได้

ผ่านเผ้าไอศวรรย์

When the two noble ones revealed
    this news,
The two ladies felt as if they had
    received a heavenly treasure.

As the attendants were nearing the palace
with the good news Phra Phuan and Phra Phaeng

saw them coming. Anxious to hear any news,
but fearful of having their secret desires
revealed, they debated about what to do and
complained about the delay.

Stanzas 461-464 (*khlooŋ 2*)

#461 ๔๖๑ มาสองราจะร้อง   ถามเถิดฤๅพระน้อง

จุ่งได้แรงใจ   หนึ่งรา

Let us then cry out,
And ask them for news, so we will
     have some encouragement.

#462 ๔๖๒ คิดนึกไปชอบเหรื๊อง   ความรั่วรู้ทุกเบื๊อง

พระย่ารู้ฤๅดี

I think we should not.
It will get out to everyone, and we
     shouldn't let grandmother know.

#463 ๔๖๓ มาจะตีตนตายจุ่งแล้ว   สองพระพี่เลี้ยงแก้ว

ยกย่างช้าเยียใด   ดั่งนี้

Oh, it would be better to kill
     ourselves!
Why do our two dear companions walk
     so slowly!

#464 ๔๖๔ ทวารวังในว่าใกล้   ฤๅและวันนี้ไสร้

ขยกออกรี๊อดูไกล   บารนี

The inner palace door is close by,
     isn't it?

But today it looks different. Have
they moved it away?

A meeting was arranged between the royal
lovers, and it too is described with elaborate
nature images, but rather than being humorous,
the tone of the scene is one of awe. The four
attendants were transfixed in admiration of
the grandeur of the scene before them as Phra
Law and Phra Phuan and Phaeng gazed at each
other in admiration. Finally, the four with-
drew quietly, leaving the royal individuals
alone. All fears and doubts were forgotten as
the three fell hopelessly in love and enjoyed
a period of intense love making.

Finally darkness approached, and the
sisters knew they would be expected back at
the palace. With a ruse devised by Run and
Roy, Phra Law and Kaew and Khwan were brought
in disguise through the palace gates and into
the private chambers of the royal sisters.
There they remained in secret for two weeks of
bliss, but eventually word of their presence
reached King Phisanukon, who came in secret to
see their treason himself. He was at first
enraged, but then was overwhelmed by Phra
Law's regal bearing. He blessed their love
and decided to arrange for a marriage, pleased
at the prestige such a son-in-law would bring.

However, word of the situation reached
the king's mother, the widow of the slain
Phimphisakhonrat, who had not forgiven her old
enemies. She protested the proposed marriage
vehemently but to no avail and so decided to
arrange for an attack on the lovers by deceit,
telling her own soldiers that the king wanted
the young people dead. The attackers meet
fierce resistance, first from the four attendants who died defending their superiors and
then from Phra Law and from Phra Phuan and
Phra Phaeng, who had disguised themselves as
soldiers. The three proved themselves most
valiant, but were eventually overwhelmed by
the force of numbers and finally succumbed to

26

poisoned arrows. News of the events quickly reached the king, who rushed to the scene.

Stanza 607 *wâk* 29 to 69 (*râay*)

#607 ๖๐๗   ข่าวขจรไปบมิมิด ถึงท้าว
พิษณุกร ภูธรด่วนเสด็จมา เห็นสองธิดาสุดสวาท แล
พระบาทลอดิลก เลือดตกอาบทั้งตน ยืนอยู่กลบมิตาย ธก็
ฟายน้ำเนตรจะไจ้ เรียกลูกไท้แลเขยขวัญ เรียกฉันใดก็บมิพร้อง
ต้องฉันใดก็บมิติง ยืนอิงกันอยู่กระด้าง เจ้าช้างจึงรู้ฉบัด ว่า
สามกษัตริย์เสวยกรรม ธก็ทำฉันธบมิโกรธ ว่าฆ่านักโทษ
ทั้งหลาย ตายตามกันหนำใจ แต่ผู้ใดกล้าสามารถ อาจอาสามา
ล้างเขา ให้มาเอารางวัล ผู้ใดอันแกล้วหาญ จะบำนาญยิ่ง
รู้หลัก เราจะให้ศักดิ์เป็นขุน ปุนเป็นหมื่นเป็นพัน เขาก็หา
กันมาบมิช้า มาถ้วนหน้าบาบหลอ ได้ ธก็ให้เอาเชือกสวมคอ ปอ
สับรัดมัดศอก แล้วให้เอาหอกร้อยขา ตรา ชื่อถ้วนทุกคน ก็
ให้ฟั่นกลฟั่นหยวก ดาบจวกกลิ้งเกลือกตาย ส่วนหมู่นายนั้น
ไสร้ ธก็ให้ค้มให้คลอก แต่ต้นย่าดอกไสร้ให้แล่ ใช่ แม่ตัวเจ้า
หล้า ธก็ให้ฆ่าให้ลำบาก ลากเอาศพเสียเสร็จ ธก็เสด็จยังลูกไท้
ให้บรู้กี่ไท้ โอ้ลูกแก้วกับตน พ่อเอย

      The news spread unchecked, and soon reached King Phisanukon. The ruler hastened to the scene, and saw his two beloved daughters, and the magnificent Phra Law, all completely bathed in blood, standing together as if still alive. He wept bitter tears, calling out to his daughters and blessed son-in-law. He called them, but they did not answer. He touched them but they did not move. They stood, leaning against each other in defiance. And then the king

knew well that the three had come to
their end. He hid his anger, saying,
"All of the guilty have gone to
their deaths, and I am satisfied.
But which brave, able ones came to
wipe them away? Let them come forward for their reward. Whichever
bold men they are, I will reward
them beyond expectation. I will give
them the rank of *khŭn*, with income
of 1,000 and 10,000." They quickly
brought [the guilty ones] to him,
leaving out no one. He had ropes
placed around their necks, and tied
their elbows together, and severed
the tendons of their legs. Listing
all of their names, he had them
sliced like the trunk of a banana
tree. Swords cut them, and they
struggled and died. And the officers
of those troops, he had boiled
alive. But as for the grandmother,
he had her flayed, saying "You are
not my mother." And she was killed
most painfully. When the bodies had
been dragged away, he returned to
his children, and sobbed ceaseless-
ly, "Oh my precious children."

The news soon reached Lady Darawadi, as
well, and she rushed to the scene of the
already completed battle. Once there she,
too, mourned the painful loss of her children.

Stanzas 612-614 (*khlooŋ 2*)

#612 ๖๑๒ ยินดีใดด่วนม้วย   เยื้อนปากปราศรัยด้วย

แม่ให้เต็มใจ   หนึ่งเรา

Why does it please you to hasten
     onto death?
Open your mouths and speak to me, so
     I may understand.

28

#613 ๖๑๓ ใดผิดใจสองเจ้า   ควรเคียดฤๅจึงเต้า

แขก*ฟ้าทั้งสอง

What displeases you two?
Should you be so angry that you go
      visit the heavens?

#614 ๖๑๔ หมองใจใดด่วนผ้าย   สองอย่าคิดยินร้าย

แก่แม่ร้าณหัว   แม่เอย

What depresses you so, that you must
      hurry away?
Don't be so angry with your mother,
      my loved ones.

After a time of expressing their great
sorrow, the king and queen found that the
intensity of their own grief lessened, and
they set about quieting the sounds of lament
from the others.

Stanzas 628-634 (*khlooŋ 2*)

#628 ๖๒๘ สองพระองค์สร่างไห้   สองบพิตรท้าวไท้

จึงห้ามทั้งหลาย

The weeping of the two rulers
      slackened,
And the two forbade the others (from
      further crying).

#629 ๖๒๙ ครั้นวายเสียงไห้แล้ว   สองราชชมใจแกล้ว

แก่นไท้ทั้งสาม

When the sound of crying abated,

29

They praised the bold hearts of the
three noble ones.

#630 ๖๓๐ ยืนตายงามเลิศแล้   รู้ว่าใจกษัตริย์แท้
บให้ใครปุน

They died standing, how admirable.
We know they truly had royal hearts,
beyond compare.

#631 ๖๓๑ ทั้งสองขุนพี่เลี้ยง   นางรื่นนางโรยเพี้ยง
เทพไสร้ไบ่ปาน

The two companions of *khŭn* rank
[that is, Kaew and Khwan]
And Lady Run and Lady Roy, are like
incomparable angels.

#632 ๖๓๒ ใจหาญตายก่อนเจ้า   เป็นเพื่อนตายคลึงเคล้า
คู่หน้ารักใจ   บารนี

Bold hearts, to die before their
lords,
Companions, embracing in death,
deserving of love.

#633 ๖๓๓ ทุกคนในแหล่งหล้า   เสียงสรรเสริญถ้วนหน้า
ทั่วทั้งเมืองมี   มีแล

Everyone in the land,
Sang in admiration, filling the city
with their praises.

๖๓๔ ธรณีลือลั่นฆ้อง   เสื่องเสนาะฟ้าร้อง
เรียกท้าวยังสวรรค์

All of the earth echoed with the
      story,
And the sky resounded with the
      melodious sound, calling
      after them in the heav-
      ens.

Preparations were begun for a fitting
funeral, and performances of various types
were arranged to mark the passing of such
great and noble people. Also, an embassy was
arranged to carry the sad news to Lady Bunlua,
Phra Law's mother. On hearing the news she,
too, was stricken with great grief, and wept
for her dead son.

Stanzas 638-641 (*khlooŋ 4*)

#638 ๖๓๘ แม่สงวนมาแต่ตั้ง   มีครรภ์ ลูกเอย
      บเบกษาสักอัน   หนึ่งน้อย
      ถึงพระผ่านไอศวรรย์   เสวยราชย์   แลพ่อ
      รักลูกรักได้ร้อย   ส่วนล้ำรักตัว

I cared for you from the moment you
      were conceived,
And never relaxed my guard, even for
      a moment.
Even until the time that you ascend-
      ed the throne of the kingdom,
I loved you completely, more than I
      loved myself.

#639 ๖๓๙ ใช่เป็นไท้ท้าวแต่   พอดี ลูกเอย
      เป็นมกุฎกษัตรีย์   ผ่านเผ้า

ท้าวร้อยเอ็ดเมืองมี มาส่วย พระนา
ทูลบาทบงกชเจ้า แม่เที้ยรทุกวัน

You weren't just an ordinary ruler,
   my son.
You were a monarch of the highest
   rank, above all others.
Rulers of 101 cities came to pay you
   tribute,
Laying it before you nearly every
   day.

#640 ๖๔๐ เสวยสุขปราสาทเพี้ยง เมืองสวรรค์ ลูกเอย
เสด็จออกโรงกษัตริย์คัล คั่งเผ้า
หัวเมืองหมื่นขุนพัน นายไพร่ พลนา
เผ้าบาทบงกชเจ้า คู่ท้าวเมืองแมน

You took your pleasures in a heavenly palace, dear son.
When you came out to the throne hall
   kings attended you, in numbers.
Heads of cities, and *mùun*, *khŭn*,
   phan, nobles, freemen and
   soldiers,
They attended you, companion to
   Indra.

#641 ๖๔๑ พิศช้างคือคู่ช้าง อมรินทร์ ลูกเอย
ม้าคู่อัศวทินกร หยาดฟ้า
ริพลเพียบธรณิน มีมั่ง เกษมนา
เมืองบพิตรเจ้าหล้า แม่เพี้ยงเมืองสวรรค์

Your elephants equaled those of the
   God Indra,
Your horses, the steeds of the Sun

God, descended from heaven.
Your numerous troops filled the
    land, and were happy.
This city of yours, ruler of the
    earth, was like a city in the
    heavens.

Finally, the grief subsided in the city
of Suang as well, as all realized that they
must go on with the business of the kingdom.
Lady Bunlua ordered that a return embassy be
prepared to go to the city of Song to participate in the funeral rites, and also to bring
gifts to the rulers of that city. When the
funeral rites were completed a great spectacle
was held. Finally, the king ordered the
remains divided into two portions, and stupas
were prepared to receive them in each city.
On the day on which the remains were interred
each ruler gave alms in a great merit making,
and peace was restored between the cities.

The final verses of the story are addressed to the audience, as this last example
shows.

Stanza 658 (*khlooŋ 4*)

#658 ๖๕๘ เป็นศรีแก่ปากผู้   ผจงฉันท์

      คือคู่มาลาสรร   เรียบร้อย

      เป็นถนิมประดับกรรณ   ทุกเมื่อ

      กลกระแจะต้องน้อย·   หนึ่งได้แรงใจ

This tale is a credit to the mouth
    of its composer,
Equal to the beauty of a heavenly
    flower.
May it always be an adornment for
    the ear,
As a sachet, only lightly touched,
    that gives strength to the
    heart.

33

The Study of the Poetic Forms of *Lilit Phra Law*

Despite the great beauty and literary significance of *Lilit Phra Law*, it is largely unknown outside of Thailand, at least in part because it presents formidable difficulties for those who wish to appreciate it. This study is both an introduction to, and a discussion of the poem, as well as the body of scholarly opinion and writing that concerns it; this study is written in the hope of lessening some of those difficulties and making the poem more accessible to modern readers.

A great deal of scholarly discussion in Thai, as well as a much smaller amount in other languages, has been devoted to *Lilit Phra Law*. That discussion tends to be devoted to three main points: the nature of the forms used by the poets to create their story; the location in which the events of the tale took place; and the identity of the author or authors of the story as we know it today. Opinions vary greatly on all of these points, and they are significant because they have direct bearing on a point of larger and as yet largely unrecognized import, the history of the development of Thai poetic art.

The position of *Lilit Phra Law* in the chronology of Thai literature is a point of uncertainty and contention, and efforts to clarify the point undertaken to date, concentrating as they do mainly on matters of theme and style, have not made much progress toward resolving the question. What has not been done previously is to examine each stanza in detail, to discover any and all patterns that the ancient poets may have followed. The present study is the result of such an examination, and the findings presented here are given in the hope that they will be instructive not only for studies of *Lilit Phra Law* itself, but also for studies of the *khlooŋ* and *râay* forms of poetry, in general.

34

Many scholars have noted numerous seem-ingly anomalous passages in *Lilit Phra Law*, most frequently in the *khlooŋ 4* stanzas, but also in stanzas composed in the other verse types, as well. Most analysts offer one of two somewhat different explanations for these problem passages. Some have suggested that the forms used in the poem are not really examples of the *sùphâap* variety, which is described in detail in the discussion of *khlooŋ* and *râay* forms given in chapter 2 of this study. According to this analysis, the poem is more accurately described as an exam-ple of composition using a type of verse known as *dân*, which is similar to the *sùphâap* vari-ety, but has somewhat different rhyme and tone placement patterns. The other common explana-tion for the apparently anomalous passages is that the composer or composers of the poem used a mixture of forms. According to this theory, the poem was created during a time of transition, when the supposedly earlier *dân* forms were developing toward more completely worked out *sùphâap* forms, which reached the height of their popularity, if not the height of their development, in the time of King Narai, who ruled from 1656 to 1688 (Sumonna-chat 1945: 22).

An assumption basic to much of this speculation is the almost universally held opinion that the authors of the poem were not as constrained by the rules of the forms as are modern authors and did not feel reluctant to violate the prescribed patterns. The idea seems to be that rather than working in an auditory form that sprang up from the rhythms of normal speech, the poets first conceived of an abstract form and then worked to arrange words to fit this abstraction, much as do present-day students of Thai poetry who are trying to master the unfamiliar patterns of centuries ago. Over the course of genera-tions, the reasoning seems to be, both the forms and the poets improved. The argument comes to its logical conclusion in statements

35

to the effect that it is poets who have had the benefit of modern education who have brought the previously imperfectly developed forms to a state of perfection.

In discussing the forms used in the poem, and the varying opinions mentioned above, we ought to keep in mind the cautionary comment of M. R. Sumonnachat Sawatdikun in his discussion of the forms used in *Lilit Phra Law*, a caution that seems to have been forgotten by many who have written about the poem. Since the first textbook was written at least 200 years after the poem was composed, he says, it is hardly appropriate to say that the poem breaks the rules (1945: 14). As the discussion will attempt to show, it is equally inappropriate to focus only on the seeming anomalies.

The poem must be examined in its entirety, not with the aim of comparing it to modern compositions, but with the aim of discovering what patterns may have guided the ancient poets. A thorough stanza-by-stanza examination of the poem will show that the poetic forms used in it, rather than being the conscious invention of a specific group in the society, were intensely auditory in nature and must have sprung out of the patterns of everyday speech. This point has been overlooked by modern scholars, who are more oriented toward visual than oral communication and seem to have conceived of the ancient poetic forms primarily as written rather than auditory entities. It will also become clear that, rather than being a transitional composition in ill-defined poetic forms, *Lilit Phra Law* was composed in fully developed *sǔphâap* forms, by poets in complete control of the medium in which they worked.

Before we deal with these specific questions, however, we will have to examine the linguistic background of the poem and also discuss the study of Thai poetry as it has been carried out to date. These points are covered in the following chapters of the present study.

NOTES

1. I received my introduction to Thai poetry in two seminars conducted by Professor William J. Gedney in Ann Arbor in 1978. This training has proven to be invaluable in my subsequent work on Thai poetry, and I wish to acknowledge with gratitude my debt to Professor Gedney. Any errors or misinterpretations of the material, however, are my own.

The phonetic transcription system used throughout the present work is the one used in the Thai teaching materials developed by J. Marvin Brown (1967, 1979).

2. For a delightful collection of graffiti gathered from trucks and buses as well as washroom and classroom walls throughout Thailand see Thawisak, et al. (1980).

3. The poem is highly praised in the program notes prepared by the Division of Music and Drama of the Department of Fine Arts for a performance on December 17th, 1948. According to those notes a version of the poem composed by Prince Narathip and dramatized and set to music by his wife, Mom Luang Tuan, in order to fulfill a wish of King Chulalongkorn, was a favorite of audiences from its first performance in 1908, and was thereafter regularly presented by many dramatic troupes (Dhanit 1963: 253-260). Evidently the original wording was also a favorite: "The singing of the words of the original play which Prince Naris has set to delectable music (vocal and instrumental) ... have achieved a popularity, with the lovers of Siamese theatrical art, which shows no signs of abating" (Dhanit 1952: 63).

4. For more on this point see Gedney (1985).

5. The published editions do not correspond to the manuscript copies, in which the direction cited in this passage is the east, not the west.

6. The text is difficult to interpret here, and there is some disagreement over just what it was that the sisters saw. Some take the wording to mean that they saw a single tiger transformed into a single cat, others say that they saw a pair of tigers transformed into a pair of cats.

Chapter 2

THE STUDY OF THAI POETRY

The *Chanthalak* Tradition

The student who wishes to appreciate the
rich and varied literary heritage of Thailand
needs, first of all, help in recognizing the
features of the various forms of Thai poetry.
Of the materials available for this purpose,
in many ways the best are the traditional
native text books on poetry, generally known
as the *chănthalăk* 'principles of versifica-
tion'. These books follow a pattern seen in
the oldest extant example of such a work, a
text known as the *Jindamani* (*Cindaamanii*),
said to date from the 17th century. The
content and format of the book suggest that
the original purpose of such works was to show
students how to compose good poetry, and to
that end the author, or authors, give diagrams
of various poetic forms, along with descriptions stating the appropriate number of syllables per line, and lines per stanza. Descriptions of rhyme placement (intra-line and
also sometimes inter-line rhyme) are given,
along with any other constraints associated
with the form, as well as sample passages.

Of the modern versions of the *chănthalăk*,
the most thorough and most influential is that
done by Phrayaa Uppakit Silapasarn as part of
his work *Làk phaasăa thay* [Principles of the
Thai Language] (1968). He set down the ideas
and attitudes of his generation, and added
much of his own, and his work has formed the
basis for many of the modern literature textbooks written for the rapidly expanding educa-
tional system of Thailand.

We will begin our discussion of *Lilit
Phra Law* with a summary of the general descriptions of the poetic forms known as *khlooŋ*
and *râay*, and the compositional style known as

39

lílít, the forms and style used in *Lilit Phra
Law*, as they are presented by Phrayaa Uppakit.
The information is given in summary form, and
only that which is of relevance to this study
has been included here. A reader wishing to
pursue the matter further would do well to
read the *chănthalăk* discussion in its entirety. The reader must also bear in mind that,
as fine as Phrayaa Uppakit's discussion is,
the material cannot be accepted without question, and there are several points with which
I will take issue.[1]

General Poetic Rules

All forms of poetry have rules, according
to Phrayaa Uppakit, but there are only two
types of rules that one encounters in all
forms of Thai poetry; these rules cover structure (*khaná?*) and rhyme (*sămphàt*). Each
poetic form has a definite structure, and each
form has rhyme, and without structure or
rhyme, there is no poetry.

Regarding structure, each form has specific requirements that define the *bòt* 'stanza', the *bàat* 'line', the *wák* 'hemistich' and
the *kham* 'word; syllable', according to the
nature of the form. The specific constraints
that make up Thai poetic forms must be discussed separately for each form, but each one
has such constraints.

Regarding rhyme, one may speak in more
general terms. There are two types of rhyme,
sămphàt sarà? 'vowel rhyme' and *sămphàt ?àk-
sŏɔn* 'consonant rhyme'.[2] Vowel rhyme requires that the syllables to be rhymed match
exactly in vowel, including length, and also
in consonant final sound, if one is present.
According to Phrayaa Uppakit, spelling is not
significant in this context, and tone is also
irrelevant. As we shall see, however, this
latter contention is not historically correct,
and the misconception will have to be recti-

fied if studies of Thai poetry are to be advanced. The following are given as examples of vowel rhyme:

kàʔ and *càʔ*, *dii* and *mii*, *khĕɛ* and *lɛɛ*

kàk and *dàk*, *chĩik* and *lĩik*, *cĕɛk* and *sĕɛk*

kan and *taŋ*, *khɯŋ* and *dɯŋ*, *tɛ̀ŋ* and *cɛ̂ɛŋ*

Consonant rhyme (that is, alliteration) is said to involve only the initial sound of the syllables involved, not the spelling of that sound. The vowel, the tone, and the final consonant, if any, of the syllables are also not significant for this type of rhyme. The following are given as examples of consonant rhyme:

khăw, *khăn*, *khuu*, and *khâm*

suŋ, *sâap*, *sâaŋsăn*, and *sɔ́ɔn*

In relation to structure, there are two categories of rhyme in Thai poetry, *sămphàt nay* 'inner rhyme' and *sămphàt nɔ̀ɔk* 'outer rhyme'. The former occurs within a given line and is in most cases optional; inner rhyme may be either vowel rhyme or consonant rhyme. The latter type, outer rhyme, is generally considered required. It occurs across line boundaries, and only vowel rhyme is acceptable (Uppakit 1968: 352-353).

There is one point with which we must take issue in the discussion summarized above, and that is the definition of vowel rhyme. In modern Thai, tone does not, indeed, play any role in rhyme. Words that match exactly in vowel, including length, and in any final consonant sound may rhyme, whether they have the same one of the five tones of modern Thai or not. The poetic form known as *klɔɔn*, which developed from modern speech with its system of five tones, does not incorporate tone placement requirements in its structure.

Also, authors who work with the modern reflections of the ancient *khlooŋ* and *râay* forms are not concerned with which of the tones is used in pronouncing a word, but with which of the tone marks is used in spelling it. An examination of the text of *Lilit Phra Law* will show, however, that this was not the case when the poem was created. At that time the ancient three-tone system was still in place, and words could rhyme only if they matched exactly in vowel, including length, and in any final consonant sound, and also had the same tone. This basic difference between the ancient and modern forms of speech is the result of a fundamental change in the phonetic structure of the language. As later discussion will show, this change has caused much confusion and misunderstanding for students of Thai poetry.

Form-Specific Poetic Rules

In his discussion of poetry Phrayaa Uppakit raises several points that, he states, are rules that apply only to specific forms of poetry. In fact, most are as much definitions as they are rules for composition. Those rules of relevance for a discussion of *Lilit Phra Law* cover the following concepts: 1) the distinction between open and closed syllables; 2) the nature and positioning of *ʔèek* tone syllables (those written with the first tone mark) and *thoo* tone syllables (those written with the second tone mark), and 3) the use of *kham sɔy* (literally "ornament" syllables). The discussion given by Phrayaa Uppakit for each of these three points is summarized below, and illustrations from his text are included.

1) Open vs. closed syllables
In the Thai system an open syllable, known in traditional terminology as *kham pen* 'live syllable', is one that ends with a voiced sound: a vowel, a sonorant (*m*, *n*, *ŋ*),

42

or a semi-vowel (*y*, *w*).[3]   The examples given
are:

   kaa, *kii*, and *kuu*

   ʔam, *ʔay*, and *ʔaw*

   kaŋ, *kan*, *kam*, *kaay*, and *kaaw*

The Thai system defines a closed syllable, known in traditional terminology as *kham
taay* 'dead syllable', as one that ends in one
of the stop sounds that occur in this position
in Thai: *p*, *t*, *k*, or *ʔ* (glottal stop).[4]   The
examples given are:

   kàʔ, *kǐʔ*, and *kùʔ*

   kàp, *kàt*, and *kàk*

In the poetic forms known as *khlooŋ* and
râay, according to Phrayaa Uppakit, a closed
syllable may be substituted whenever the rules
call for a syllable with the first tone mark.
A detailed examination of the text of *Lilit
Phra Law* shows that substitution of a closed
syllable for one spelled with the first tone
mark is common in the poem. But, contrary to
the impression given by modern commentators,
this substitution is not haphazard, nor is it
motivated by the need to find an appropriate
word for a line. As later discussion will
show, the substitution is part of a pattern
that strongly suggests that the poet, or
poets, who created *Lilit Phra Law* were working
in a form that was strictly oral in nature,
unlike the modern reflections of those forms,
which require nearly perfect mastery of the
intricacies of the spelling system used to
represent modern Thai speech.

2) First tone vs. second tone syllables
     A *kham ʔèek* 'first tone syllable' is
defined as one spelled with the symbol known
as the *máy ʔèek* 'first tone mark', " ˈ ". A
kham thoo 'second tone syllable' is defined as

43

one spelled with the symbol known as the *máy thoo* 'second tone mark',"˝".[5] Examples of each are given in the text, and they are repeated below. Syllables written with the first tone mark are in the right column and those written with the second tone mark are in the left column.

ข่า	(*khàa*)	ข้า	(*khâa*)
ก่อน	(*kɔ̀ɔn*)	ช้า	(*cháa*)
น่า	(*nâa*)	ค้าน	(*kháan*)
ว่าย	(*wâay*)	เศร้า	(*sâw*)

The forms known as *khlooŋ* and *râay*, as described by Phrayaa Uppakit and virtually all others who have written about the forms, have strict "rules" calling for syllables spelled with one or the other of the two tone marks in various places in the stanza. The so-called rules were so strict, according to the author, that the poets even purposely misspelled particular words so that the required tone mark would appear as dictated by the form.

At this point it is necessary to add a clarification. Modern presentations always discuss the *khlooŋ* and *râay* forms in terms of spelling conventions. As later discussion will make clear, however, the forms must originally have been completely auditory in nature, and the positions in the stanza were characterized not by the spellings of words, but by their pronunciations. Fundamental changes in the nature of speech following the composition of the poem have hidden this fact from modern scholars, but it is a crucial one for a proper understanding of ancient poetry. As the discussion of the linguistic background of the poem will show, the idea that the poets have purposely misspelled words in order to obey the constraints of the forms, although almost universally accepted, is actually incorrect.

Examples of the supposed alteration of spelling to produce the required tone mark are given by the author. Interestingly, although there are many words in *Lilit Phra Law* with seemingly anomalous spellings, the examples given in Phrayaa Uppakit's text, and repeated below, do not actually appear in the poem. This discrepancy between the analysis of the text and the actual wording found in it is a small illustration of a problem that has great implications for all modern studies of *Lilit Phra Law* and also of *khlooŋ* and *râay* as verse forms. Modern scholars have paid far too little attention to what the ancient texts actually say and do not have sufficient evidence on which to base either their formulations of the "rules" for the poetic forms, or their judgments of the quality of ancient texts.

เข้า	(*khâw*)	spelled	เค่า	(*khâw*)
ข้าม	(*khâam*)	spelled	ค่าม	(*khâam*)
ช่วย	(*chûay*)	spelled	ฉ้วย	(*chûay*)
สุ่ย	(*lûy*)	spelled	หลุ้ย	(*lûy*)

As Phrayaa Uppakit explains, words that appear in the poem with apparently anomalous spellings are known to modern analysts as *ʔèek thôot* 'incorrect first tone mark' words, and *thoo thôot* 'incorrect second tone mark' words (1968: 355ff). The first spelling in each of the four pairs above is the one considered correct in modern Thai, and the second is considered incorrect, but both spellings in each pair represent the same modern tone, the falling tone. Thus, there are two different spellings available with which to represent a single pronunciation. The common misconception that the poets have deliberately distorted words in order to achieve the desired tone pattern must have developed first around this ambiguity in the tone system of modern Central Thai and the necessary overlap in the spelling

45

system used to represent it.

3)   The *kham sɜy*

Extra syllables, or *kham sɜy*, are found added to various positions in a stanza. According to Phrayaa Uppakit, they may be added to a *wák*, to a *bàat*, or to a *bòt* (that is, to a hemistich, a line or a stanza), depending on the form of poetry being used. Stanzas of *râay* may have *kham sɜy* added following the individual *wák* and also following the entire stanza. Stanzas of *khlooŋ* may have *kham sɜy* added following the individual *bàat*. In such cases the *kham sɜy* are generally two single syllable words and often are vocatives or mood particles. The *kham sɜy*, he says, are added to make the poetry more pleasing to the ear.

This material is correct, but we will have to add to it later in a discussion of the poetic forms as they are used in *Lilit Phra Law*. In fact *kham sɜy* did not simply add euphony to the poem; they had a significant structural role as well, one that has been overlooked by modern authors.

The Poetic Forms *khlooŋ*, *râay*, and *lílit*

In chapter 4 of his *chǎnthalák* Phrayaa Uppakit gives long and detailed descriptions of all of the varieties of the forms known as *khlooŋ* and *râay* (1968: 379-430). The author includes without distinguishing them both the ancient forms that sprang up from the speech of centuries ago, and also the more artificial varieties that have been developed as a result of the modern attention to written language. The discussion below that covers this material is a general summary of the points that are made about specific forms that are of relevance to a discussion of *Lilit Phra Law*. More will be added later from this source as the need arises.

46

The *khlooŋ* Forms

All types of *khlooŋ* verse consist of lines of five syllables each. The most frequently encountered forms are *khlooŋ 2*, *khlooŋ 3*, and *khlooŋ 4*, each so named because of the number of five-syllable lines contained in each stanza. Constraints require rhymes between specific syllables and also placement of designated tones in specific places in the stanza. There are also rules regarding extra syllables, the *sɔ̌y* words mentioned above, which apply to each stanza. Diagram 1 shows the structure of the *khlooŋ 2* stanza by indicating the essential points in traditional diagram form. Circles are used to represent syllables, and the Thai tone marks are placed above those positions said to require syllables spelled with them. Lines connect those syllables that, according to the conventional rules, are required to rhyme. The optional *kham sɔ̌y* are enclosed in parentheses.

Diagram 1: *khlooŋ 2*

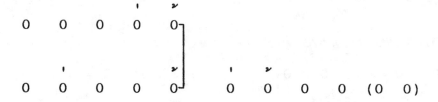

Included in the *chǎnthalák* is an example stanza of *khlooŋ 2* that happens to be from *Lilit Phra Law*. The stanza is number 18 according to the numbering system of the edition of the poem published by the Ministry of Education. It is given below.

Example 1: *khlooŋ 2*

thamnɔɔŋ naasìk thǎy
way   nose   title

khɯ̀ɯ	*thêep*	*níramít*	*wáy*	*prìap*	*dûay*	*khɔ̌ɔ*	*kaam*
be	god	create	keep	comp.	with	hook	love

His nose was as though created by
the gods; it was like the hook of
the god of love.

The structure of the form known as *khlooŋ*
3 is similar to that of *khlooŋ 2*, except that
an additional *wák* is placed at the beginning
of the stanza. The first *wák* in *khlooŋ 3* has
no tone placement rules, but it is said that
it must be connected to the second *wák* by a
vowel rhyme link between the last syllable of
the first *wák* and the first, second, or third
syllable of the second *wák*. The first syllable in such a rhyme is known as the *sòŋ* 'send'
syllable, and the second is known as the *ráp*
'receive' syllable. Diagram 2 shows the
structure of the *khlooŋ 3* stanza, again following the traditional diagram format of using
circles to represent required syllables,
connecting them with lines to indicate rhymes,
and using Thai tone marks to show positions of
specified tone placements.

Diagram 2: *khlooŋ 3*

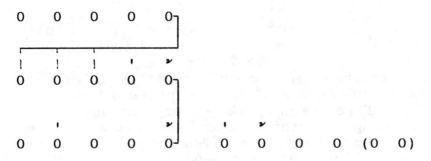

One of the example stanzas given in
Phrayaa Uppakit's text is, again, from *Lilit*
Phra Law. It is stanza number 362 of the text
published by the Ministry of Education.

Example 2: *khlooŋ 3*

sɔ̌ɔŋ yàa   praarom krasǎn
two neg. worry   yearn

mɛ̂ɛ mí   wan   phrûŋ   cháaw
if   neg. today tomorrow morning

lɔɔ râat càk sadèt tâw   sùu sɔ̀y   sǔan   khwǎn
Law king pt. go   go   to   orna- garden spirit
                                  ment

     Don't you two worry. If not today,
     then tomorrow morning Phra Law will
     come to the royal garden.

     As the diagram and explanations show, the
khlooŋ 2 and *khlooŋ 3* forms are nearly the
same. The *khlooŋ 4* stanza, while following a
similar pattern, is more complex both in terms
of tone placement and rhyme pattern. Diagram
3 shows the various aspects of the structure
of that form and follows the same conventions
used in the previous diagrams.

Diagram 3: *khlooŋ 4*

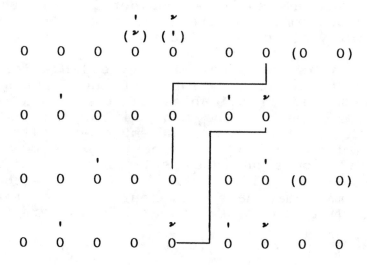

Example 3: *khlooŋ 4*

sĭaŋ	*luu*	*sĭaŋ*	*lâw*	*ʔâaŋ*	*ʔan-day*	*phîi*	*ʔəəy*
sound	rumor	sound	tell	aver	which	sib.	pt.

sĭaŋ	*yɔ̌m*	*yɔɔ*	*yót*	*khray*	*thûa*	*lâa*
sound	sure	lift	honor	who	cover	earth

sɔ̌ɔŋ	*khŭa*	*phîi*	*làp-lǎy*	*luum*	*tùun*	*ruu*	*phîi*
two	you	sibling	sleep	omit	wake	?	sib.

sɔ̌ɔŋ	*phîi*	*khít*	*ʔeeŋ*	*ʔâa*	*yàa*	*dây*	*thǎam*	*phŭa*
two	sib.	think	self	voc.	neg.	get	ask	we

> What are all these tales and rumors
> talking about?
> Who do they praise from one end of
> the earth to the other?
> Have you two slept so that you have
> forgotten to wake?
> Figure out for yourselves (what's
> bothering us). Don't ask us.

The example stanza of *khlooŋ 4* given here is the one given in nearly all textbooks that discuss the forms. The wording happens to match exactly the conventional description of the form, and so it is considered an excellent illustration. The stanza is number 30 in the Ministry of Education edition.

It is said that the rhyme links formed between the last syllable of the first line and the fifth syllables of the second and third lines must be made with syllables in which no tone mark is employed, although closed syllables with short vowels may be used. Tones on these syllables, it is explained, may differ, since syllables with no tone mark may have different tones.[6] Examples given in Phrayaa Uppakit's text are:

กิจ   (*kìt*), มิตร (*mít*), and ติด (*tìt*)

กัน   (*kan*), หั้น (*hǎn*), and มัน (*man*)

An additional rule stated in Phrayaa Uppakit's text is that the same rhyming syllable may not be repeated in sequence; thus, the first pattern given below is acceptable, but the second, containing the same syllables, is not.

การ (*kaan*), สาร (*săan*), and การ (*kaan*)

การ (*kaan*), การ (*kaan*), and สาร (*săan*)

The final syllable of the stanza, it is said, must be one with either the modern rising tone or the modern mid tone. Phrayaa Uppakit says that this stipulation allows for elongation of the syllable when it become necessary in performance. Elongation of syllables in modern performance is common, but it is not just the modern mid-tone or rising-tone words that are altered in this way. As the discussion of poetic forms as they are used in *Lilit Phra Law* will show, there is a more fundamental reason for this characteristic of the *khloon* and *râay* stanza.

The comments summarized above are meant to cover all of the forms of the *khloon sǔphâap* variety. Another variety of *khloon*, known as *khloon dân*, differs from the forms explained and diagrammed above mainly in rhyme and tone placement. These differences are not relevant at the moment, and discussion of them will be postponed until later, when the nature of each form as it actually appears in the poem is examined in detail.

The *râay* Forms

The description of *râay* given by Phrayaa Uppakit is quite simple. The structure constraint given in his analysis specifies that each *wâk* should have five syllables. The rhyme pattern requires that the last syllable of each *wâk* rhyme with an early syllable of the following *wâk*. The author also notes that

51

the rhyming syllables should be of the same "sort," that is, if either syllable has a tone mark, both must have that same tone mark. Although Phrayaa Uppakit does not seem to recognize the fact, this point is connected with the ancient tone categories of Thai and the nature of rhyme at the time that *Lilit Phra Law* was composed. This point is crucial for a full understanding not only of this poem but also of all other compositions done in *khlooŋ* and *râay*; however, significantly, it is overlooked in nearly all modern work on Thai poetry. Those that do note the point simply mention it and do not seem to see the real significance of it. We will return to this point frequently throughout the discussion.

Two forms of *râay* discussed in this section of Phrayaa Uppakit's work are of importance for a study of *Lilit Phra Law*: *râay booraan* and *râay sùphâap*. The form *râay booraan* (literally "ancient *râay*") is described as usually having at least five syllables per *wâk*. It is said that while five syllables per *wâk* is the correct number, the ancient poets often had more and often had fewer than the "proper" number. The rhyme pattern as described above for all *râay* is used in *râay booraan*, and the only stipulation is that the stanza end in a syllable that does not have a tone mark. Diagram 4 shows the conventially accepted structure of the form.

Diagram 4: *râay booraan*

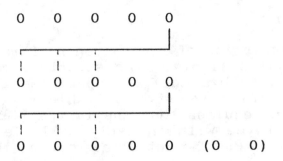

52

In connection with the example of *râay booraan* given here, it should be noted that the text published by the Ministry of Education includes an alternate reading for the stanza that is found in one of the old manuscripts. The reading is in fact not *râay booraan*, but the form known as *râay sùphâap*, which is discussed below. This discrepancy casts doubt on the accuracy of both the manuscripts and the published texts.

The example given by Phrayaa Uppakit is stanza 43 of the text of *Lilit Phra Law* published by the Ministry of Education. Due to the length of the English glosses, each *wák* is placed on a separate line.

Example 4: *râay booraan*

> *chom   khâaw sɔ̌ɔŋ phîi-nɔ́ɔŋ*
> praise news two siblings
>
> *tɔ̂ŋ   rúthay cɔɔm râat*
> touch heart   great king
>
> *phrá-bàat hây   raaŋwan*
> king   give reward
>
> *pan   phâa-sûa sanɔ̀ɔp*
> divide garment garment
>
> *khɔ̀ɔpcay sûu ʔaw khâaw*
> thank   you take news
>
> *maa klàaw tɔ̂ŋ   tìtcay (baaranii)*
> come tell touch like   pt.

"He praised the news of the two sisters, which touched his heart. He gave them garments as a reward. 'Thank you for bringing this news to tell me. I am impressed by it.'"

The form known as *râay sùphâap* as described by Phrayaa Uppakit is based on a *wâk* of five syllables in length, and any number of *wâk* may be used, but the form requires that the stanza end in the pattern of *khlooŋ 2 sùphâap*. As with *râay booraan*, it is said, rhymes must be between syllables having either no tone mark, or the same tone mark. Permissible extra syllables are included in parentheses in diagram 5, and the positions of the rhymes and tone placements are indicated as in previous diagrams.

Diagram 5: *râay sùphâap*

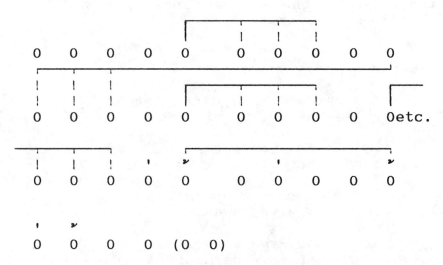

The example given below is also taken from the Ministry of Education text of the poem. It is stanza 349. Due to the length of the English glosses, each *wâk* has been placed on a separate line.

Example 5: *râay sùphâap*

phrá² lɔɔ mii harúthay
Phra   Law have heart

ramayyaa phírom
mood   pleased

chầunchom kham phîilíaŋ
like   word attendant

sɔ̌ɔŋ phîi klàaw klɔɔn klîaŋ
two sib. say poem all

klɔm thâaw nítthraa
sing king sleep

Phra Law was very pleased with what
the two attendants said. The
two of them sang to lull Phra Law to
sleep.

The *lílít* Style of Composition

The compositional style known as *lílít* is
described as a combination of stanzas of
poetry written in the various *khlooŋ* and *râay*
forms, used alternatingly as the poet sees
fit. According to Phrayaa Uppakit, each
stanza in a *lílít* composition must have a
rhyme link with the following stanza (1968:
427ff). In *lílít* using the *sùphâap* forms of
poetry, this inter-stanza rhyme link is between the last syllable of a stanza and the
first, second, or third syllable of the first
line of the next stanza. According to the
author, all stanzas should be joined in this
way, and the "common" tone (that is, the
modern mid tone) is preferred, although the
4th tone (that is, the modern rising tone) is
permissible, as is the use of some checked
syllables. Described as absolutely forbidden
is the use of syllables with tone marks in the
stanza-linking rhymes.

In a footnote to the above material
Phrayaa Uppakit states that these rules are
carefully followed in modern works. But in
older works, he says, there are places in
which rhyme links exist and places in which
they do not. He also states that there are
even places in which rhyme links begin with a
syllable that has no tone mark, but end with

one having the first or second tone mark, or even a checked syllable. Phrayaa Uppakit concludes that the older poets were not as strict about following the methods described in the rules as were the poets of later generations (1968: 428). Far from being unique with Phrayaa Uppakit, this opinion is, unfortunately, very common among those who write about Thai poetry.

Later, I will discuss the *lǐlít* style as it is used in *Lilit Phra Law* and address in detail the presence of stanza rhyme links and the supposedly faulty links. At this point it is sufficient to say that the unfavorable comparison between ancient and modern poets is inappropriate. What Phrayaa Uppakit notes is not evidence of weakness on the part of the ancient poets, but a written reflection of the features of *lǐlít* as it was originally conceived. The supposed preference for modern mid-tone words over modern rising-tone words is simply a reflection of the distribution of words in the ancient A-tone category.

The *chǎnthalǎk* tradition has produced a great deal of fine scholarship, and much useful information, but these works are limited by their very nature. That is, the books seem to have been intended as instructional manuals designed to teach students how to compose good poetry. But such work cannot form the basis for analytical studies, because it provides only brief treatments of each form, and no single version is comprehensive.[7] The greatest problem is lack of historical perspective. As M.R. Sumonnachat Sawatdikun points out in his discussion of *Lilit Phra Law*, the first textbooks, the first attempts to give written descriptions of poetic forms, were written at least 200 years after the poem was composed, and under such circumstances it is hardly appropriate to say that the poets broke the rules (1945: 14). And yet, nearly all modern analyses make just that assertion. In order to correct the situation we must examine the entire text of the poem in detail. The textbook formulations will be a useful framework from which to work, but we will have to be aware that the "rules" found in the textbooks are really only descriptions of patterns that were noted long after the ancient poets had completed their work and departed the scene. In fact, we will see that the patterns are far more complex than has been previously noted, and a careful examination of the text clears away any doubts about the skill of the ancient poets. Before proceeding to an examination of the text, however, we should first consider the sources of information other than the *chănthalăk* books that are available to the student of Thai poetry.

General Works on Thai Poetry

In addition to the textbooks, based directly or indirectly on the *chănthalăk* tradition and devoted mainly to presentation of the poetic forms, there are other works that are available to the student of Thai poetry that place emphasis on considerations other than the nature of the forms. Some of these works give excerpts of the classics accompanied by summaries and comments on the various works. The extensive *Prawàt wannákhadii thay sămràp náksùksăa* [History of Thai Literature for Students], by Pluang Na Nagara (1974), for example, devotes considerable attention to *Lilit Phra Law*. Some of these works are scholarly articles that discuss a variety of interesting points, "Investigation into the Composition of *Lilit Phra Law*" by M. R. Sumonnachat Sawatdikun (1945), for example.

There are a very few sources in Western languages that deal with the study of Thai poetry. One of the most extensive is the 1951 work *Etude sur la littërature siamoise* by P. Schweisguth. Others are brief introductions to each of the poetic forms, usually with example stanzas taken from a variety of sources, and sometimes written by the author as illustrations. *Introduction to Thai Literature*, by R. B. Jones, et al. (1970), and *Interpretative Translations of Thai Poets*, by M. R. Seni Pramoj (1986), are examples. Some of these materials also give background, but often they repeat or even elaborate on the misconceptions found in Thai sources.[8] One indispensable article for students of Thai poetry is "Siamese Verse Forms in Historical Perspective," by William J. Gedney (1978), in which the author discusses historical background for each of the forms of Thai poetry, free of the common misconceptions. Only one text written in English, *Phra Lo, a Portrait of the Hero as a Tragic Lover*, by Wibha Senanan Kongkananda (1982), is devoted completely to *Lilit Phra Law*, giving extensive discussion of thematic considerations.

Some of the Thai materials are guides or introductions to published editions of the classics. Unsigned introductions to *Lilit Phra Law*, for example, precede the editions of the poem prepared by the Ministry of Education (1975, 1984) and by the Fine Arts Department (1971) of the government of Thailand. Two separate handbooks for the poem have been prepared by noted scholars, one written by Phra Worawet Phisit (1961, 1974) and one by Chanthit Krasaesin (1954).

These various works address a variety of points concerning *Lilit Phra Law*, but two concerns raised most frequently are the desire first to determine the approximate date of composition and the identity of the author or authors, and second to locate the scene of the events of the story. As part of the latter concern, the vocabulary of the poem is frequently mentioned as evidence of a northern origin, by which is always meant the northern part of Thailand. There are no studies, however, that present lists of specific vocabulary items to support the contention, and so we cannot be sure if the words referred to are truly regionalisms or are simply forms that are archaic in the central region. Without detailed analysis the contention must be considered tentative, at best.

M. R. Sumonnachat, in his lengthy study of the poem mentioned above, takes another approach. He compares the events of the story and the geography of Thailand and comes to the conclusion that the events must have occurred in the areas around the modern city of Lampang. This often quoted study is the only one of its kind.

The most frequently voiced opinion regarding the date of composition and authorship of *Lilit Phra Law* is that the poem was composed during the reign of King Narai the Great, who ruled the Kingdom of Ayutthaya during the period 1656-1688 A. D., and who is noted in part for the literary work produced during his reign (Pluang 1974: 80). This period is famous for the number of works produced in the form *khlooŋ 4 sùphâap*, one of the forms used in *Lilit Phra Law*, and it is a natural assumption that the work ought to date from this period. The question is not of crucial significance for this study of *Lilit Phra Law* and I will not address it directly except to say that the historical evidence suggests a much earlier date. Also, as Gedney (1985: 15) points out, even as recently as the early part of the last century, poetic composition in the court was primarily a group effort involving the skill of a number of individuals working together over extended periods of time. The attempt to identify one specific author of *Lilit Phra Law* is probably destined to be unsuccessful and is most likely irrelevant as well. However, part of the controversy is valuable in demonstrating the need for a new approach to the study of the classic texts of Thai poetry. Below is a brief discussion of this point.

Three stanzas that appear in the published editions of the poem, numbers 4, 659, and 660, are cited by nearly every commentator who mentions the question of authorship. Stanza 4 says that the poem was composed to be presented to the king, but the name of the king is not mentioned. Stanza 659 says that the *mahǎarâat* 'king' composed (*níphon* is the term used) the poem. Stanza 660, the last in the published versions of the poem, says that the *yawwarâat* 'son of the/a king' wrote down (*bancoŋ* is the term used) the poem.

The first of these three stanzas is part of the preliminary matter that precedes that actual story of *Lilit Phra Law*. The section in which the stanza appears extols the greatness of the capital city and of the ruler thereof, but it is clearly not part of the story being related by the poem. Nonetheless, the section does mention that the work was to be given to a ruler. The final stanzas, as they appear in the published texts, mention a ruler and the son of a ruler. It is not clear whether the stanzas refer to the same ruler or not.

Differing explanations are advanced for these stanzas. They are used as the basis for speculation about the likelihood that one or another historical figure was the ruler to whom the work was to be presented, or perhaps was the ruler who composed while his son wrote down what was said, or may even have been the prince who composed the poem and thereafter himself became king, necessitating an additional reference that would reflect his new status, and so on.

Part of the discussion sometimes revolves around the term *mahǎarâat* and whether it was intended as a name or as an honorific, but more often than not the age of this term as an honorific is not taken into account. Also not considered is the possibility that the poem as we know it today is only one version of a tale that developed as part of an oral tradition and that these stanzas may have been added to that tale only after it had been set down on paper. In fact, some of the manuscript copies also contain other additional closing verses that have clearly been added recently, by the one who either undertook to make the copy in question, or perhaps was the patron who commissioned the copy. This practice suggests that even in recent times the addition of material to a text was not considered inappropriate, as it no doubt would be to today's scholars, and it calls into question the age of the two stanzas that end the text as it appears in published form, and on which so much speculation has been focused.

All of the speculation overlooks a crucial fact: not one of the extant manuscripts on which the printed editions are said to be based uses the term *yawwarâat* in the last stanza. Those manuscripts that have this stanza, and not all of them do, use the term *mahâarâat* 'king', the same term as used in the previous stanza. The point is that all of the carefully and elaborately worked out theories, designed to account for all of the references in the poem, do not take into account the possibility that parts of the text may have been added over the course of the centuries since the poem was first set down on paper. Also, the speculation that we find in modern analyses is based on wording that first appears no earlier than 1902, which is at least 250 years, and probably a great many more years than that, after the poem was composed.

The introduction to the Fine Arts Department edition notes this important discrepancy between the manuscripts and the published versions and calls for a new edition, based directly on the old manuscripts as soon as it can be arranged; but the needed correction is not made in that text. The preference stated is that no changes be made until all the needed corrections can be completed (1971:

viii). Left completely unanswered is the question of how the spurious wording came to be used in the edition of 1902, evidently the first mechanically produced edition of the poem.

The Available Texts of *Lilit Phra Law*

The oldest extant copies of the poem are currently held in the collection of the National Library of Thailand. They are written in traditional style on books that are folded in such a way as to give the appearance of an accordion. Most of the books are made from a raw material derived from the *khɔ̌y* tree, which produces a black paper that is a good and durable writing surface. Such books are known as *samùt khɔ̌y*, '*khɔ̌y* (tree) books', from the name of the most commonly used raw material, or as *samùt thay* 'Thai-style books'.

According to the numbering system currently used by the National Library, there are now fifty-two individual manuscript books in the collection. Each of these books contains from about 120 up to 250 or so of the stanzas of the text, and most stanzas appear in from twelve to eighteen of the books. Some of the books are identified by the former owner, or by the individual from whom it was obtained by the library, although for many no identifying matter is available. One of the books carries a note saying that that particular copy was completed in 1860, and while the others are not dated their appearance and condition suggest that they are generally of comparable age, with some among the collection perhaps a few decades more recent. Some of the books have suffered damage from water and insects, others from great use. Only one complete set is numbered consecutively, but at least one other complete set is in the collection, although it has somehow been given non-consecutive catalog numbers. Most of these books are legible, but working with them is a cumbersome process since the stanzas are not numbered, and each book contains a different amount of material. No critical edition has as yet been attempted.

Several of the printed editions of the poem give brief printing histories, which indicate that all of the currently available printed editions are based on one completed in 1926, and commonly referred to as *Chabàp hɔ̃ɔ phráʔ samùt wáchíráyaan* [Edition of the Wachirayan Royal Library]. This edition was itself based on another said to be dated 1915, which was in turn based on another said by the introduction of the Ministry of Education text to have been done in 1902. This 1902 text was evidently the first edition done by mechanical means and was the only one not based on a previously published version. What this means is that none of the editions of the poem now available is based exclusively on the oldest, extant manuscript copies.

There are several published editions of *Lilit Phra Law* available in library holdings, and one or two are generally available for purchase at any given time in Thai bookstores. All editions present the entire text of the poem, and some add a bit of introductory matter. All of these texts have their own strengths, but the one published by the Thai Ministry of Education, although it does not include any interpretation, is especially good for several reasons.

The Ministry of Education text numbers each stanza of the poem consecutively, no matter what form of verse is used. This practice is an important innovation in the presentation of Thai literary works that greatly simplifies the comparison of different versions. Also, the editors have included many variant readings that resolve some of the questions about the text, and they have added a glossary that identifies the location of problematic vocabulary items. These additions represent significant advances over other editions, which seldom number the stanzas and usually provide no interpretation or glossary material.

There are also two large companion volumes for the poem. The more commonly known of the two, *Khûu mʉʉ lílít phrâʔ lɔɔ* [Handbook for *Lilit Phra Law*], was written by Phra Worawet Phisit. It was first published in 1961 as a single volume, and then again in 1974 as a two volume set, although without changes or additions to the original material. The author includes both a complete text of the poem and interpretation of passages that he felt were difficult or obscure. One is left with the impression that the work is partly a collection of notes and observations made by the author during his many years of teaching at Chulalongkorn University in Bangkok. Unfortunately, the work is now out of print, although it can be found in some libraries.

The second companion volume, *Prachum wannákhadii thay phâak sɔ̌ɔŋ: phrâ lɔɔ lílít* [Thai Literature Collection Part Two: *Lilit Phra Law*], written by Chanthit Krasaesin, was published in 1954. It includes a full text with numerous interpretive passages and also gives many variant readings from both published and unpublished sources. This work, too, is out of print.

A significant drawback for each of these texts is the decision to number stanzas by type rather than consecutively, which makes them very cumbersome for comparative work. Also, neither author was trained in linguistics, and many of the interpretations given suffer from this lack.

The history of the poem leaves one uncertain about the accuracy of any of the available texts, either in manuscript or printed form. First, even the oldest extant manuscripts are fairly recent copies, in all probability not pre-dating the founding of Bangkok. The books are perishable and are subject to deterioration in the hot and humid climate of Thailand, and one must assume that no copy could have survived normal use for very long. The written texts that we have today must be the products of repeated copying over the course of several centuries, and it is more than likely that passages have been altered in the process.

It is commonly believed that all of the written materials of Ayutthaya perished in the attack and destruction of the city by Burmese armies in 1767. If, in fact, the destruction was complete, it may be that the oldest texts we have were reconstructions done by memory in the early decades of the last century. The potential for unintended alteration in such a situation is, of course, great.

We must assume, therefore, that manuscript copies have been changed over the course of time, and we know that the printed versions have also been changed further. It has been the habit of editors who have compiled editions of all of the classics for publication to alter the spelling of the older texts (Gedney 1978: 39) and even to make substantial changes in content to conform to modern ideas of correctness or propriety. There are no printed editions of *Lilit Phra Law* presently available in which the oldest known versions of the poem, those done by hand in the *samùt khɔ̀y* manuscripts, are used as the sole source.

The texts published by the Ministry of Education and the handbook for the poem prepared by Chanthit Krasaesin take a step in the right direction. Both texts include variants found in some of the *samùt khɔ̀y* copies, although one wishes that the work had been even more faithful to the manuscripts. In the preface to Ministry of Education edition, the editors state that they based their text on the edition compiled by the Royal Library in 1926 and consulted the manuscripts whenever they were in doubt (1975: ii). They do not, however, specify which of the manuscripts they consulted, or just what sort of situation was sufficiently doubtful to require that consultation. They also include a number of variant readings in footnote form, but do not specify which of the manuscripts, or even how many of them, contain the variant reading. Moreover, there are numerous anomalous passages that were evidently overlooked for which the manuscripts contain solutions not noted in the Ministry of Education text. The Krasaesin handbook goes an important step further by including some details of which manuscripts include a particular reading and by offering interpretations of the different available readings. It seems from the lists given by the author, though, that not all of the manuscripts then in the library collection were consulted, and acquisition information shows that some of the copies now in the collection were obtained after that handbook was completed. Also, the handbook omits discussion of some passages that are clearly anomalous.

CONCLUSIONS: THE STUDY OF THAI POETRY

The main problem in nearly all of the sources of information presently available for the study either of *Lilit Phra Law* specifically, or of *khlooŋ*, *râay*, and *lílít*, in general, both those sources written in Thai and the very few written in Western languages, is a lack of historical perspective. The language and the forms of poetry that have sprung up from it are treated as separate entities. The fact that language changes over the course of time, with consequent changes in the poetic arts, is not taken into account.

Thus, nearly all modern commentators, who speak a language with five tones, have overlooked the fact that the ancient poetic forms

66

were created by speakers of a language with three tones. Whenever differences are noted between ancient and modern uses of a particular form, the opinion expressed is nearly always that modern authors, due to superior knowledge and education, have perfected forms only imperfectly used in the past. Rather than trying to put ancient works in their proper context, and seeking for explanations for the seemingly anomalous passages, modern commentators have simply assumed that work done in the present surpasses that of the past. This assumption is incorrect, but in order to see the point clearly, and to understand fully the implications of the misunderstanding, we will have to examine the text of the poem itself, while trying to set aside a great deal of what has been written about it.

NOTES

1. Editor's notes accompanying the text show that the author died without having had an opportunity to edit his work (Uppakit 1968: ix), and one suspects that he would have clarified some points had he had the chance to do so.

2. For a detailed discussion in English of rhyme in all types of Thai poetry, see Hudak (1986: 38-61).

3. The Thai situation differs somewhat from the linguistic convention that generally defines an open syllable (also known as a "smooth" syllable) as one ending with a vowel, and a closed syllable (also known as a "checked" syllable) as one ending with any consonant. For general information on terminology, see Crystal (1980: 58, 64, 248).

4. In modern citation forms, short vowels not followed by any other consonant are followed by a glottal stop. This is a modern pattern

not present in the ancient language, which did not use the glottal stop as a final consonant.

5. In discussing the structure of Thai poetry the word *kham* can be translated as either "syllable" or "word," and this can be confusing to a reader new to the subject. In the present study I have tried to use the translation "syllable" when discussing the poetic forms as independent entities, and the translation "word" when discussing individual lexical items that are used in those forms. The distinction is, at times, difficult to maintain, and I hope that I have been consistent enough to be clear.

6. The same is true, of course, of syllables written with the first and second tone marks, but the point is not expanded to include such syllables. If it had been expanded in this way some of the confusion about the nature of the ancient forms might have been clarified long ago. The inevitable conclusion, which parts of the present study will attempt to demonstrate, is that the tone categories were once unambiguous and that the forms were once strictly auditory in nature.

7. There are many literature text books available in Thailand today, most written to be used in specific high school and college classes. These books are either consciously or unconsciously based on the traditional texts, but most do not improve on them, and some make matters more difficult. Generally, the traditional material is simply reorganized so that it fits comfortably into a modern course syllabus. Unfortunately, in reorganizing the older material, modern authors have sometimes blurred distinctions and inadvertently created confusing books. For example, several volumes have copied each other in repeating what Phrayaa Uppakit describes as the two general rules of poetry (that is, structure and rhyme requirements) and the several other constraints applicable only to

specific forms. However, these rules are presented as though they were of equal status and importance, all under the heading of "Characteristics of Good Poetry." Thus, students are required to memorize a set of seven or more points that are described as universals, of which only two actually apply to all Thai poetry.

8. See, for example, Schweisguth (1951: 84), in which *Lilit Phra Law* is described as having stanzas not only of the forms mentioned previously, but also of a form known as *khlooŋ 5*. In fact, there are no stanzas in the text that actually resemble this form. Also, see Cooke (1980: 421-437), which repeats without correction or comment many of the misconceptions regarding the nature of *khlooŋ* poetry found in native Thai work.

Chapter 3

THE LINGUISTIC BACKGROUND OF *LILIT PHRA LAW*

Modern Thai treatments of the classics do not take into account linguistic studies. The long and thoughtful discussions of poetry done by the previous generations of scholars were completed prior to the beginning of comparative linguistic studies of the Tai language family, and recent reworkings of the older analyses have overlooked crucial facts because they have overlooked modern linguistics. This chapter will set out some of the basic findings of linguistic studies of Thai and the Tai family in order to cast some light on the oldest of the poetic classics, and particularly on *Lilit Phra Law*.

Attitudes Toward Language in Modern Thailand

The language that is known today as "Thai" is only one member of a large and widespread language family whose speakers live in an area extending on the west to Assam in India, on the south to Southern Thailand, on the east into Vietnam, and on the north into the southern provinces of China. In this area are people who speak some 300 or more dialects that are members of the language family known, in the manner of the early French scholars, as "Tai." The member of the family most widely know in the Western world, of course, is Thai, the official language of modern Thailand, which was known as Siam until 1932.

In modern Thailand it is the speech of the central plain of the country that is the prestigious dialect.[1] Commonly referred to as Central Thai, it is the native dialect of most areas in and around Bangkok. The educated form of this dialect is the speech that is taught in the schools throughout the country, and it is the language of the government and the public media. So important is this dialect that unless one can function well in it, many avenues of advancement in Thai life are closed.

While the speech of the capital city and the surrounding plain is the prestigious dialect, the dialects of the other areas of the country are held in lesser esteem. The attitudes are similar to those that motivate speakers of American English who denigrate the speech of those with different regional pronunciation patterns, except that the differences between the major regional dialects of Thailand tend to be more of a barrier to communication than are differences between the dialects of American English.

That the speech of the central plain is held in high regard is not surprising. The city of Bangkok has been a center of political power for 200 years, and the nearby city of Ayutthaya preceded that city as a seat of power for a period of approximately four centuries. For many generations of Thai speakers the source of power, and wealth, and learning has been located in the area in or near the present capital city. Although recent increases in international travel have changed the picture somewhat, most residents of Thailand still know little of the many Tai-speaking groups located elsewhere, with present day Laos the only real exception.

The frequent wars between the Tai kingdoms of the central plain and their neighbors have not been one sided, but the people of the region do tend to have the impression that they and their ancestors have long dominated the area, and recent history has supported this feeling. Bangkok has been the starting point for the water, land, and air routes by which first Christian missionaries and then technology, two of the more visible aspects of modern foreign presence in this part of the world, reached the up-country areas of Thailand and Laos.

There is a strong feeling among many of the Thai that the Lao, and the Northeastern Thai who speak Lao, are rather backward country cousins. The economic situation of those in up-country areas of Thailand is not as strong as is that of the residents of the central plain, and attitudes that have developed around the political and economic situation are reflected in attitudes about language as well. Many in Thailand consider the speech of the various other regions within Thailand, and of all of Laos as well, to be mispronunciations of the "correct" language of the central plain. They have come to see the dialect of the present capital city as the standard by which both the present and the past may be judged. As we shall see below, this attitude is not supported by the facts.

Historical Change and the Thai Language

It is generally agreed that the languages of the Tai family as we know them today are all related to a common parent language, known to linguists as Proto-Tai, and it is from this source that all of the varieties of Tai have developed (Gedney 1972: 423-437). Available evidence does not support the contention that the place of origin of the family is in central China, although this has long been the popular conception,[2] but points instead to the area near the border between present day North Vietnam and the southeastern part of China. As for the nature of the proto-language, it is agreed that a tone system was employed, although the phonetic nature of the tones is still very much a point of speculation. It is clear that there were three distinct pronunciations for those syllables having a vowel or sonorant as the final element, called open or "live" syllables in traditional Thai grammatical terms. Those syllables that ended in a stop consonant (*p*, *t*, *k*), known as closed or "dead" syllables in traditional Thai grammatical terms, had a

72

fourth pronunciation.[3] The three pronunciations for open syllables are known in the
comparative Tai literature by the letter
designations A, B, and C; the letter D is used
for the pronunciations of closed syllables.

This system of three pronunciations for
open syllables and one for closed syllables
lasted until at least the time of the invention of the Thai writing system, which is
attributed to King Ramkhamhaeng who ruled in
the city of Sukhothai toward the end of the
13th century, and is based on the script then
in use by the Khmer of present-day Cambodia.[4]
Similar scripts were devised for other members
of the language family, but this development
is independent of the history of the family in
general. Even those members for which no
written system was devised can be shown to
have undergone a process of development identical in its general outline to the one recon-
structed for the language of Siam.

In general, one finds that the words that
linguists place into the A category are written in modern Thai with no tone mark. Most of
the words placed in the B category are written
with the tone mark known as *máy ʔèek* 'first
tone mark', and most of those placed in the C
category are written with the *máy thoo* 'second
tone mark'. If one compares words from a
great many members of the family one finds
that there are very clear patterns of corre-
spondence in this matter. That is, those
words that can be grouped into the classes A,
B, and C in Siamese have large numbers of
corresponding words, called cognates, in linguistic terms, that can be grouped in similar
classes in the other languages. Words that
belong in the A category in Thai, for example,
will be found to belong in the A category of
Lao, as well as Lue, Shan, White Tai, and all
other members of the Tai family. Words in the
B category will also be found in the B category in other dialects, and the same is true for
C-category words.

There are occasional exceptions, but they are generally recent borrowings, or stem from other unusual circumstances, and the vast majority of words will fit into the pattern described here. Comparative studies clearly demonstrate the existence of a common parent language, from which all the modern dialects developed. No one modern dialect is older, or more pure, or more faithful in its likeness to that parent language than is any other. And, at least as far as the history of the language family is concerned, no one dialect is any more deserving of a place of prestige than is any other. Pronunciation differences do exist, of course, and the cognate words may not appear to the native speaker of either language under consideration to be at all similar. Why, the question will be asked, if these languages are so closely related, do they seem to be so different to the non-linguist? Here, in brief, is what must have happened to bring about the situation as we know it today.

At one point the members of the language family must have all had similar sound systems, that is, three distinctly different, and lexically significant, pronunciations for open syllables, and another one for closed syllables. Within each dialect, all A-category words must have been pronounced in one way, all B-category words in another, all C-category words in a third way, and all D-category words in a fourth way. The precise phonetic characteristics of the pronunciations used in any particular dialect may have differed from any other, but the pattern must have been the same throughout the family. In all probability the pronunciation systems did not make distinctions based on pitch height as the modern tone systems do, but the term "tone" is still generally used to refer to the ancient system, and I will now follow that usage here, as well.

Chart 1: Original Sound System

A	B	C	D
(None)	'	˅	-*p* -*t* -*k*

This ancient pattern is shown in chart 1. The original tone categories are designated by a letter across the top of the chart, and also with the traditional Siamese tone marks, placed within the boxes.

At some point, some time after the development of the writing system, the tones of all of the languages began to change, in a general phenomenon that affected the languages of other language families of Southeast Asia, both tonal and non-tonal, as well. The reason for the massive and wide-spread changes is not clear, but the fact that they did occur is not doubted by linguists familiar with the area.

In the Tai family, the system of three tones on open syllables split, and there came to be two or more tones in each of the categories designated A, B, and C. The split in tones on open syllables developed along lines determined by the phonetic nature of the initial consonant of the syllable. Most often this split was between the voiced and voiceless consonants. For example, while a particular dialect had one tone for the A category before the split, it came to have two tones in that category after the split, with one of the new tones found only on words that originally began with a voiceless consonant, and the other of the new tones found only on words that originally began with a voiced consonant. Chart 2 shows this type of tone split, with each of the categories again represented by letters and by the traditional Siamese tone marks.

While the split was most often based on the distinction between voiced and voiceless consonant sounds in the initial position of the syllable, it was sometimes based on other distinctions, the presence or absence of aspiration, for example. Sometimes a particular dialect made two distinctions in a single category, giving rise to not two, but to three tones in a category where only one had existed before the tone changes took place. In some dialects the split was made according to one distinction in one category and according to another distinction in other categories; this is the case for Siamese, as is shown in chart 4, which will be discussed below.

Chart 2: Proto-Tai Tones[5]

	A	B(')	C(ˇ)
Originally Voiceless Initials	1	3	5
Originally Voiced Initials	2	4	6

Closed syllables behaved somewhat differently in that the pronunciation changes they underwent were based not only on the nature of the sound of the initial consonant but also on the length of the vowel in the syllable. That is to say, syllables with a short vowel developed one set of tones, while those syllables with a long vowel developed another set of tones, as is shown in chart 3.

Chart 3: Proto-Tai Tone D

	Short	Long
Originally Voiceless Initials	7	9
Originally Voiced Initials	8	10

It is clear to linguists that the tone splits developed along the lines of phonetic differences in the initial consonants of the syllables. But the loss of distinction between sets of consonants, and subsequent mergings within the new tone systems, have hidden the original simplicity of the system from those not familiar with comparative linguistic studies. In some cases, for example, initial consonants that were originally voiced have lost their voicing, becoming phonetically identical to other voiceless consonants. As an illustration of this process, we might imagine two words in the proto-language with the original A tone *pha* and *ba*, differentiated only by initial consonant. We might imagine further that because of the tone splits in their dialect the words came to have different tones, which we can indicate by number as *pha*$_1$ and *ba*$_2$. As part of the changes in the dialect some voiced consonants lost their voicing, becoming phonetically identical to originally voiceless consonants. Thus, the initial *b-* became *ph-*, and the word *ba*$_2$ became *pha*$_2$ meaning that our hypothetical example words were now *pha*$_1$ and *pha*$_2$, differentiated only by tone, the details of their origin obscured from later generations of speakers of that dialect.

A process of coalescence also sometimes occurred with the tones, which also obscures the simplicity of the original system.[6] Sometimes some of the different tones that developed from the pronunciations of the old A, B, or C categories fell together, becoming phonetically the same. Thus, words that at one time were differentiated by the old tone categories (we might imagine a pair of words, *kii*_A and *kii*_B, for example) each came to have new, but still different tones, (which we can indicate by number, *kii*₄ and *kii*₅, for example). In time, however, some of the new tones came to be the same, and some words thus came to be homophones (the hypothetical *kii*₄ and *kii*₅ merged, for example, into *kii*₂), with the result that there were now two sources in the parent language for one pattern of initial consonant, plus vowel, plus tone in the modern dialect. This sort of merger across the old tone boundaries happened in modern Central Thai, or Siamese, as is shown in chart 4.

The letters across the top of chart 4 indicate the original tone categories of A, B, C, and D, with the last of the categories divided into two sections to reflect the differing behavior of closed syllables with short and long vowels. Along the side of the chart are the phonetic categories of the syllable-initial consonants that determined the tone splits in this particular dialect. As stated above, voiceless unaspirated sounds in the ancient language behaved differently in different categories; this is not uncommon. Within the boxes are letter designations representing the names most commonly used by linguists for the modern tones (M = mid tone; L = low tone; F = falling tone; R = rising tone; H = high tone).

	A	B(')	C(ʌ)	Ds	Dl
Voiceless friction sounds: *h*, *ph*, *hm*, etc.	R				
		L	F	L	L
Voiceless unaspirated sounds: *p*, *ʔ*, etc.	M				
Voiced sounds: *b*, *m*, etc.		F	H	H	F

There are two points to be made with the help of this chart that are of particular importance for the study of older Siamese poetry. The first is that there is no place in the pattern of development of Siamese for those words that are currently written with the tone marks known as *máy trìi* 'third tone mark', or *máy càttawaa* 'fourth tone mark'. Such words must be the product of changes that took place after the tone splits were completed, or recent borrowings, either from other members of the Tai language family or from unrelated languages.

These two tone marks, and the words written with them, have no role in *khlooŋ* or *râay* forms as they were developed by the ancient poets, or in *Lilit Phra Law*. And yet, it seems illogical to assume that the ancient poets would have invented a poetic system that employed some of the tones available to them, but not others. This absence of a part of the modern pronunciation system is a clear indication that the forms were conceived of, and the poem composed, prior to the time that the tone splits occurred, when the ancient and unambig-

79

uous system of three tones on open syllables was still in place.

As we shall see in the discussion of each of the poetic forms as used in *Lilit Phra Law*, we must conclude that the modern emphasis on the visual aspect of these ancient poetic forms, on whether the proper spelling is used, is an unrecognized modern response to changes in the spoken system that rendered ancient conceptions of poetry unworkable. Spelling could not have been an issue for the ancient poets who were working in a spoken system that did not have the overlaps of tone categories that exist in modern Thai, causing such a separation between spoken forms and their written representation.

The second point is that there are two sources in the ancient language for words that are pronounced in Siamese with what is known as the falling tone. That is, words from the B category that originally began with a voiced consonant, and words from the C category that originally began with a voiceless consonant, now have phonetically identical tones. Since other dialects of the family developed other patterns, comparisons of these words with their cognates in other dialects can establish for us quite definitely which of the two categories the words came form. This point of ambiguity in the modern tone system has been particularly important in giving rise to the idea that the ancient poets resorted to dis-torting words (the so-called *ʔèek thôot* 'in-correct first tone' and *thoo thôot* 'incorrect second tone' words) in order to meet the dictates of the form they were working in. This unfortunate misconception is the next major point that we must consider in our treatment of *Lilit Phra Law*, and it will be discussed in detail in the next section.

Finally, returning to the original point of discussion in this section, comparative analysis shows that the dialect of the central plain underwent a process of development identical in its general pattern to that of all other dialects of the language family. No one member of the Tai family of languages can be said to be older than any other, or more worthy of a position of prestige than any other. To judge one dialect by the patterns of another is inappropriate. It is equally inappropriate to judge the speech or poetic arts of one point in the history of the language family by the preferences or standards associated with another; and yet, this is exactly the situation that has developed in modern Thailand. Unaware that a dramatic change in language separates modern speech from the speech of the early poets, scholars have inadvertently made such inappropriate comparisons the basis of much of the current thinking about the oldest literary classics. The most glaring example is the idea that the ancient poets were reduced to purposeful distortion of words in order to follow the constraints of their own poetic forms. With the background material now covered, we are ready to take up this important point.

The Concept of *thôot* 'incorrect' Forms

Nearly all of the analytical material dealing with *Lilit Phra Law* has been written by speakers of Thai who were thoroughly familiar only with their own dialect, and had little awareness of the changes that have taken place in all members of the Tai family since the poem was composed. Because of basic misunderstandings about the linguistic facts, modern commentators have fallen into a regrettable, if understandable, pattern of erroneous interpretations, most notably in the concept of the *ʔèek thôot* 'incorrect first tone' words and *thoo thôot* 'incorrect second tone' words.

The *thôot* Concept and the Modern Falling Tone

The term ʔèek thôot is applied to a word
that in modern Thai is normally spelled with
the second tone mark but appears in older
works spelled with the first tone mark. The
term *thoo thôot* is applied in the opposite
situation. It refers to a word that is normally spelled in modern Thai with the first
tone mark but appears in older works spelled
with the second tone mark. These terms are
used in most published sources, although one
also encounters other labels, with some authors preferring the term *baŋkháp* 'required'.
Thus, a particular spelling referred to elsewhere as a *thoo thôot* 'incorrect second tone'
is generally called *baŋkháp thoo* 'required
second tone' in the Ministry of Education
text. One also finds other terms, such as
sǎmphàt baŋkháp 'required rhyme', used to
explain vowel lengths that differ from accepted modern usage.

Such seemingly anomalous words are to be
found in all the verse forms used in *Lilit
Phra Law* and are most frequently identified in
positions that call for a specific tone mark,
although they also appear in rhyme links that
connect *wák* of *râay*, which do not have a
specific required tone. Whatever the term
used to describe these words, the explanation
offered for the unusual spellings is that the
poets, anxious to use the tone mark required
by a particular position, or anxious to complete a required rhyme, but unable to come up
with a wording that gave the desired result,
purposely resorted to spelling a word in an
aberrant way. The glossary of the Ministry of
Education text identifies almost four dozen
different words that are said to be examples
of this purposeful misspelling and lists
almost 150 stanzas in which they appear.

The vast majority of the so-called *thôot*
words have the modern falling tone, which, as
has been explained, developed from two differ-

82

ent sources in the ancient tone chart: from B-column syllables that originally began with a voiced consonant, and from C-column syllables that originally began with a voiceless consonant. In modern Thai orthography the consonant symbols are divided into three categories: high, mid, and low. Consonant letters from the high category represent originally voiceless, aspirated sounds. Consonant letters from the mid category represent originally voiceless, non-aspirated sounds, and those from the low category represent originally voiced sounds. The combination of a high- or mid-category letter and the second tone mark indicates that the syllable in question is to be pronounced with the falling tone. Similarly, the combination of a low-category letter and the first tone mark also indicates that the syllable is to be pronounced with the falling tone. Because of duplication between the high-category and low-category initials in modern speech, one can represent many sounds in two different ways (although convention normally recognizes only one of the possible spellings as correct). It is this ambiguity that forms the basis for the entire concept of *thôot* words.

The word that appears most frequently as a *thoo thôot* is the word *thâa* 'wait' pronounced in modern Thai with the falling tone and spelled with a low-category consonant and the first tone mark (ท่า). The word appears in twenty-one stanzas in the Ministry of Education text in positions that are said to require a syllable spelled with the second tone mark. In such cases the word is spelled with a high-category consonant and the second tone mark (ถ้า). Comparison of this word with cognates in other dialects shows that it developed from the C column of the ancient tone chart. That is, the word was pronounced originally with an aspirated initial sound and the C tone and, therefore, really ought to be spelled as it is in the twenty-one stanzas noted in the Ministry of Education text. This means that the modern Thai spelling is a relatively recent development that is not historically correct.

Another example of a word thought to be purposefully misspelled is *lên* 'play' also pronounced in modern Thai with the falling tone and normally spelled with a low-category consonant and the first tone mark (เล่น). The word as it appears in twelve of the stanzas of the Ministry of Education text is spelled with a high-category consonant and the second tone mark (เหล้น), and in such cases the spelling is called a *thoo thôot*. Comparison of this word with its cognates in other dialects shows that the so-called *thôot* spelling is historically correct. Prior to the tone splits, the word must have begun with an aspirated sound, and the tone must have been that of the C category. Again, the modern Thai spelling is historically incorrect.

In the two cases cited above the problem is easily resolved by comparing the words in question with cognates from other dialects, which establishes the fact that the modern spelling is historically inaccurate and the spelling found in the text is actually correct. In most cases both spellings represent the modern falling tone, and the question is only over the correct source in the ancient system for the modern pronunciation.

Chart 5: Cognates for So-Called *'thôot'* Forms

Modern Form	Modern Spelling	Ancient Spelling	Source
1. *khwâm*	คว่ำ	ขว้ำ	Li p. 240
2. *khâa*	ฆ่า	ข้า	Li p. 192
3. *thâa*	ท่า	ถ้า	Li p. 120
4. *thâw*	เฒ่า	เถ้า	Li p. 102

Modern Form	Modern Spelling	Ancient Spelling	Source
5. *fân*	ฟั่น	ฝั้น	Li p. 77
6. *nâa*	น่า	หน้า	Li p. 113
7. *mân*	มั่น	หมั้น	Li p. 352
8. *yɔ̂ŋ*	ย่อง	หย้อง	Donaldson p. 262
9. *yâam*	ย่าม	หย้าม	Donaldson p. 257
10. *lôm*	ล่ม	หล้ม	Li p. 133[8]
11. *wâay*	ว่าย	หว้าย	Li p. 182
12. *yîam*	เยี่ยม	เหยี้ยม	Li p. 181
13. *lên*	เล่น	เหล้น	Li p. 137

For thirteen of the words identified in the glossary of the Ministry of Education text as *thôot* words, there are cognates that establish the historical accuracy of the supposedly incorrect spelling. These thirteen examples are given in chart 5. Provided for each is the modern spelling, the old spelling, and one source of information about cognates.

It must have been with words such as these that the *thôot* concept had its origin, and it is easy to see how the misunderstandings could have developed. The word *lên* 'play', for example, which now begins with a voiced consonant sound, must once have had a voiceless initial, as is indicated by the so-called *thôot* spelling (เหล้น), with the initial consonant cluster "หล-", *hl-. After the tone splits, and the coalescence of voiceless *hl- with the voiced *l-, the initial " ห " no longer had any phonetic value and served only as part of the orthographic system, similar to the now silent "k" in the English word "know."

Over many generations, as writing was passed from teacher to pupil in the traditional temple schools of Siam, the orthographically less complex spelling became preferred for some words. Why this happened for some words and not others is difficult to say, but it is probable that by the time dictionaries were being written many words had already come to be spelled in a way that was phonetically correct but that did not conform to historical fact. When speakers of modern Thai, familiar only with modern spellings, examined the older poems they assumed that the modern way of spelling words like *lên* was correct. In seeking for an explanation for the unfamiliar spellings they assumed that the older way, with its seemingly superfluous, silent initial was a curious device resorted to by poets of only limited skill who needed to obey the rules of the poetic form.

The greatest problem with the concept of the *thôot* words is that it has been expanded to explain situations that have nothing to do with the origins of the modern falling tone. While comparative analysis shows that the *thôot* concept is historically groundless, we can see that on the surface, at least, it is not an entirely implausible idea when applied to words with the modern falling tone. It appears that once the idea became accepted, however, it was used to explain away many other unrelated situations. The availability of any easy solution to complex problems probably hid the need for more thorough analysis and thus prevented much progress in the study of the ancient works. The remainder of this section will address briefly those situations that do not involve the origins of the modern falling tone, but to which the *thôot* concept has been applied in *Lilit Phra Law*.

The *thôot* Concept and Other Modern Tones

The *thôot* concept has been used to explain the differences in tone between the ancient and modern forms of the modern word *kĭi* 'how many; several', a difference that cannot have its basis in the merger of parts of the B and C columns. The accepted modern spelling of the word is written with the first tone mark and a mid-category consonant (กี่), and the tone is low, suggesting that the word comes not from the lower part of the B column, as with previous examples, but from the middle of that column. In the poem the word is spelled with the same consonant initial but with the second tone mark (กี้), and in four of the five cases it rhymes with *nĭi* 'this', which is also spelled with the second tone mark (นี้).

Cognates in other dialects show that the spelling found in the poem is correct. The word actually originates from the middle part of the C column and in modern Thai ought to have the falling tone instead of the low tone.[9] The modern form must be the result of a secondary change that took place after the tone splits, perhaps connected with the use of the word in unstressed position (Gedney 1964: 41). Whatever the source of the modern pronunciation might be, the poets knew what they were doing when they used the second tone mark. It is the modern dialect that has made the change.

In one case the *thôot* concept is used to explain what, at first glance, seems to be a spelling change in an A-column word. The word is *khláa* (คล้า), spelled with a low-category initial and the second tone mark, and said in the Ministry of Education text glossary to be a misspelling of *khlaa* (คลา) 'go; walk'. The word appears in *wák* 51 of stanza 144, in the expression:

yàa khláa kham kuu
neg. (?)   word I

Don't deviate(?) from my order.

The use of either *khlaa* or its supposed
misspelling *khláa* is not satisfactory. The
sense of the order is clear from context, but
the word used is only distantly connected with
the meaning of the passage. The *samùt khɔ̀y*
text number 2 gives another reading, however,
in which *khláa* is replaced by *khlɛ́ɛw*, (แคล้ว),
also spelled with a low-category initial and
the second tone mark. This commonly used Thai
word better fits the sense of the passage,
because one of its meanings is to "escape" or
"avoid," giving a reading something like
"Don't try to avoid my orders," which is
semantically acceptable and does not depend on
any forced spellings.

The *thôot* Concept and Vowel Length

In two cases, a change in vowel length
has been explained away by saying the poets
altered a word in order to create an appropriate rhyme. One of the words is *khâaw* 'rice',
which in both spoken and written modern Thai
has the long vowel *aa*, and is spelled with the
second tone mark and a high-category consonant
(ข้าว). The word also appears in the poem
spelled with the same tone mark and initial
consonant, so there is no confusion about the
proper tone, or about the place of origin in
the tone chart. In five cases noted in the
Ministry of Education text glossary, however,
the word is spelled with a short vowel (เข้า).
Comparison of the word with its cognates in
other dialects shows that the short vowel is
historically correct and the word in modern
Thai is the product of secondary vowel lengthening (Li 1977: 207,213), which must have
taken place after the poem was composed. In
each case the word rhymes with the word

"lord," which is pronounced *câaw* in modern Thai, with a long vowel even though its normal spelling indicates a short vowel (เจ้า). The modern form of this word is also a product of secondary vowel lengthening although the commonly accepted modern spelling does not reflect this fact. Curiously, one finds in the *Phôtcanaanúkrom chabàp râatchabandìt-sathǎan* [Dictionary of the Royal Institute] an alternate long-vowel spelling, but it is labeled as an ancient and archaic form (1983: 225); this must be the reverse of the actual situation.

The second case of change in vowel length noted in the Ministry of Education text is the word *yâw* 'home' spelled and pronounced in modern Thai with a short vowel, and spelled with the second tone mark and a high-category initial in a consonant cluster (เหย้า). The word appears in the poem spelled with the same initial and tone mark, but the glossary notes five cases in which it is spelled with a long vowel (หย้าว) and rhymes with the word *thâaw*, a title of noble or royal rank. The word appears in other dialects with a long vowel (Li 1977: 181), which means the spelling found in the poem is historically correct. In this case, the vowel has been shortened in modern Thai, perhaps because modern speakers almost always use the word in the weak stress posi-tion of the compound *yâw rᴻan* 'home'.[10]

The *thôot* Concept and Manuscript Variation

Following the concept of the *thôot* words, some copiers and editors have disregarded variations in the manuscripts and selected aberrant spellings even when the commonly accepted and historically accurate spellings are to be found in the manuscripts. The word *lâw* 'liquor' is pronounced in modern Thai with a short vowel and falling tone. Unlike the word *lên* 'play', *lâw* has retained its histori-cally accurate spelling, with the second tone

mark and an initial (and, in modern Thai,
silent) *h-, which is a high-category consonant (เหล้า). This spelling indicates that
the word comes from the upper part of the
ancient C column, which is confirmed by dialect comparisons (Li 1977: 290).

Stanza 320 of the Ministry of Education
text, however, and the same stanza from the
Royal Library edition (1926: 87), show the
word spelled with the first tone mark and an
initial voiced *l* (เล้า), indicating that it
comes from the lower section of the B column.
It appears as the fourth syllable of the first
wâk of a *khlooŋ 2* stanza, a position that
usually is filled with a B-column word. This
does indeed seem to be an *ʔèek thôot*. However, six of the eleven manuscript copies have
the word spelled in the historically correct
manner, which is reproduced in one printed
edition (Worawet 1974: 1,230).

As later comments on the *khlooŋ 2* forms
will show, it is actually not uncommon to find
a C-column word in this position. It is,
therefore, quite possible that the poet did
use a C-column word here, despite what modern
formulations of the "rules" might say, and
that in the preparation of both the Ministry
of Education and the Royal Library editions
the normally accepted spelling was ignored in
favor of its opposite. In effect, an *ʔèek
thôot* was created by a modern editor.

> *khlûan phon daa dooy dùan*
> move troops numerous hastily
>
> *thûan thúk mùu thúk mùat*
> complete every section every group
>
> (The signals) moved the numerous
> troops hastily, all sections and
> divisions.

A similar but somewhat more complex set of circumstances probably brought about the creation of another modern *ʔèek thôot*. Stanza 228 of the Ministry of Education text of the poem uses the word *thûan* (ห้วน) 'complete' and spells it with the first tone mark and a low-category consonant. Comparison with other dialects, however, shows that the word actually developed from the upper part of the C column, and the modern spelling reflecting that origin is correct (Li 1977: 119). The problem does not lie with *thûan* but with the word with which it is said to rhyme. The two *wák* of *râay* involved are given below; they are the third and fourth of the stanza.

This stanza describes the activities of the army raised by Phra Law as it begins its procession out of his city. The first two *wák* of the stanza say that signals given with flags were used to direct the march. The *wák* quoted here describe the way the troops moved in response to the signals, and the reading says that each unit moved hastily. It is thought that *thûan* was purposely misspelled by the ancient poets who used the first tone mark in order to create a rhyme with *dûan* 'urgent', commonly spelled with the first tone mark. In fact, all of the *samùt khɔy* that contain these *wák*, as well as the Royal Library edition (1926: 62) which is the supposed source for the Ministry of Education text, spell *thûan* with the second tone mark. The Ministry of Education text spelling of the word is an *ʔèek thôot* created by a modern editor to make the two words rhyme.

The alteration should have gone in the opposite direction; instead of changing the spelling of *thûan* the editors should have sought a replacement for *dûan*, one with the second tone mark. An examination of the fourteen legible *samùt khɔy* shows that the expression *dooy dûan* 'hastily' is a modern invention that does not appear in any of the manuscripts. In ten of the manuscripts one finds the expression *dooy khabuan*, which provides for a semantically correct reading of 'in procession' or 'in ranks' or the like, but *khabuan* (ขบวน) is spelled with no tone mark, and this would make for a different but still incorrect rhyme. Four other manuscript copies have the expression *dooy phayûu*, which is both semantically and structurally appropriate. The word *phayûu* (พยู่ห์) is of Indic origin and like *khabuan* is used in Thai to refer to groups of troops, or armies. It is spelled in Thai with the first tone mark meaning that it is treated as a B-column word and thus forms an appropriate rhyme link with *mûu* (หมู่). The wording makes for a reading of something like, "(The flag signals) moved the many troops in formation." In all probability, the availability of a ready solution to the problem in the form of the *thôot* concept has prevented modern scholars from pursuing an investigation along these lines.

The *thôot* Concept and Archaic Words

In one case the *thôot* concept has been used to explain a word that, it seems, was not recognized. The word *sûay* appears in the text three times spelled with the second tone mark and a high-category consonant (สร้วย). In each case the word rhymes with *dûay* (ด้วย), also spelled with the second tone mark, and the expression in which the word appears is *nâa sûay*. The Ministry of Education text glossary says that *sûay* is a purposeful misspelling of *sǔay* (สวย) 'pretty', and that the expression is the equivalent of *nâa sǔay* 'pretty face', which seems semantically acceptable. However, White Tai uses a word that appears to be a cognate of *sûay*, from the upper part of the C column. The word is defined by Donaldson (1970: 333) as "thin, tapering" and an example expression given is *nâa sûay* 'oval shaped face'. This word is not used in modern Thai and must have fallen out of use in the dialects spoken in the area before dictionaries

92

were written and so evidently has not been recognized by modern scholars. The spelling used in all of the published editions, and repeated above, includes an unpronounced consonant letter that suggests a pronunciation of *srOay*, as though the word had actually been borrowed from Khmer. This spelling may be part of the confusion. Significantly, it does not appear in any of the manuscript copies of the poem and so must be a recent invention.

The idea that the ancient poets were somehow less constrained by communicative conventions seems to be part of the reasoning behind Phrayaa Uppakit's opinion regarding the apparently aberrant spellings of the words *tháŋ* (ทั้ง) 'all' and *tàaŋ* (ต่าง) 'differ' that are found in the poem. Both words appear in rhyme positions that require the use of syllables spelled with no tone mark, although in modern Thai *tháŋ* is spelled with the second tone mark and *tàaŋ* is spelled with the first tone mark. In order to account for these words Phrayaa Uppakit suggests that the tones were "not yet stabilized" at the time the poem was written (1968: 385). In fact the spelling *thaŋ* (ทง), which suggests an origin in the A column is historically correct. It is modern Thai that has an unusual pronunciation, most likely due to stress in emphatic expressions (Li 1977: 104).

The word *tàaŋ* 'differ' is normally spelled with the first tone mark, suggesting that it originated in the B column, and other Tai dialects have cognates for this word that show the historical accuracy of the spelling. However, White Tai has a different word that originated from the A column, *tàaŋ* 'substitute for' (Donaldson 1970: 342). Given below are the two lines from *Lilit Phra Law* in which *tàaŋ* appears in a position requiring an A-tone word. The first example is the second line of stanza 257, which is a stanza of *khlooŋ 4*.

chom   mâannaaŋ wǎŋ tàaŋ   mâan   nɔ́ɔŋ
admire flower   wish substitute   curtain sib.

> He admired the Lady's Curtain (a
> kind of flower), but wished instead
> to see the curtain of his lady.

This line is built on a play on words
involving the names of a flower, the sight of
which is said to call to mind the absent
lover. The next example, also the second line
of a *khlooŋ 4* stanza, is from stanza 271.

wâay   yùu salɔ̌ɔn taaŋ   dɔ̀ɔkmáay
salute stay ample substitute   flower

> They raised their hands in salute
> like the flowers sending out blos-
> soms.

In both cases it is clear that the meaning is not the common meaning for *tàaŋ*, which
is 'differ'. In fact, the modern Thai form
tàaŋ can also mean something like "to substitute for", and the presence of the A-column
word in White Tai suggests an explanation. At
an earlier stage the language may have had two
words, one from the A column and one from the
B column, with two different meanings, that
have fallen together in modern Thai but have
remained distinct in other dialects. Thus, we
can assume that the poets were not changing
the spelling of a word in order to fit the
poetic convention. They were using a different word that has not survived in modern Thai.

The *thôot* Concept and Speech Particles

The *thôot* concept is also used to explain
spellings for which no explanation is really
required. There are nine speech particles
identified in the Ministry of Education text

glossary as *thoo thôot* words. They are listed below, spelled as they appear in the published editions of the poem, with the pronunciation indicated by that spelling shown in phonetic transcription.

เท้อญ (*thə́ən*) รื้อ (*rɯ́ɯ*) ร้า (*ráa*)

เย้อ (*yə́ə*) แล่ (*lɛ̂ɛ*) แล้ (*lɛ́ɛ*)

หน้อย (*nɔ́ɔy*) หน้อ (*nɔ́ɔ*) เล้ย (*lə́əy*)

It is not necessary, however, to say that the poets were misspelling words in order for us to understand these forms. Particles in all of the dialects of the family show great variation in speech, and modern attempts to represent the particles of Thai orthographically show similar variation from author to author. One finds different vowel lengths, different tone marks and different consonant symbols used in modern writing in attempts to represent all of the sounds used as particles. There is every reason to believe that the ancient language used similarly varied particle forms also, and there is no reason to suppose that any one spelling is more correct than any other.

The *thôot* Concept and Speech Variation

The *thôot* concept is also used to explain other spellings that, rather than being errors, are probably reflections of normal phonological patterns of the language. In stanza 201 the name *naaraay* (นารายณ์), a name for the god Vishnu, is spelled such that the first syllable has a short vowel, giving the pronunciation *naraay* (นรายณ์). The Ministry of Education text glossary says that the spelling was altered to conform with the poetic requirement. Actually, the spelling also conforms to normal modern speech. The first syllables of disyllabic words are frequently given reduced stress and have short-

95

ened vowels. The Ministry of Education text spelling reflects a normal pronunciation, a reduction in the length of the vowel that probably would have taken place in performance whether the written representation of the text indicates that reduction or not. In fact, in half of the old manuscripts one finds the short-vowel spelling, while in the other half one finds the long-vowel spelling preferred by modern writers.

CONCLUSIONS: LINGUISTIC BACKGROUND

Modern linguistic studies of Central Thai and the Tai language family show that much of the analysis that has been done of ancient Thai poetic forms in general, and of *Lilit Phra Law* in particular, has been based on misconceptions. Inappropriate comparisons have led to incorrect conclusions, and while it is easy to see how part of the situation came about, the mistakes must be corrected before real progress can be made in the study of Thai poetic arts.

This discussion of the *thôot* concept has not covered all of the words identified by modern commentators as purposeful misspellings, and there are a few that are puzzling, but they are too few in number to hide the obvious conclusion. The entire *thôot* concept, the idea that the authors of *Lilit Phra Law* were reduced to altering their speech or writing, or both, in order to conform to poetic constraints, has absolutely no basis in fact.

Much of the modern dissatisfaction with the ancient poetic works concerns these seem- ingly anomalous words, and they serve as justification for those who wish to praise modern work and fault the older poets for supposed carelessness or lack of discipline. At first glance the *thôot* concept does seem reasonable enough, at least when one considers only words with the modern falling tone. But a close examination of the facts shows that the idea is completely groundless and must be abandoned, along with any idea that the ancient poets were not every bit as skillful as those of the present day.

NOTES

1. There is great variation within the central plain region, of course, and the idea of a "standard" speech is as much of a misconception in Thailand as it is an any country of the world. The present discussion greatly simplifies some points that would be more significant and would require more detailed attention in other contexts.

2. For a thorough and convincing refutation of the popular theory that the Tai peoples had their origin in the Nan-chao kingdom of China, see Backus (1981: 46-52).

3. Syllables that end in a short vowel and final glottal stop are the result of secondary changes in modern Thai. For additional information on the point, see Li (1977:207, 213).

4. For a discussion of the historical development of the Thai writing system, see Brown (1979:107-115).

5. Charts 2, 3, and 4 are adapted from Gedney (1972), pages 429, 431, and 433, respectively.

6. For an indication of the complexity of this point, see Brown (1975).

7. A chart of this type can be constructed to represent the tone system of each of the dialects of the family. Students of Thai linguistics in Thailand can often be heard to refer to a chart of this type as "Gedney's boxes," a clear acknowledgement of the influ-

ence of Professor William J. Gedney on the
field.

8. Originally a voiced initial and a C tone.

9. See Li (1977:34), for information on cognates. Note also the modern Thai expression
mûa kîi níi 'just a moment ago', in which the
historically correct pronunciation is retained.

10. Personal communication, Professor William
J. Gedney.

Chapter 4

THE *khlooŋ 4* STANZAS OF *LILIT PHRA LAW*

In this chapter, as in the others that follow, we will be guided by many of the points raised by Phrayaa Uppakit. These points, however, will be regarded not as "rules" that must be followed, but as general patterns noted in the ancient poetry by modern authors attempting to understand archaic forms. As we shall see, much of what has been noted has been misunderstood, and there is also much of significance that has not yet been noted. Studying each of the forms of poetry individually will help to clarify a number of the seemingly troublesome points, and it will also help to show how closely related the forms found in the poem actually are. We will, in fact, be led to the conclusion that the different forms are actually only slightly different manifestations of the same poetic phenomenon, but first we must look at each stanza type separately. In this chapter we will deal only with *khlooŋ 4*, and in later chapters will take up the *râay* form, followed by *khlooŋ 2*, and *khlooŋ 3*, turning finally to the *lílít* compositional style.

The *khlooŋ 4* Stanza

The diagram of the *khlooŋ 4* variety known as *sùphâap* is given in diagram 1. It is accompanied by diagram 2, which shows the structure of the variety known as *khlooŋ 4 dân*. A comparison between these two forms is essential since much of the confusion about the poem, and criticism of its author or authors, centers on the supposed mixing of *sùphâap* and *dân* patterns, which in work of recent periods were not used together. We must first see to what extent, if at all, these forms are mixed in *Lilit Phra Law*. Discussion will cover the differences between the two types of verse and will compare the stanzas of *Lilit Phra Law* to

99

the two idealized stanza forms shown in the diagrams.

Diagram 1: *khlooŋ 4 sùphâap*

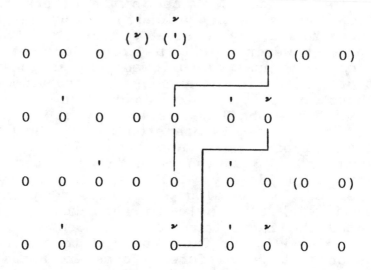

Diagram 2: *khlooŋ 4 dân*

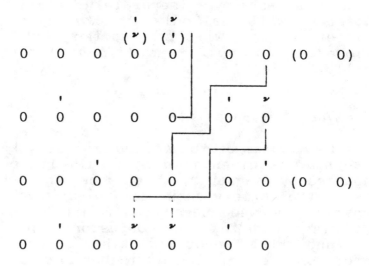

According to the textbook descriptions the two types of *khlooŋ* differ in four respects:

1)   The length of the final line of the stanza

2) The use of *kham sɜy*
3) Tone placement
4) Rhyme pattern

The final line of a stanza of *khlooŋ 4 sùphâap* is said to require nine syllables, divided into two *wâk*, the first with five syllables and the second with four. The final line of a stanza of *khlooŋ 4 dân*, on the other hand, is said to allow only seven syllables, divided into two *wâk*, the first with five syllables and the second with two.

Textbook formulations allow for the use of extra syllables, known as *kham sɜy*,[1] following the first and third lines of the stanza of both the *sùphâap* and *dân* varieties, but forbid their use following the second or fourth lines. The textbooks offer no explanation for this supposed rule, but an examination of the stanzas of *Lilit Phra Law* will show that there is strong motivation for avoiding the use of *kham sɜy* at the end of the second line of this stanza type, at least in so far as the *sùphâap* stanza is concerned.

Tone placement in the first three lines of the stanza is the same in both varieties of *khlooŋ 4*. It is in the last line of the stanza that the forms are said to differ. The textbook formulations of the *sùphâap* variety call for syllables spelled with the first tone mark in the second and sixth positions and for syllables spelled with the second tone mark in the fifth and seventh positions. Formulations of the *dân* variety differ in calling for syllables with the second tone mark in the fourth and fifth positions while leaving the seventh position without a required tone mark.

Rhyme placements differ somewhat more noticeably. The *khlooŋ 4 sùphâap* stanza links the first, second, and third lines together in one rhyme pattern, and links the second and fourth lines together in another, as is indicated in the diagram. The *khlooŋ 4 dân* stanza

101

does not link more than two lines together with rhyme, unlike the *sùphâap* variety with its three-position rhyme link. There are also differences in the manner in which stanzas of the two varieties are linked together by rhymes. The textbook formulations require that stanzas of *khlooŋ 4 sùphâap* be joined by a rhyme link between the last syllable of the stanza and the first, second, or third syllable of the first line of the following stanza, although as the following discussion will show I will have to disagree strongly with the textbooks on this point. Stanzas of *khlooŋ 4 dân* are said to be linked by a rhyme between the final syllable of the stanza and the fifth syllable of the second line of the following one.

These modern rules for the composition of *khlooŋ 4 sùphâap* and *khlooŋ 4 dân* are those used by various authors who attempt to categorize the forms used in *Lilit Phra Law*. Each of the four "rules" is discussed below in light of a stanza-by-stanza examination of the poem itself.

1) Length of the final *wâk* of the stanza
A careful examination of the stanzas of *khlooŋ 4* in *Lilit Phra Law* shows that each stanza has the number of syllables characteristic of the *sùphâap* variety. In all of the 294 stanzas of *khlooŋ 4* in the poem, the final line has at least nine syllables, with the expected division into two *wâk*. None of the published editions of the text, or commentaries on it, indicate the existence in any of the *samùt khɔ̀y* copies of stanzas in which the final line has fewer than the nine syllables that, the textbooks all state, are required in *khlooŋ 4 sùphâap*. Also, a thorough check of the manuscripts held in the National Library failed to discover any shorter than normal lines. It is possible that there are some extant manuscript copies that are not in the National Library collection, but we can be sure that a shorter than expected final line,

if one existed, would be so conspicuous that it would have been noted by one of the scholars who have studied the poem, and brought to the attention of the scholarly community. Thus, there is no evidence, on this point at least, to support the argument that *Lilit Phra Law* is anything but well-formed and carefully worked out *sùphâap* poetry.

There are many stanzas in which some *wâk* have more rather than fewer than the expected number of syllables, in the strict linguistic sense, and this may be a cause of confusion for some. An example is given below.

khân càak sŏŋ sadèt   nay ʔàat thǎy
rise from bath go   in   bed royal

... got out of the bath and went into the bedroom.

The passage quoted here is the second line of stanza 298. Although there are six syllables in the first *wâk*, they may easily be read as five, simply by giving the syllable *sa* in the word *sadèt* light stress and reduced duration.[2] It has been noted elsewhere (Bidyalankarana 1926: 126; Compton 1977: 30) that modern performers working with poetic forms may shorten lines in this way to obtain the appropriate number of syllables for the line. There is no reason to believe that this was not the case in ancient poetry as well, especially if one assumes that *Lilit Phra Law* was intended to be performed orally. Thus, the *wâk* in question has six syllables on paper, but only five syllables would be given full stress in normal speech or, it is reasonable to assume, in normal poetic performance. Extra syllables that can be disposed of in this way are common in stanzas of *khlooŋ*, but they are even more common in passages of *râay*, and so this point will be addressed in detail below, in the discussion of that form.

103

2) The use of *kham sɜy*

    According to the textbook descriptions of *Lilit Phra Law* poets are free to add extra syllables, called *kham sɜy*, to specific lines in the stanza in both *khlooŋ 4 sùphâap* and in *khlooŋ 4 dân*. The syllables, it is said, may be added to the first and third lines, and if they are to be added to a line, there must be two of them. In *Lilit Phra Law* the poets exercise this option a great deal. In many cases the syllables are vocatives or are particles that serve to define the mood of the speaker. In some cases they are independent lexical items that serve to complete the meaning of the line, but often they are syntactically unnecessary.

    In the poem as it is available to us today, *kham sɜy* have been added to the first line of the *khlooŋ 4* stanza in 123 (42%) of the 294 stanzas. A total of 273 (93%) of the stanzas have *kham sɜy* at the end of line three. Ten stanzas (not quite 4%) have *kham sɜy* at the end of the final line of the stanza, although the textbooks all agree that their use at this point in the stanza is not permissible. It is only in the second line of the stanza that one finds no *kham sɜy* used at all.

    Judging from the number of cases in which *kham sɜy* are used in the third line of the stanza it might be best to rephrase the standard "rule" and say that the poet had the option of omitting the *kham sɜy* at the end of the first and third lines, and of adding them to the final line if so desired. Also, it should be noted that addition of *kham sɜy* to line 2 would cause *wâk* 4 to become structurally identical to *wâk* 8. While this would have no detrimental effect for a primarily visual form, it would create an ambiguity in a primarily auditory form and so would most likely be avoided. More will be said of this point below in the discussion of the *khlooŋ 4* stanza as an auditory phenomenon.

3) Tone placement

Tone placement in the stanzas of *khlooŋ 4*
found in *Lilit Phra Law* follows the textbook
description of the *sùphâap* variety, but a
close examination of the stanzas shows that
there is a more complex pattern than has been
noted previously, one that involves substitutes for syllables spelled with the first
tone mark. In is clear that the poets were
concerned with tone placement in the positions
noted by the textbook authors. Those positions that are said to call for a syllable
spelled with the second tone mark do indeed
have such a syllable in all the *khlooŋ 4*
stanzas in the poem. Also, those positions
that are said to require a syllable spelled
with the first tone mark do have either such a
syllable, or a closed syllable (that is, one
ending with a stop consonant), which is recognized in the textbooks as an appropriate
substitute.[3]

The pattern that has not been noted
previously is that this substitution occurs
significantly less frequently at the structural boundaries of the stanza. Positions in the
middle of a *wák*, in other words, frequently
are filled with a closed syllable instead of
one with the first tone mark, while positions
that appear near the *wák* or *bàat* boundary are
filled by substitute syllables far less frequently, and when substitutions do occur near
a boundary, there is a clear preference for
long-vowel closed syllables. I will discuss
each *wák* in the stanza with this point in
mind.

The textbook descriptions of the first
wák call for the last two positions of the *wák*
to be filled with one syllable spelled with
the first tone mark and one spelled with the
second tone mark, and all of the stanzas of
the poem follow this pattern. The totals for
wák 1 also support the textbook contention
that the positions of the syllables with the
first and second tone marks in this *wák* may be

reversed. In sixty-one (21%) of the *khlooŋ 4* stanzas, a syllable with the second tone mark appears as the fourth syllable of the *wák*, and one with either the first tone mark or with a stop consonant in final position appears as the fifth syllable. There are no stanzas in the poem in which one or the other of these positions does not have a syllable of the expected type.

Two example lines are given below. In the first, which is line one of stanza 290, the fourth syllable, *thâw* (เท่า), is spelled with the first tone mark, and the fifth syllable, *núa* (เนื้อ), is spelled with the second tone mark.

> *rɔ́ɔy chúu rʉʉ thâw núa mía ton*
> 100 lover neg. equal flesh wife self

> A hundred lovers cannot equal one's own
>   wife.

The second example is line one of stanza 22. Here the fourth syllable, *tháaw* (ท้าว), is spelled with the second tone mark, and the fifth syllable, *thûa* (ทั่ว), is spelled with the first tone mark. This line is thus an example of the optional reversal of the primary pattern.

> *lâw lʉʉ chǒom tháaw thûa mʉaŋ sɔ́ɔŋ*
> tell fame figure title all city Song

> The fame of the regal bearing of the
> king [that is, Phra Law] spread
> throughout the city of Song.

Syllables that are spelled with the first tone mark are used in the appropriate position in the first *wák* of 156 (53%) of the *khlooŋ 4* stanzas. Another 118 (40%) of the stanzas

106

have a closed syllable with a long vowel,
while only twenty (slightly less than 7%) of
the stanzas have a closed syllable with a
short vowel. All of the *khloon 4* stanzas of
the poem follow the expected pattern.

The third *wâk*, in which the *sùphâap* form
is said to require that the second syllable be
one with the first tone mark, does in fact
comply with the stated rule in every stanza.
Syllables with the first tone mark appear a
bit more often (54% of the stanzas) than do
closed syllables, which may substitute for
them. When a substitution is made, closed
syllables with a long vowel appear somewhat
more often (26% of the stanzas) than those
with a short vowel (17% of the stanzas). The
examples below illustrate each situation. The
first example is line two of stanza 141 and
thus contains both the third and fourth *wâk* of
that stanza. The second syllable of the line,
and therefore the second syllable of the third
wâk, is the word *pùu* (ปู่), which is spelled
with the first tone mark.

> *thăam pùu   pen chănday   dàn níi*
> ask   title   be how   like this
>
> ... to ask him [that is, Saming
> phray] why it is this way.

In the next example, which is line two of
stanza 36, the second syllable is the word
prìap (เปรียบ), a closed syllable with a diphthong as the vowel. In the Thai system a
diphthong is by definition considered a long
vowel, at least in so far as determining the
position in the tone chart is concerned.

> *bɔ̀   prìap   sɔ̆ɔn kasàttrii   phîinɔ́ɔn*
> neg. compare two   lady   siblings
>
> (None) could equal the two royal sisters.

The third example is line two of stanza 60, in which the second syllable is closed and has a short vowel.

mɔ̌ɔ   càk   ʔaw ʔanday   rêŋ   hây
doctor will take which   hurry give

Hurry and get the doctor whatever he
    wants.

Syllables with nasal finals appear in *wâk* number 3 in a total of nine (3%) of the *khlooŋ 4* stanzas in the position said to require a syllable with the first tone mark. The number is, of course, quite small, but there are enough cases to suggest that it may have been a purposeful substitution and not simply the result of recent corruptions of the text. The syllables that appear in such positions in *Lilit Phra Law* include all three of the Thai nasal sounds, *m*, *n*, and *ŋ*, in the various spellings that the Thai system uses to represent them. The example given below is line two of stanza 494 and therefore contains the third and fourth *wâk* of that stanza. The second syllable of the line as it appears in the manuscripts is *baŋ* (บ้ง), which ends with the nasal *ŋ*.

sɔ̌ɔŋ baŋkhom khawróp   kràap-wâay
two   attend respect   prostrate

The two attended [Phra Law], pros-
    trating themselves to show
their respect.

The textbook descriptions of *wâk* number 4 call for only two syllables, the first one having the first tone mark, or its equivalent, and the second having the second tone mark. In this position of the stanza as it appears

108

throughout the poem, there is a predominance of syllables that are spelled with the first tone mark over those that may be used as substitutes. In 195 (66%) of the stanzas the first syllable of the *wák* is one written with the first tone mark. In seventy-five (26%) of the stanzas the syllable in this position is a closed syllable with a long vowel, and in only twenty-four (8%) of the stanzas does the syllable have a short vowel and stop final. There are no cases in which a syllable with a nasal final substitutes for one with the first tone mark, and there are no cases in which the tone mark requirement is ignored entirely. All 294 of the stanzas have a syllable with the second tone mark in the second position.

The three examples quoted above have been given in full so that they may serve as illustrations of tone placement in *wák* 3 and also in *wák* 4. The lines from stanzas 141, 36, and 60 each end in two syllables of which the first is spelled with the first tone mark, *dàŋ* (ดั่ง), *phîi* (พี่), and *rêŋ* (เร่ง), respectively. The second syllable of each of the *wák*, *níi* (นี้), *nɔ́ɔŋ* (น้อง), and *hây* (ให้), respectively, is written with the second tone mark. In the line from stanza 494 the second last syllable, *krâap* (กราบ), has a long vowel and a stop consonant in syllable-final position, and the last syllable, *wâay*[4] (ไหว้), is spelled with the second tone mark.

Unlike the final position of the first *wák* of the stanza, there are no instances of a reversal of position in the fourth *wák*. In all probability the fact that the tone placements are not reversed, like the absence of *kham sɔ̌y* at this point, has to do with the need to avoid structural ambiguity in the stanza. The frequency of a substitute for first-tone syllables is probably constrained by the same need, as well. The point will be raised again below in the discussion of the stanza as an auditory phenomenon.

The fifth *wâk* is said to require a syllable with the first tone mark as the third of
the required five syllables. Of the 294
stanzas, 154 (52%) do have a syllable spelled
with the first tone mark. Another fifty-two
(18%) of the stanzas have a closed syllable
with a long vowel in this position. A total
of seventy-two (24%) of the stanzas have a
closed syllable with a short vowel, and sixteen (5%) have a syllable with a nasal final.
The example given below is line three of
stanza 341 and therefore contains the fifth
and sixth *wâk* of the stanza. The third syllable of the line, *yùu* (อยู่), is spelled with
the first tone mark.

sadèt-maa yùu ʔaasăy sŭan   râat (níi naa)
come   stay reside garden   king this pt.

    ...(Phra Law) has come to stay in
      this royal garden.

The next example is from stanza 297. In
it the third syllable of *wâk* five is *ra* (ระ),
which ends in a short vowel and substitutes
for a syllable with the first tone mark.

hàrúthay rathót thon   thúk yày   (lŭaŋ naa)
heart   sad   bear   pain large   great pt.

    His heart was saddened; he bore a
      great distress.

The textbook descriptions state that *wâk*
6 requires a syllable with the first tone mark
in the second of its two required positions.
In 189 (64%) of the stanzas the syllable in
this position is spelled with the first tone
mark. In 101 (34%) of the stanzas a closed
syllable with a long vowel appears in this
position, and only four (slightly more than
1%) of the stanzas have a closed syllable with

a short vowel. No syllables with a nasal final appear in this position.

The examples given above from stanzas 341 and 297 contain the entire third line of those stanzas and so will serve as examples for both the fifth and sixth *wák* of the stanza. In both cases two *kham sɔ̀y* appear at the end of the line. Thus, in each case the second syllable of *wák* six is the third syllable from the end of the line. In stanza 341 the sylla-ble is *râat* (ราช), which is closed and has a long vowel, and in stanza 297 the syllable is *yày* (ใหญ่), spelled with the first tone mark.

The seventh *wák* is said to require a syllable with the first tone mark in the second position and one with the second tone mark in the fifth position. In 163 (55%) of the stanzas, the second syllable does have the first tone mark. In sixty-one (21%) of the stanzas a closed syllable with a long vowel appears in this position, and in an equal number of stanzas the syllable is closed, but with a short vowel. In ten (3%) of the stan-zas the syllable in this position ends with a nasal. The fifth syllable in the line in all 294 of the stanzas is one that is written with the second tone mark. The example below, from stanza 269, is the fourth line of the stanza, and so it contains both the seventh and eighth *wák*. The second syllable of the line, and also of the seventh *wák*, is *sìi* (สี่), which is spelled with the first tone mark, and the fifth syllable is *câaw* (เจ้า), which is spelled with the second tone mark.

sǎam sìi wan phrácâaw   cɯ̀ŋ hây phon mɯa
three four day lord   then let troop return

    (Wait) a few days before sending the
        troops back.

The next example is the fourth line of

111

stanza number 268. The second syllable of *wák*
seven as it appears in the text is *kham* (คำ),
which ends with a nasal consonant sound, and
the fifth syllable is *tháaw* (ท้าว), which is
written with the second tone mark.

kuu khamnuŋ-thйŋ tháaw phйan tháy pheeŋ thɔɔŋ
I   think of   title PN   title PN   gold

    I think of the two precious prin-
        cesses, Phuan and Phaeng.

    In *wák* 8, the final one of the stanza,
the textbooks call for four syllables, the
first one with the first tone mark or an
appropriate substitute, and the second one
with the second tone mark. In 209 (71%) of
the stanzas the first syllable does have the
first tone mark.[5] In another seventy-six
(26%) of the stanzas the first position is
filled with a closed syllable with a long
vowel, and in nine (3%) of the stanzas it is
filled with a closed syllable with a short
vowel. In all 294 of the stanzas the second
syllable of the *wák* is one written with the
second tone mark. The examples above also
illustrate tone placement in *wák* eight of the
khlooŋ 4 stanza. In each case the first syllable of the *wák*, *cùŋ* (จึ่ง), and *phйan* (เพื่อน),
respectively, is one spelled with the first
tone mark. In each case the second syllable,
hây (ให้) and *tháy* (ให้), respectively, is
one spelled with the second tone mark.

    The use of tone marks in the final two
wák of the *khlooŋ 4* stanzas as they appear in
the poem shows that, according to the textbook
descriptions, the *khlooŋ 4* stanzas of *Lilit
Phra Law* are all of the variety known as
sùphâap. It is said in the textbooks that
khlooŋ dân stanzas have syllables with the
second tone mark in the fourth and fifth
positions of the fourth line in what is called
thoo khûu 'paired second tone'. Of the 294

stanzas of *Lilit Phra Law* a total of 117 (40%) have this *thoo khûu* pattern in the seventh *wâk*. This arrangement is the only part of the tone placement pattern of the poem that follows the pattern described in the textbooks as being that of *khlooŋ dân*. The example line below is the fourth line of stanza 201, which is one instance of the *thoo khûu*. Both the fourth and fifth syllables of the line, and thus of the seventh *wâk*, are written with the second tone mark.

chûay	*ráksăa*	*câw-cháaŋ*	*yàa*	*hây*	*mii*	*phay*
help	protect	Title	neg.	let	have	danger

> Please protect the King. Don't let
> him fall into danger.

M. R. Sumonnachat points to this aspect of the tone pattern of the poem as evidence that *Lilit Phra Law* is actually a transitional piece, occupying an historical position between *khlooŋ dân* and the more finely worked out *khlooŋ sùphâap* form, used during the great literary era of the reign of King Narai the Great, in the middle of the Ayutthaya period. As the foregoing discussion shows, however, there is no real structural evidence to suggest that the poets were using anything but an already carefully defined and well worked out form at the time that *Lilit Phra Law* came into being. Discussion of other points below will show that the so-called *thoo khûu* is the only feature of the stanzas of *Lilit Phra Law* that is reminiscent of *khlooŋ dân*. In every other respect the forms fit the pattern of *sùphâap* varieties. There is simply insufficient evidence to posit a state of transition. One may be able to say that later poets avoided the use of the *thoo khûu* when working with the *sùphâap* forms, but it would not be proper to turn this change in preference back on the ancient poets and redefine their work based on modern developments of taste.

113

What is clear from this examination of tone placement in the *khlooŋ 4* stanzas is that the poets were following patterns not noted in the textbook treatments. Continued examination of the *khlooŋ 4* stanzas, and then of the other stanza types, will show previously unrecognized patterns in many other aspects of the forms, as well. We will see that the ancient conception of both the *khlooŋ* and *râay* forms must have been quite different from that of modern times. That difference in conception stems, however, not from a difference in skill between ancient and modern poets, but from a difference in emphasis, with the ancient poets emphasizing auditory considerations, and modern poets emphasizing visual ones.

4) Rhyme pattern

Nearly all of the stanzas of *khlooŋ 4* in the poem follow the rhyme pattern commonly associated with the *sùphâap* variety. In all, only seventeen of the stanzas given as the main reading in the Ministry of Education text differ in some way from this pattern, and the manuscript copies lower this number further by providing alternate readings that match the normal pattern for all but six of the stanzas in question. But there remains sufficient divergence to fuel speculation about whether or not the poem belongs in the *sùphâap* or *dân* category, or is a mixture of those forms.[6] A close examination of the text shows that the question is not an "either/or" proposition, nor is it a question of mixing two supposedly mutually exclusive varieties.

Diagram 3 repeats the form of the *khlooŋ 4 sùphâap* stanza, but it is modified to show only the rhyme patterns of the stanza. The first pattern links three syllables located in three separate lines. The first syllable in the pattern is known as the *sòŋ* 'send' syllable, and it is always the last required syllable of the first line of the stanza. The second syllable is known as the *ráp* 'receive'

114

syllable and is normally the fifth syllable of
the second line of the stanza, although in a
variation of this pattern discussed below it
sometimes is placed fourth in the line.   The
third syllable of the pattern is known as the
rɔɔŋ 'underlay' syllable and is always the
fifth syllable of the third line.   This is the
pattern found in all but seventeen of the 294
khlooŋ 4 stanzas found in the poem.

Diagram 3: The Rhyme Patterns of
            khlooŋ 4 sùphâap

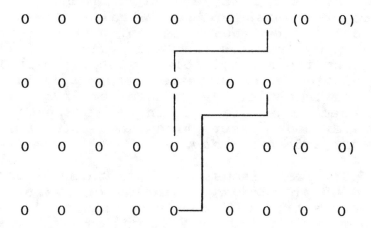

Diagram 4: Variation of the *sɔ̀ŋ-ráp-rɔɔŋ*
            Rhyme Pattern

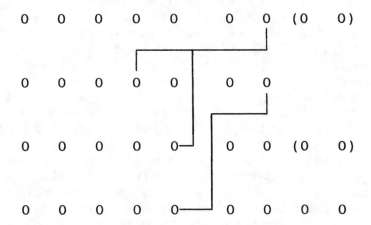

115

The variation of this *sǒŋ-ráp-rɔɔŋ* rhyme pattern is given in diagram 4. The only difference between the primary pattern and the variation of it is the change of the position of the *ráp* syllable from the fifth to the fourth position in the second line of the stanza. The textbooks describe yet another variation of this pattern, in which the *ráp* syllable is placed third in the line, but there are no stanzas in *Lilit Phra Law* in which this variation occurs, so we need not be concerned with it in this discussion.

The second rhyme pattern found in the *khlooŋ 4* stanzas in *Lilit Phra Law* links two syllables from the ancient C-tone category. The *sǒŋ* syllable is the last syllable of line two, and the *ráp* syllable is the fifth syllable of line four; there is no *rɔɔŋ* syllable in this pattern. All 294 stanzas of *khlooŋ 4* in the poem have this pattern as it appears in the textbook descriptions of both *khlooŋ sùphâap* and *khlooŋ dân*.

Critical discussion of the rhyme patterns found in the *khlooŋ 4* stanzas of *Lilit Phra Law* deals only with the three-place *sǒŋ-ráp-rɔɔŋ* pattern and the variations on it that are found in the poem. The presence of the variations is cited as evidence that the poem was written at a time when the form was in a state of flux, not yet as fully worked out as it would come to be in the time of King Narai, in the middle of the Ayutthaya period of Thai history. The variations are also, in all probability, part of what has given some authors the idea that the poets were not as sophisticated or disciplined as more modern writers, and that they mixed stanzas of *sùphâap* and stanzas of *dân* either out of ineptitude or ignorance. The point thus requires a full investigation, and a close examination of the rhyme patterns in the divergent stanzas is in order, but first a brief consideration of rhyme links between *khlooŋ 4* stanzas in compositions of *lílít*, since this point is relevant

116

to the question of rhyme patterns used within the stanza.

The term *lílít* refers to narrative works composed in a combination of stanzas of *khlooŋ* and *râay*. A *lílít* composition, according to the textbooks, may use either *sùphâap* or *dân* forms, but should not mix the two types of poetry in a single work. The stanzas of verse in a *lílít* composition, it is said, should be linked by rhyme from stanza to stanza from the beginning to the end of the poem (Uppakit 1968: 428).

The textbooks say that in the rhyme links between stanzas of *lílít sùphâap* the *sòŋ* 'send' syllable should be the last one of the preceding stanza and the *ráp* 'receive' syllable should be the first, second, or third one of the first line of the following stanza, no matter what type of stanza may be in the recipient position. Stanzas of *lílít dân*, however, are said to be joined this way except when the *ráp* stanza is *khlooŋ 4*. In this case, the *sòŋ* syllable is still the last of the preceding stanza, but the *ráp* syllable is in the second line of the recipient stanza, and is usually the fifth, but sometimes the fourth syllable of that line. It seems to be primarily due to this point that the rhyme patterns in the seemingly divergent stanzas of *Lilit Phra Law* have raised doubts about the nature of the forms used in the poem.

We will again take up the question of stanza linking rhymes below, when we discuss the *lílít* style in detail. At this point we need to focus primarily on *khlooŋ 4*; and so, with this brief background material regarding rhyme links in *lílít* compositions, I will now return to the question of the seventeen divergent stanzas.

Ten of the seventeen seemingly divergent *khlooŋ 4* stanzas as they appear in the printed editions of the poem match exactly the variation of the three-position rhyme commonly identified as a characteristic of *khlooŋ 4 sùphâap.*[7] In each case the *sòŋ* syllable is the last of the required syllables of the first line of the stanza, and the *rɔɔŋ* syllable is the fifth of line three. The *ráp* syllable, which is the second of the three syllables in the pattern, is in the fourth position of line two. There is no rhyme link at all between these stanzas and those that precede them in the poem, so while they do differ from the common *sùphâap* pattern somewhat, they do not follow what the textbooks identify as the *dân* pattern of linking each stanza with a rhyme. Nor is the change in position of the *ráp* syllable evidence of ineptitude on the part of the poets. The example stanza given below is number 162.

tùun khûn wɔɔn wâa khâa càk pay
awake ascend beg say I will go

praphâat chom phray phlaaŋ lây cháaŋ
travel view woods while chase elephant

chom phanom phanaalay phlaaŋ lây marúk na
view mountain forest while hunt deer pt

chom pàa-doŋ-phoŋ kwâaŋ thùan thâm sàʔ sǐi
view dense woods wide wilds cave pond great

> (Phra Law) awoke begging (his moth-
> er) "I wish to go,
> To travel, to admire the woods and
> hunt elephants,
> To look at the mountains and chase
> after deer,
> To view the dense jungle, the wil-
> derness, and caves and ponds."

The syllables that form the variation of the *sòŋ-ráp-rɔɔŋ* rhyme pattern in this example stanza are *pay* (ไป) in the first line, *phray*

(ไพร) in the second line, and *-lay* (-ลัย) in the third; for convenience they are under- lined.

Two of the seventeen divergent stanzas, numbers 268 and 657, are also written with the alternate rhyme pattern illustrated above. They differ from each other in that these stanzas are preceded in one case by a stanza of *khlooŋ 4* and in another case by a stanza of *râay*. They also differ from the ten stanzas noted above in that in each case there is a definite rhyme link with the previous stan- za.[8] In both links the *sòŋ* syllable is the final syllable of that stanza, and the *ráp* syllable is the second syllable of line one of the verse of *khlooŋ 4*. This pattern, accord- ing to the textbook descriptions, is not permitted in stanzas of *khlooŋ dân*. Again, there is no real support for the suggestion that these verses are anything but *khlooŋ sùphâap*.

Stanza number 248 also has the variant rhyme pattern for *khlooŋ 4 sùphâap*, with the *ráp* syllable taking the fourth position in line two. However, the fifth syllable of line two seems to form a rhyme link with the last syllable of the previous stanza, suggesting a *khlooŋ dân* pattern. This seeming rhyme link probably should be disregarded, however, for two reasons. First, the syllables that seem to form the *sòŋ* and *ráp* pattern are the same lexical item (*cay* 'heart'). Throughout the rest of the poem it seems clear that the use of a word in consecutive positions in a rhyme link is purposely avoided, to the extent that Phrayaa Uppakit surmises that such rhymes were forbidden.

Second, if this were a genuine stanza- linking rhyme, we would have a situation that does not occur elsewhere in the poem, that of a rhyme link between stanzas crossing over another rhyme pattern. The overlap of rhyme patterns within the stanza is characteristic

119

of *khlooŋ 4 sùphâap*. That is, the *sɔ̀ŋ* sylla- ble of the two-position rhyme falls between the *ráp* and *rɔɔŋ* syllables of the three-sylla- ble rhyme. But the textbook descriptions do not mention any pattern in which a stanza-link rhyme overlaps with a rhyme within the stanza, and there are no other cases of such a pattern in the text itself. For these reasons it is probably best to disregard the possibility that the poets intended to link this stanza in the fashion characteristic of *khlooŋ dân* and to assume that it is simply another example of *khlooŋ sùphâap*, perhaps even an instance of corruption of the ancient text.

There remain three stanzas that are written in a pattern that differs noticeably from the pattern described for *khlooŋ sùphâap*. Significantly, however, they each differ from the other stanzas of the poem in the same way, and they all appear in sequence. It is proba- bly these three stanzas that are the most troublesome to those who feel that the poets who composed *Lilit Phra Law* were either not sure of their forms, or were not truly expert in their use, or perhaps were in the habit of mixing the *khlooŋ sùphâap* and *khlooŋ dân* forms. However, a closer examination will show that such conclusions are at least hasty.

The stanzas in question are the second, third, and fourth of the poem, and it is true that these three stanzas are significantly different from the others of the poem. The example stanza is number 3. The syllables *chaay* (ชาย) and *-yaay* (-ยาย) rhyme, and the syllable *lɔɔ* (ลอ) in the second line rhymes with the last syllable of the previous stanza.

rúu malǎk sòp sàat thûan yǐŋ chaay
know much all rule all woman man

càk klàaw klɔɔn phrá?lɔɔ lâət phûu
pt. tell poem Phra Law surpassing person

phayrɔ́? rîap banyaay phrɔ́? yǐŋ phrɔ́? naa
beuatiful neat narrate pretty pt. pretty pt.

sǒm pìi-lûu sǐaŋ lûu lɔ́ɔ lǎw-loom cay
fit flute sound flute tempt soothe heart

> Being fully versed, Oh men and
>   women,
> I will recite the poem of Phra Law,
>   surpassing man,
> A euphonious and well-arranged tale
>   of great beauty,
> Fit to be played on a pipe, beguil-
>   ing to the heart.

The number of syllables in each line and the tone placement pattern of each stanza are those of *khlooŋ sùphâap*. However, these stanzas do not have a rhyme pattern with three participant syllables, the *sòŋ-ráp-rɔɔŋ* pattern discussed above. They have instead a two-position pattern in which the *sòŋ* syllable is the last one of the first line and the *ráp* syllable is the fifth one of the third line; the second line does not participate in the rhyme pattern. Moreover, in each case there is a rhyme link between the previous stanza and the second line of the stanza in question. In stanzas two and three, the *ráp* syllable is the fifth one of the line, and in stanza four it is the fourth syllable. Although there is some variation in the wording of these stanzas in the old manuscript copies, the rhyme patterns that are used do conform to the textbook descriptions of *khlooŋ dân*.

Despite the patterns found in these stanzas, it does not seem at all appropriate to say that the poets were mixing the *sùphâap*

121

and *dân* forms together. It is only these three stanzas out of a total of 294 *khlooŋ 4* stanzas that resemble the *dân* pattern, and all three of them are grouped together at the beginning of the poem. Nor should this be taken as evidence of inability on the part of the poets, or of instability of the poetic form.

Along with being structurally different these stanzas are also thematically different from those of the rest of the poem. They actually appear prior to the beginning of the story itself, and prior to the passages describing the circumstances by which the two cities became enemies before the birth of the main characters. These three stanzas -- along with the first, which is written in *râay*[9] -- are less concerned with advancing the story at hand than with praising the glory of the king and the city of Ayutthaya, which of course is located far to the south of the commonly accepted location of the events of the tale. For both poetic and thematic reasons, therefore, it seems reasonable to suggest that these stanzas were added to this version of the story after the task of composition had been completed or, if all of the stanzas do date from the same period, that special conventionalized wording was used in an otherwise unmarked prologue.

A detailed examination of the rhyme pattern of the *khlooŋ 4* stanzas produces no evidence that the poets were working with an undeveloped form or that they were at all inept in their work. Nor is there evidence that they were mixing forms. There is only the possibility that the poets purposefully set off the prologue from the body of the tale by using a slightly different form, or perhaps that a prologue was added at a later date, when other patterns were in vogue.

The *khlooŋ 4* Stanza as an Auditory Phenomenon

It is now appropriate to return to a point first raised in the discussion of the Thai tone system in chapter 3 and mentioned again briefly several times in the present chapter. This point is the concern with the visual as opposed to auditory aspects of Thai poetry.

Visual Considerations

If one is to compose good *khlooŋ* and *râay* poetry in modern Thai, one must be aware of what a particular syllable looks like on paper, that is, of what symbols are used to represent it in writing, in order to know if it is appropriate for use in a particular position in a poem. This concern for the visual came about at least in part due to the pattern of the tone splits that occurred in what we know today as Central Thai, discussed in chapter 3. It is this pattern of splits, and later coalescence, that resulted in two sources in the Proto-Tai tone chart for the modern falling tone, as well as two tones each for the three ancient tone categories, the A column, the B column, and the C column in the tone chart. The visual requirements are now so significant that one cannot easily discuss *khlooŋ* poetry except in terms of the writing system and must make continual reference to the tone marks, not the spoken tones themselves.

This need for attention to the written form would not have existed prior to the tone splits. Anyone would have known simply by listening to a syllable whether it was appropriate for use as, for example, the first syllable of the fourth *wâk* of a *khlooŋ 4* stanza, since all syllables with the B tone sounded the same. There could have been no confusion about which syllables could appropriately have been used in the first position

in that *wák* and which in the second, because
all syllables with the B tone sounded different from all those with the C tone. And, of
course, these spoken differences were unambig-
uously reflected in the use of tone marks. It
was only after the tone splits that some B-
column syllables and some C-column syllables
came to have the same tone, although spelling
conventions still captured the old distinctions. It was only after the tone splits that
the tone mark used to spell those syllables,
that is, their visual representation, became
more significant for the integrity of the
khlooŋ and *râay* forms than the way the syllables sounded in speech.

There is no evidence in the *samùt khɔ̌y*
copies that visual form was at all important
to the ancient poets, or to the succeeding
generations of scribes who copied and recopied
their work. The page format used in those
books was clearly designed for economy of
space. Each stanza usually follows immediately after the preceding one, often with no
indication that one stanza has ended and
another begun. In most of these books the
written line, or *banthát*, contains as much
material as is convenient and comes to an end
when there is no more space, not necessarily
at the end of any of the poetic units. In
modern printed editions, however, the poetic
line, or *bàat*, consisting of one five-syllable
wák 'hemistich' and another of two or four
syllables, always appears alone and complete
on a single, printed line. The poetic and
typographical units are made to coincide,
which provides for the modern student of
poetry a visual clarification of what has
become, on auditory grounds, an ambiguous
structure. For the composer or composers of
Lilit Phra Law, however, a *bàat* of *khlooŋ 4*
poetry must have been a strictly auditory
structure intended to be perceived as such
without any visual assistance or reinforce-
ment. Of course we cannot be sure that the
page format used to record the text in the

124

extant *samùt khɔ̌y* copies is exactly that used at the time that *Lilit Phra Law* was first set down in writing, but most likely it is at least similar. What the manuscripts make clear is that the modern written representation, with its emphasis on visual format, does not predate modern printing technology.

This modern attention to the visual, to whether something looks right, is probably behind much of the modern dissatisfaction with the ancient poets and the common notion that they did not follow the rules very carefully. In all probability, modern writers have come to feel that, since using the visually correct tone mark is so important, it is also equally important to have what appears to be the visually correct number of syllables. The feeling seems to be that if the ancient pattern appears to call for five syllables in a *wâk* then it should, wherever possible, be five written syllables.

Auditory Considerations

As was noted earlier, there are often more than the prescribed number of syllables in a *wâk* of *khlooŋ 4* as found in *Lilit Phra Law*, particularly in those *wâk* said to require five syllables. Generally the extra syllables are the first syllables of disyllabic words; they often have a short vowel and, in modern citation form, a glottal stop in final position. Many such words are found frequently in the poem, for example: *kasàt* 'king'; *sadèt* 'go' (royal); *sawɔ̌əy* 'acquire' (royal); and *samɔ̌ə* 'equal'. Such extra syllables appear far more frequently in *râay*, and so the point will be taken up again in the discussion devoted to that form, but some remarks about the significance of these syllables are appropriate here.

According to the textbooks the first *wâk* of each line of *khlooŋ 4* should have exactly

125

five syllables, and many do. One never finds fewer than five, and nearly all those *wâk* having more than five syllables can easily be read as though they did have only five, by reducing the stress and duration of syllables such as those pointed out above, in exactly the way that modern speech de-emphasizes such syllables in normal conversation. This resemblance to speech suggests that *khloong 4* poetry as found in *Lilit Phra Law* is first and foremost an oral phenomenon, with a rule that these *wâk* should have five predominant or stressed or emphasized syllables, and as many others as required to convey the meaning, provided that the extra can be squeezed in without disturbing the normal flow of the recitation or singing. A similar rule would also hold for those *wâk* requiring only two syllables.

If, pursuing this train of thought, we think of the *khloong 4* of *Lilit Phra Law* as an exclusively oral phenomenon, we note that several interesting points suggested by the textbook descriptions of the poem are not fully expanded. One such point is the use of substitutes for syllables with the first tone mark or, to put it more conveniently, for syllables with the B tone. There are no instances of substitution of any kind for the C tone, but syllables with a stop final do often appear in a position requiring the B tone. This substitution is not haphazard, as a look at the tone placement chart in appendix 1 and the various stanza diagrams will show.

Substitution seems to have been acceptable to the ancient poets in all positions requiring the B tone, but it is far more common in the odd numbered *wâk*, and it is only in *wâk* three, five, and seven that nasal consonant sounds are also substituted. When substitution does take place, the syllable is generally more likely to be a long-vowel, closed syllable than a short-vowel, closed syllable, or an open syllable ending with a nasal final, particularly in the even-numbered *wâk*, those that complete each *bàat* 'line' of poetry. The presence of these substitution patterns suggests that the end points of the ancient poetic units were conceptually more significant than were beginning points, as is the case with ancient musical patterns in much of Southeast Asia. This would only have made sense, of course, if the poetic units were primarily auditory in nature. Visual considerations would have placed primary importance on the first position in each unit. More will be said of this point in the discussion of the *khlooŋ 2* and *khlooŋ 3* forms.

Another point is interesting in this connection, one that concerns the three-position rhyme pattern of the *khlooŋ 4* stanza, which connects the last syllables of the second, third, and fifth *wâk* of the stanza. This rhyme pattern is made up almost exclusively of syllables that are from the A column, that is, ones that are spelled with no tone mark. The only exceptions are rhymes made up of short-vowel, closed syllables, and of the 294 stanzas of *khlooŋ 4* only thirty-one (11%) have a pattern composed of syllables of this type. But the fact that this substitution does occur, albeit rarely, is a puzzle. We know that in other positions syllables with a stop final were substituted for those with the B tone, suggesting that the two types of syllables were phonetically similar in the ancient language. And the clear preference for substitute syllables with long vowels suggests that they may have resembled syllables with the B tone more than those with a short vowel and a stop final. What is puzzling is how rhymes formed by syllables with a stop final can also appear in a position normally filled by syllables from the A column. The point is worth further attention, and a critical edition of the poem may well show that some, if not all, of these rhymes are relatively recent additions to the poem, inserted after the sound changes had obscured

the original structural constraints. For the
moment, however, it is significant to note
that a total of 263 (89%) of the stanzas have
rhyme links formed by syllables from the A
column.

If we conceive of the stanza of *khlooŋ 4*
only in terms of the ancient tones, and if we
also include in our considerations the tone
found in nearly all of the three-position
rhymes, we have a different picture of the
form than that given in the textbooks. Diagram 5 represents a stanza of *khlooŋ 4* in
terms of the ancient tones. In a break with
the traditional method, however, the circles
and tone marks have been replaced by letters
indicating the ancient tone category in those
positions in which syllables with specific
tones are said to have been required. The
three-position rhyme is represented by the
letter 'A' since that tone appears in these
syllables with such regularity.

**Diagram 5: Rhymes of *khlooŋ 4* by Ancient
Tone Categories**

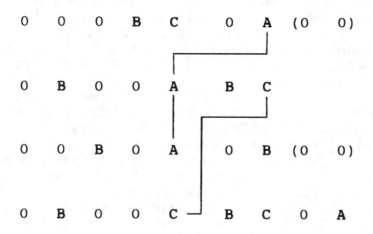

We do not know how these stanzas were
read or sung, of course, but it is reasonable
to assume that the ancient method was similar

to the modern one. If the diagram of a *khloong* *4* stanza is expanded to include these features as well, as is done in diagram 6, we have an even more complex structure. In modern performance *wǎk* of five or more syllables are read or sung as two syntactically separate phrases of two or three syllables, each with a brief pause following the first phrase (represented by a comma in the diagram) and then a somewhat more pronounced pause following the second phrase (represented by a semicolon) to indicate the end of the *wǎk*.[10] Those *wǎk* of only two syllables are followed by the more pronounced pause unless *kham sɔ̌y* are added, in which case the less pronounced pause follows the required syllables and the more pronounced one follows the *kham sɔ̌y*, to indicate the end of the *wǎk*. The completion of the stanza is marked by a pronounced lengthening of the final syllable, which is always one from the A column, and by a slowing of the pace of recitation, both of which is represented in the diagram by a period (Nuphuk 1939: 188).

Diagram 6: *khloong* *4* **Recitation Style**

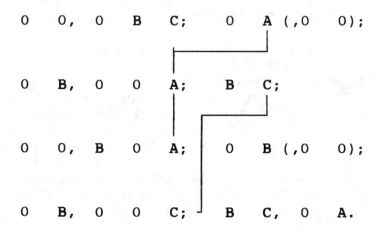

```
0   0,  0   B   C;      0   A (,0   0);


0   B,  0   0   A;      B   C;


0   0,  B   0   A;      0   B (,0   0);


0   B,  0   0   C;      B   C,  0   A.
```

What emerges is a pattern of great auditory richness and complexity composed of syllable count, rhyme, tone placement, and

129

recitation style. In many ways the stanza resembles traditional Thai music, and the similarities are more apparent if one conceives of the tone placement pattern as a network of three unambiguous tones. In performance one would hear in each stanza the same phonetic realization in each position requiring the C tone, for example. And the lack of ambiguity in tones would have made each section of the stanza distinctly different in structure from any other.

In this context it becomes clear why the poets never used *kham sɔ̌y* after *wâk* 4. The addition of extra syllables at that point would have rendered *wâk* 4 and *wâk* 8 identical, bringing ambiguity into the stanza at the least desirable spot, at the end. Because each part of the stanza was clearly different from the others, all those involved in a performance, whether they were musicians, dancers, singers, or audience, would have known exactly what point had been reached in the stanza strictly on auditory grounds without reference either to the content of the stanza or to the writing system.

CONCLUSIONS: THE ANCIENT *khlooŋ 4* STANZA

The rich and unambiguous auditory structure described above would not have confronted the ancient student of poetry with anything like the difficulties that the modern reflection of that structure poses for those of us in the present day, attuned as we are to a different type of tone. The original structure of the stanza is now obscure at best, and we must memorize complex diagrams that we constantly refer to, at least mentally, in order to read or compose in these poetic forms.

If we apply the insights of linguistic analysis to the study of the *khlooŋ 4* stanza, however, we see that we must conceive of the form as a strictly auditory phenomenon. We are then lead to surprising but inescapable conclusions. Among these conclusions is the fact that the ancient forms of poetry, just like the ancient forms of speech, differed fundamentally from their modern counterparts, and the differences are far greater than writing, the visual representation of speech, would seem to suggest. We must also conclude that, prior to the massive sound changes that forever separated ancient and modern spoken forms, one could have fully appreciated the beauty of *khlooŋ 4* poetry, and could also, no doubt, have been adept at creating such poetry, without ever having seen a visual representation of the ideal stanza. To both the ancient poet and the ancient audience, literacy, which is so necessary for dealing with the modern reflection of the ancient poetic forms, must have been irrelevant.

NOTES

1. As I have mentioned previously there is a sometimes confusing ambiguity involved in translating into English the Thai word *kham*, which is the equivalent of both "syllable" and "word." In the present study I have tried to use "syllable" when discussing the structure of the poetic forms, and "word" when discussing individual lexical items that are used in those forms. In the present context, however, it seems clearest to use the Thai term without translation.

2. This light stress and reduced duration are, of course, characteristic of ordinary modern speech styles. For a thorough discussion of this point see Patcharin Peyasantiwong (1986).

3. Although the textbooks do not speculate on just why this type of substitution was used by the ancient poets, it was most likely because of a phonetic similarity between syllables

from the ancient B-tone category, written in modern Thai with the first tone mark, and closed syllables, those that end with a stop consonant. In this context note the similar tone patterns that developed for B-column syllables and long vowel, D-column syllables, as part of the change from the ancient system to that we know today. The similarity between these two columns in the tone chart is widespread in the Tai language family.

4. In modern speech the word is pronounced with a long vowel, although the written form represents a short vowel pronunciation.

5. Stanza 196 as it has appeared in earlier editions of the Ministry of Education text is clearly incorrect. The first syllable of *wák* 8 was written out as *tháaw* (เท่า), but in thirteen of the fourteen *samùt khɔ̀y* copies in which the *wák* is legible the word appears as *tháw* (เท่), which makes better sense, and also provides for the expected tone pattern. The wording of the stanza in the 1984 edition (see p. 52) is changed, without comment, to match the manuscript wording.

6. The seventeen stanzas with differing patterns of rhyme placement are numbers 2, 3, 4, 25, 109, 141, 162, 246, 248, 260, 268, 271, 514, 558, 563, 641, and 657. Most of the stanzas have alternate readings that follow the expected rhyme pattern. Stanza 260, for example, appears legibly in twelve manuscripts, all of which agree on a wording that follows the normal rhyme pattern, showing that the wording in the published editions is specious. In other cases only three or four, or sometimes only one, of the manuscripts have the alternate reading. Detailed study of the manuscripts may one day help to develop a chronology of when they were written and perhaps allow us to date some of the wording changes. At present we have to deal with some conflicting wording and must remain open to different possible interpretations. Only six

of the stanzas have no alternate reading in the manuscripts. They are stanzas 2, 3, 4, 271, 514, and 563. And the first three of this latter group appear to be part of an otherwise unmarked prologue purposefully different from the rest of the poem, further undermining the contention that the poets mixed forms.

7. The stanzas are numbers 25, 109, 141, 162, 246, 271, 514, 558, 563, and 641.

8. The significance of the presence or absence of a rhyme link between stanzas is addressed in detail in chapter 7, which discusses the *lilit* style of composition as used in the poem.

9. This point is raised again in chapter 5 in the discussion of the types of *rǎay* found in *Lilit Phra Law*.

10. For the sake of simplicity the diagram assumes that all the five-syllable *wǎk* begin with a phrase of two syllables. In fact, however, the three syllable phrase often appears first, but this does not contradict the conclusions drawn here regarding the stanza structure.

Chapter 5

THE *râay* STANZAS OF *LILIT PHRA LAW*

The textbook discussions of *râay* identify three varieties of the form that need concern us in our examination of the verse forms of *Lilit Phra Law*. The three are differentiated mainly by the pattern of the last few *wâk* 'hemistich' of the stanza.[1] Stanzas that close with the tone and rhyme patterns of *khlooŋ 2 sùphâap* are considered to be *râay sùphâap*. Those that close with the tone and rhyme patterns of *khlooŋ 2 dân* are considered *râay dân*, and those that close with a rhyme and tone pattern that cannot be classified as either *sùphâap* or *dân* are generally referred to by the term *râay booraan* 'ancient *râay*'. One gets the impression from the textbook treatments that the so-called *booraan* variety is held in rather low esteem; the implication seems to be that the ancient poets often lacked sufficient skill or discipline to bring their work to a stylish close.

Of the 113 stanzas of *râay* in *Lilit Phra Law*, 108 are clearly of the *sùphâap* variety, all ending in stanzas of *khlooŋ 2 sùphâap*. Despite the suggestions of many textbook authors, there is really very little in the poem that can be called *râay booraan* and less that can be considered *râay dân*. At most four, and possibly only three, of the 113 stanzas can be classified as *râay booraan*, and only one ends in a pattern that resembles *râay dân*. The patterns found in those *wâk* that close the various stanzas of *râay* will be discussed in detail in chapter 6. First we will discuss those *wâk* that form the bulk of each stanza and, according to the textbooks, are the same in all three varieties of *râay*.

As in the discussion of *khlooŋ 4*, we will again be guided by the points laid out in Phrayaa Uppakit's discussion, regarding them not so much as "rules" that the ancient poets

134

placed upon themselves, but as general patterns noted in the ancient poetry by modern authors attempting to understand archaic forms. This approach will help to distinguish between the nature of the forms as they sprang up from the language spoken by the ancient poets and the nature of the forms as seen by speakers of the very different form of speech that we know as modern Thai.

Structure of the *wǎk*

The first general "rule" that the various textbooks give for *râay* poetry is really a definition of the structure of the *wǎk*. Some textbooks say that each *wǎk* of *râay* has from five syllables up to nine, and some simply say that each has five syllables, without addressing the variation in syllable count noted by others. Both descriptions are actually true, although from different points of view. A close examination of the text of *Lilit Phra Law* shows that the vast majority of the more than 2,000 *wǎk* that appear in the stanzas of *râay*[2] (exclusive of those *wǎk* in *khlooŋ 2* ending patterns) have five syllables, although many do have six or seven and a few even have eight or nine.[3] However, nearly all of the *wǎk* with what appear to be extra syllables can be read in a manner that places stress on only five of the syllables, de-emphasizing any others that might appear. Although it is seldom mentioned in the textbooks, the *wǎk* is generally divided syntactically into two phrases, one of three stressed syllables and one of two.

In his discussion of Thai oral poetry Prince Bidyalankarana (1926: 126) states that "In singing, a syllable missed out is substituted by a draw which serves to bridge the gap, while a syllable too many is hurried over so that it is not too noticeable." In her discussion of Lao oral poetry Carol Compton (1977: 30) refers to "generally accepted patterns for 'squeezing' or 'stretching' these syllables to fit in with the poetic require- ment. . . and musical structure." The former discussion deals with a variety of oral Thai forms, and the latter with one specific Lao form. While neither author was speaking specifically about *râay* poetry, and both were discussing extemporaneous composition, their comments apply nonetheless. If one counts all of the syllables in a *wâk* of *râay* in *Lilit Phra Law*, the number will sometimes be more than five, but if one counts only those that are normally stressed in ordinary speech, the number is almost always five. An example of a five-syllable *wâk* of *râay* is given below; it is taken from stanza 229 of the Ministry of Education text.

khìi săan   sŭuŋ klêɛw klâa
ride elephant tall daring bold

(The nobles) ride the tall   coura- geous elephants.

Another example is given below. It is taken from stanza number 7 of the Ministry of Education edition, and it has six syllables.

wâa mɯaŋ sɔ̌ɔŋ kasàt klâa
say city Song king bold

(He) said, "The city of Song has a bold king."

Although the *wâk* does have six syllables, the first syllable of the word *kasàt* (กษัตริย์) 'king' can easily be ignored as far as rhyme count is concerned since in normal speech syllables of this type are usually given less stress than the other syllable or syllables in the word. Thus, a piece of poetry to be read or sung aloud can be made to fit the prescrib-

136

ed pattern, and syllables can be altered to suit the needs of the performer by a process common to ordinary conversation.

Some words seem to lend themselves to reduction more than others. The word *kasàt* is one, and it appears frequently in the poem. Another example is given below, this one from stanza 379.

pen naaŋ phayaa naaŋ mɯaŋ
be   lady royal   lady city

(She) was a noble woman of the city.

In this *wák* there are also six syllables, but *pha*, which is the first syllable of the word *phayaa* (พญา), a royal or noble title, may be "squeezed" by the performer, leaving the required five primary stress points.[4] As is the case with the word *kasàt*, this example shows a disyllabic word in which the first syllable has a short vowel and, in modern citation form, a glottal stop. The glottal stop in such syllables is a modern innovation that is always dropped in normal speech and was not present in the ancient form of the word. In the fast speech of modern Thai a syllable of this type is often reduced by shortening of the vowel, so that it is, in fact, shorter than the normal length for short vowels in citation form.[5] The text of *Lilit Phra Law* contains a great many *wák* of this type, suggesting that the ancient language employed a similar syllable reduction technique.

Syllables that in the modern citation form end in a short vowel and a glottal stop that is dropped in normal speech seem to be the ones most likely to be reduced, especially when those syllables appear at the beginning of a disyllabic or polysyllabic word.[6] Sometimes, however, such syllables have stress and length equal to syllables with different vowel and final consonant configurations. The example below is from stanza number 611.

sàn   rúthay tháthǎaw
shake heart distress

(She) was overwhelmed with distress.

In this wǎk the first syllable of each of the disyllabic words was probably intended to be treated as a full syllable and was, therefore, given full stress even though similar syllables are reduced elsewhere.

In some cases the syllable count can be adjusted by a reduction of the stress and duration of syllables that stand as independent lexical items. Generally, however, such content morphemes are not de-emphasized, and do not undergo the processes of reduction by which syllables that begin disyllabic words often lose a final glottal stop or come to have shortened vowels. The example below is from stanza 8.

cháaŋ   phá? cháaŋ   chon kan
elephant hit   elephant crash together

The elephants crashed into one another.

In modern citation form the monosyllable phá?, with its short vowel and glottal stop, appears to be structurally identical to the previous examples. In fact, the structural elements of such monosyllables usually have a different status than they do in word-initial syllables. Thus, the glottal stop is retained, and the tone is not neutralized. In order to achieve five stressed syllables in this wǎk, then, the word must be given its normal full stress and length in recitation.

There are also many cases in which a *wâk* has more than five syllables, but none of them have a short vowel followed by a glottal stop, suggesting that speakers of the ancient form of the language reduced other types of syllables as well, just as do speakers of modern Thai. The example given below is from stanza 198.

yàa   hây yâak kɛ̀ɛ cay   phrây
neg. let hard for heart citizens

Don't oppress your followers.

The word *kɛ̀ɛ* 'for', which functions like an English preposition, is likely to be reduced in stress and duration in modern conversational speech. A similar reduction of the word in the example above would leave five emphasized syllables.

There are many variations and often there are differing ways in which a given *wâk* can be read in order to produce the expected five stressed syllables. Certainly there are *wâk* in the poem with more than five syllables for which there is no obvious reading that provides for only five stressed syllables. Some such *wâk* contain long personal names or complex reduplications, and it is difficult to know how the ancient poets would have handled them in performance. In some cases alternate readings can be found in the *samùt khɔ̌y* copies that solve the problem, but just as often the manuscripts are contradictory, and, in all probability, the original wording has been lost.

There are a few other problem *wâk*, however, that must be read with six stressed syllables, and while they are not numerous, there are enough of them to add to the impression that the poets were inconsistent in their

work. But a close examination of these *wâk*
suggests another explanation. Many of them
break syntactically into two phrases of three
syllables each, unlike the vast majority of
wâk, which have five stressed syllables and
break into two phrases of unequal syllable
count. In addition, the two phrases of these
six-syllable *wâk* are often connected by rhyme
links between the final syllable of the first
phrase and the first syllable of the next, and
they often contain internal rhyme, neither of
which is characteristic of the great majority
of *wâk* in the poem, in all the poetic forms.
In each of these points they are reminiscent
not so much of *khlooŋ* and *râay* forms, but of
modern *klɔɔn* poetry. In all probability these
wâk are either "improvements" of the ancient
wording or insertions of new material into the
text, done by later generations of poets
attuned to the tastes and preferences of
speakers of the modern, five-tone system and
the *klɔɔn* forms of poetry that sprang up from
that type of speech.

The main point to be made here is that
the vast majority of the *wâk* have five syllables, or can easily be read with only five
stressed syllables. While it is more common
in *râay* than in *khlooŋ* to have "extra" syllables like those discussed above, it is by no
means uncommon in the *khlooŋ* forms. On this
point, therefore, it is appropriate to think
of *râay* and *khlooŋ* as being structurally
similar in a way that is not mentioned in the
textbook treatments. That is, both the *râay*
and the *khlooŋ* forms are built on a five
syllable unit, which is embellished and manip-
ulated in different ways. Rather than thinking of them as two entirely different forms it
is more accurate to think of *râay* and *khlooŋ*
as different manifestations of the same linguistic or poetic phenomenon: a preference in
speech for units of five syllables broken into
two phrases.[7]

At any rate, an examination of the sylla-

ble count and structure of the many stanzas of
râay in the text of *Lilit Phra Law* shows that
the poetry is quite consistent. If it was
composed primarily for oral performance, and I
believe that it was, then much of what is
criticized by the modern commentators is
evidence not of a lack of sophistication on
the part of the ancient poets but of a goal
different from that of more recent poets. A
few poets have continued to work with the
modern reflections of the ancient *khloog* and
râay forms, and they strive to achieve absolute precision in the manipulation of idealized poetic forms, giving at least as much
attention to the visual as to the auditory
aspects of their work. The ancient poets, on
the other hand, were creating entertaining
narratives, with no thought of demonstrating
their own erudition. They must have been
working to with what to them were strictly
auditory poetic forms that sprang up directly
from the language of their audience, and so
contained many of the features of everyday
speech, in this case, stress-related syllable
reduction.

Rhyme in the *râay* Stanza

The second general "rule" that the textbooks give for *râay* of all types is that the
wâk of a given stanza should be linked together by a rhyme between the last syllable of a
wâk and the first, second, or third syllable
of the following *wâk*. As with *khloog* forms,
the first syllable in the rhyme link is called
the *sòg* 'send' syllable, and the second is
called the *ráp* 'receive' syllable. Although
the textbooks do not mention the point, when
the *ráp* syllable is the second or third of the
wâk it generally marks the boundary between
the two phrases of that *wâk*, which would have
served to emphasize the rhythm of the passage
in recitation.

Not only is the position of a rhyme

important, so àlso is the nature of the syllables that form the rhyme. According to Phrayaa Uppakit, the general "rules" for *râay*
include the stipulation that the rhymes be
between syllables of the same kind. That is,
if the *sòŋ* syllable is spelled with no tone
mark, the *ráp* syllable must also be spelled
with no tone mark, and if the *sòŋ* syllable is
spelled with either the first or second tone
mark, the *ráp* syllable must be spelled with
that mark as well (Uppakit 1968: 417). In
terms of the linguistic background discussed
in chapter 3, this "rule" can be rephrased to
indicate that rhymes must be between syllables
from the same column in the ancient tone
chart. Thus, A-column syllables must be
rhymed with other A-column syllables, and so
on. The great regularity of this pattern in
the poem suggests that it was far more than a
"rule" of poetry, however, but was a phonetic
fact; A- and B- and C-column syllables must
have been phonetically distinct from each
other in such a way that they could not have
rhymed. This point is a crucial one especially in connection with the idea of *ʔèek
thôot* 'incorrect first tone mark' syllables
and *thoo thôot* 'incorrect second tone mark'
syllables. The examination of the rhyme links
found in the text of *Lilit Phra Law* given
below should clarify this point.

The 113 stanzas of *râay* in the Ministry
of Education version of *Lilit Phra Law* range
in length from five *wák* up to 135 *wák*, and
there are 2,149 *wák* found in stanzas of *râay*
in this edition of the text. At this point we
will be concerned only with rhyme links between those *wák* that are not part of a *khlooŋ*
ending pattern of the stanza. There are,
therefore, 1,818 opportunities for rhyme links
between these *wák*, and the Ministry of Education text wording shows appropriate links
between the *wák* in all but fifty-one of the
cases. An "appropriate" rhyme, that is, one
in which the *wák* are linked by a rhyme within
the ancient tone categories, is generally, but

142

not always, reflected in modern Thai orthography with the tone mark system.

A total of 883 (49%) of the links between *wâk* are formed by syllables that are written with no tone mark in the modern system (A-column syllables). A total of 201 (11%) of the links are formed by syllables with the first tone mark (B-column syllables), and 233 (13%) are formed by syllables with the second tone mark (C-column syllables). Links are formed by long-vowel, closed syllables (D-long column syllables) in 219 (12%) cases and by short-vowel, closed syllables (D-short column syllables) in 231 (12%) cases.

There are fifty-one (3%) cases in which there are rhymes that do not fit any of the patterns above, indeed they do not fit any pattern. Significantly, in nearly every case the vowel and the final consonant, if one is present, of the syllable in the *sòŋ* position is the same as the vowel and final of the syllable in the *ráp* position, but the tone marks do not match. In terms of the Proto-Tai tone chart discussed in chapter 3, we might say that these *wâk* have rhymes that cross over columns, from A to B, or A to C, and so forth. The fact that these are perfectly acceptable rhymes in modern Thai has no doubt led to confusion about the nature of rhyme in ancient *râay* and *khlooŋ* poetry, and in ancient Thai itself.

These problem cases are few in number and are probably not noticed by the average reader, especially since modern Thai rhyme patterns do not require agreement of tone. The commentators do not speak directly of the cases in which the poets seem to violate their own "rule" that *wâk* of *râay* should be linked by rhymes between syllables that have the same tone mark; but these supposed flaws must be at least part of the reason for the opinion, stated most explicitly by Prince Bidyalankarana (1926: 105), and shared by many present-day writers and teachers, that ancient poets "were not obliged by the rules of poetry of their day to be as careful as we are today [and] judged by present day standards, their works are more or less crude." Since this opinion is widely accepted, it seems wise to examine closely these seemingly aberrant passages of *Lilit Phra Law* for a solution to the problem. And, as the discussion will show, there is a solution available.

We know that there are many places in which the various published texts of *Lilit Phra Law* differ. There are clear typographical errors, some copied and recopied from the Royal Library edition of 1926, others introduced in subsequent editions and reprintings. There are also clear examples of editors modernizing the spellings of words to match current ideas of correctness. And there are also readings in the printed texts that do not match any of the manuscript copies of the poem. Unfortunately, the printed texts are the only ones available to the average reader, and even consulting the *samùt khɔ̀y* manuscripts does not solve all of the problems since there are many places in which the different manuscripts do not agree among themselves. For these reasons one must not be content with studying only a single edition of the poem. One must look to all of the available sources for solutions to the problem of what I have chosen to call cross-column rhymes.

In many of the fifty-one cases of what appear to be problem rhymes it is not difficult to locate a reading that solves the problem by providing an appropriate rhyme. For example, in stanza 83 the thirteenth *wák* ends in the word *taa* 'grandfather', but no early syllable in the fourteenth *wák* has the vowel *aa*; thus, there is no rhyme link at all. The *wák* are given below.

khɔ̌ɔ dây phâŋ bun   taa
ask   get rely merit grandfather(?)

(They) asked to rely on his(?)
power.

pùu   duu sèt   cùŋ wâa...
grandfather look finish so say

When Samingphray finished his
meditation he said...

The thirteenth *wâk* closes a series of *wâk*
that relate the meditative vision of the
powerful magician named Samingphray, who is
often referred to by both the protagonists and
the narrator of the poem with the respectful
titles *pùu* 'paternal grandfather' and *pùu câaw*
'lord paternal grandfather'. The use of the
title *pùu* in the fourteenth *wâk* signals a
return to the narration of events, since that
term is usually not used by Samingphray to
refer to himself but only by others to refer
to him.

The first problem in interpreting the
passage is choosing between the two Thai homophones *taa*, which translate as 'maternal
grandfather' and 'eye'. The term *pùu* 'paternal grandfather' is the only one of the two
kinship terms that is used elsewhere in the
poem, making the choice of the *taa* 'maternal
grandfather' a doubtful one. An interpretation could be offered for the line in which
taa is the noun 'eye', but context makes this
possibility unlikely and, as we shall see
momentarily, the wording found in the manuscript copies of the poem further diminishes
the likelihood of this interpretation. The
other problem is, of course, that the wording
does not provide for any rhyme link between
the two *wâk*.

This instance is one of only three in the

145

poem in which two *wák* of *ráay* do not rhyme at all, and the wording of the *wák* as they stand is not at all satisfactory. Thus, we are justified in assuming that the problem lies not with the poem but somewhere in the editing or printing of it and that we may have a better and more accurate version available somewhere, even though the Ministry of Education text does not give any alternative readings. One possible solution can be found in the Royal Library edition, from which the Ministry of Education text editors say they copied their own text.

The Royal Library edition reading does not have *taa* and has instead the now archaic first person pronoun *tuu* 'I' as the final word in *wák* thirteen (1926: 22). This provides an appropriate rhyme link between *tuu* (ฎ) and *duu* (ฎ), both of which are spelled with no tone mark. The use of the first person pronoun also allows for a much more satisfactory reading; the *wák*, now clearly the words of Samingphray himself, becomes "...they asked me for my help." But the problem is not solved yet. Another possible solution is in Phra Worawet Phisit's *Handbook* text, which has the first person pronoun *kuu* (ฎ) 'I' in the final position of the *wák*, which is also acceptable both in terms of the rhyme pattern and the meaning of the passage.[8]

An examination of the manuscript copies of this passage is most helpful in resolving the problem, and it is also instructive in the matter of reliability of the published editions. Of the eighteen *samùt khɔ̀y* in which the passage is present and legible, only one uses *tuu*, and the other seventeen all have *kuu*. One is left to wonder why *tuu* was chosen for the *Handbook* text, and even more, why such a glaring error as the substitution of *taa* for *kuu* was left uncorrected in recent revisions of the Ministry of Education text. All the more interesting is the fact that the Ministry of Education text does not acknowledge that

146

there is any problem here at all and does not
include any reference to alternate readings.

   Many of the other problem links are more
easily corrected. Often the problem is solved
by the wording given in the Ministry of Education text footnotes, usually with no change of
meaning, and so the average reader does not
have to go to the old manuscripts to find
solutions to the problems. An example is
given below. The two *wâk* are the 27th and
28th of stanza 144.

   sêεŋ   pen hŭa sŭa   hŭa châaŋ
   disguise be   head tiger head elephant

   (The ghosts) had the heads of tigers
        and elephants,

   pen hŭa   kwaaŋ hŭa chamăn
   be   head deer   head stag

   and deer and stags.

   The Ministry of Education text reading
matches that of the Royal Library edition and
requires that *châaŋ* (ช้าง), written with the
second tone mark, rhyme with *kwaaŋ* (กวาง),
written with no tone mark. This rhyme would
not be considered incorrect in modern Thai
verse forms, but it does violate the textbook
"rule" that the *wâk* be linked by *sòŋ* and *ráp*
words with the same tone mark, or in modern
linguistic terms, words from the same column
of the Proto-Tai tone chart. The Ministry of
Education text footnote for this line, however, indicates that of the extant manuscripts
"some copies" have the word *săaŋ* (สาง) instead of the word *châaŋ* in the *sòŋ* position.

   This alternative reading is more satisfactory in several ways. First, *săaŋ* is
semantically appropriate. In the *Dictionary of*

147

the Royal Institute (1984: 901) several definitions for the word are given, one of which is 'elephant' and another is 'mythical tiger', each of which is acceptable here. Second, *sǎaŋ*, which has the modern rising tone, and *kwaaŋ*, which has the modern mid tone, both originate from the A column of the tone chart, thus satisfying the so-called "rule" regarding rhyme. Also, although not so importantly, the word *sǎaŋ* provides for a pleasing alliteration within the *wâk*: *sêɛŋ*, *sǔa*, *sǎaŋ*, which probably would have been present in the ancient pronunciation. Finally, turning to the *samùt khɔ̌y* we find that all seventeen of the manuscripts that are legible at this point have the word *sǎaŋ*. The reading with *chǎaŋ* must be a modern invention, one that actually introduced an error into the text.

Some problems with the *wâk* linking rhymes are solved by the text as it appears in the *Handbook*, which, as has been said, often differs from the Ministry of Education text reading even when there are no footnotes in that text indicating the existence of possible alternate readings. Below is an example of a reading taken from the *Handbook* text that solves a problem rhyme link for which the Ministry of Education text offers no alternatives. As we shall see, the *samùt khɔ̌y* copies are helpful in resolving the conflict, but in this case some interpretation is necessary. The two *wâk* are presented as they appear in the Ministry of Education text; they are the fourth and fifth *wâk* of stanza 49.

rúu chít chǎy kon   khlɔ̌ɔŋ[9]
know near use   trick fluent

(They sought one) who knew [magic]
        tricks intimately and fluently

bɔ̀ɔk thamnɔɔŋ thǔk ʔan
tell way   every one

148

         (and they) told (her) all the de-
         tails.

    The wording in the Ministry of Education
text requires that *khlɔ̀ɔŋ* (คล่อง)[10] spelled
with the first tone mark, rhyme with the
second syllable of *thamnɔɔŋ* (ทำนอง), spelled
with no tone mark.   This rhyme of a B-column
word and an A-column word can be made a rhyme
between two A-column words if *khlɔ̀ɔŋ* 'fluent'
is replaced with *khlɔɔŋ* (คลอง) 'way; canal',
spelled with no tone mark.   Modern Thai usually uses the word *khlɔɔŋ* to refer to the once
ubiquitous canals of the country and sometimes
uses the word in an abstract sense, meaning a
way of doing things.   An often repeated phrase
from modern speech that illustrates the point
uses the word *thaaŋ*, meaning 'path' or 'road'
or the like, and used in an abstract sense in
expressions referring to a manner or way of
doing things.   The common expression is *mây*
mii thaaŋ 'not have way' usually used to mean
something like, "It can't be!"   Thus, it is
not at all difficult to make a case on semantic grounds for the plausibility of the change
proposed here.   The use of *khlɔɔŋ* would change
the reading of the first *wák* in the example
above to "(They sought one) familiar with the
tricks and the ways [of magic]..."

    This reading fits the stanza well and
also seems to be that intended by Phra Worawet
Phisit in his *Handbook* (1961: 29).   The interpretation he gives for this stanza is closer
to the reading proposed here than to the
reading of the Ministry of Education text.[11]
And the interpretation is most welcome since
the *samùt khɔ̌y* texts are not uniform.   Of
eighteen legible copies, seven have *khlɔɔŋ* and
the rest have *khlɔ̀ɔŋ*.   Thus, many, but not
all, contain the proposed reading.

    As this discussion shows, none of the
printed texts can be used as the only source
for individual readings, and even consulting

the manuscripts can give inconclusive results.
When problems develop, however, an examination
of all sources of both text and interpretation, including modern linguistic studies, can
help to solve the problems with the rhyme
links and thus eliminate many instances of the
supposed crudity of ancient poetic works.

In some cases an alternate reading solves
the problem of the cross-column rhyme, but the
solution is not so apparent because problems
other than simple copying or printing errors
are involved. The example given below is from
stanza 423; the link is between *wâk* 4 and *wâk*
5.

> *nât-kan maa ca khâa*
> agree   come pt. trade
>
> (We) agreed to come here on business.

> *phlât   maa thâa thaaŋ thóp*
> separate come wait way   fold
>
> Separated from one another, (we)
>   came to the crossroads to wait.

This pair of *wâk* comes from a description
of the meeting between Kaew (*kêɛw*) and Khwan
(*khwǎn*), the two men who accompany Phra Law on
his journey, and the two women Run (*rûɐn*) and
Roy (*rooy*), attendants to the royal sisters.
The men, wishing to conceal their identity and
that of Phra Law who is coming after them,
offer a false story to explain their presence.
The example has a rhyme link between the word
khâa (ฅ) 'trade', spelled with the second
tone mark, and *thâa* 'wait', spelled in the
Ministry of Education edition with the first
tone mark (ฅ). The link is thus between a
word from the C column and one from the B
column, a violation of the "rule." The *Handbook* text addresses the problem by spelling

150

the word *thâa* 'wait' with the second tone mark
(◌้), but includes a note in the text saying
that it should really be spelled with the
first tone mark (1974: v.2, p.38). In fact,
the word is from the C column and an historically correct spelling would use the second
tone mark, as was explained in the section of
chapter 3 dealing with the effects of the tone
splits on modern Thai. The spelling used in
the Ministry of Education text, and accepted
as correct in modern Thai, is historically
aberrant. The link between these *wák* is
actually correct according to the "rule"
requiring rhyme links within columns, and the
seeming mismatch has been created by modern
editors and their preference for the current
spelling conventions. Thus, the author of the
Handbook included the historically correct
spelling in his edition, but thought it was a
thoo thôot, a purposeful error.

Of the fifty-one cases of apparently
missing or improper rhyme links between *wák* in
stanzas of *râay*, twenty have an alternate
reading reproduced from the manuscript copies,
and available in printed form in the Ministry
of Education text footnotes, the Royal Library
edition, the *Handbook* text, or the Krasaesin
text, that solves the problem, generally with
little or no rewording, although occasionally
with substantial rewording of the text. In
general, the alternate readings are as acceptable as those given as the main readings of
the Ministry of Education text, and in some
cases the alternate is better. Appendix 2
lists the cases of seemingly improper rhym'e
links, that is, links that cross the Proto-Tai
tone columns. The first list includes the
twenty cases for which there is an alternate
reading available in a published edition that
provides an appropriate rhyme link. The
alternate rhyme link is given along with its
source and the number of manuscript copies in
which it is to be found. In the interests of
economy of space and time, these examples will
not be discussed individually, but there is

sufficient information provided so that an
interested reader may locate the problem
stanzas and the alternate reading for each in
the printed editions.

There are thirty-one other cases in which
the rhyme link between the *wâk* as they appear
in the published editions violates the "rule"
governing the nature of rhyme that is given in
the textbooks, but for which no alternate
reading that solves the problem is available
in published form. For twenty-three of these
cases it is possible to reason to a satisfactory rewording of the printed edition of text
that is supported by at least some of the
manuscript copies. In each case the alternate
is as appropriate semantically as the main
reading, and sometimes is better, and also
provides a rhyme link that matches the textbook "rule." These twenty-three cases are
also listed in appendix 2, along with the
words that form the alternate link and the
number of manuscript copies that contain the
wording.

Proposed Rewording of Some Passages of *râay*

Given below are several examples of
passages in which rhyme links appear to be
formed in violation of the "rules." The
passages that are discussed below were chosen
as illustrations of the availability of solutions to the seeming problem passages. They
also give an indication of both the benefits
and the difficulties involved in working with
the manuscript copies of the poem. They are
discussed individually in the order in which
they appear in the text.

1)   Stanza 8 - *wâk* 18 and *wâk* 19

    rum   kan phûŋ kan thɛɛŋ
    gather pt. hurl pt. stab

(The armies) mingled together hurl-
    ing and stabbing [with their
    weapons].

khâw tɔɔ yέεŋ tɔɔ yút
enter oppose oppose oppose war

(They) came together opposing and
    making war.

    This early stanza tells of a ferocious
battle between the cities Suang (*sǔaŋ*) and
Song (*sɔ̌ɔŋ*), which began the enmity that
eventually resulted in the deaths of the five
most prominent characters of the story. The
two *wâk* quoted above describe some of that
battle. The *sòŋ* word, *thεεŋ* (แทง) 'stab', is
written without a tone mark, and the *ráp* word,
yέεŋ (แย้ง) 'oppose', is written with the
second tone mark, which means that the rhyme
link is from the A column to the C column in
the tone chart. However, a more likely *ráp*
word is *yεεŋ* (แยง) 'insert; prod', which is
written with no tone mark. In this case the
reading would be changed only slightly; the
second sentence would become something like
"They came together in opposition, mingling
together in making war." This change in
wording would create a rhyme link between two
syllables with no tone mark, that is, two
syllables that originated from the A column in
the Proto-Tai tone chart, which obeys the
"rule" stated for *râay* rhyme links. Eight of
the manuscript copies have this wording.

2) Stanza 53 - *wâk* 6 and *wâk* 7

    thǔŋ carɔɔk lέεw yaay   maa
reach lane   pt. grandmother come

(After leading them) to the lane,
    she returned.

khâa kɔ̀ khâw pay sùu
I   pt. enter go toward

I went in toward (him).

This passage is from a section of the poem that relates the efforts of the court ladies Run and Roy to help the royal sisters, Phra Phuan and Phra Phaeng. The two hope to entice Phra Law to their mistresses through the use of magic spells. Their search leads them to a magician who says that she herself is not powerful enough to cast a spell on one as exalted as the young king, but knows of one who might be able to help, a disciple of the greatest of magicians, Samingphray. The wâk quoted above come from the stanza in which the old woman leads Run and Roy to the home of Samingphray's disciple.

The alternate reading for wâk 6 given in the Ministry of Education text footnote as well as in the **Handbook** text (thǔŋ carɔ̀ɔk mɔ̌ɔ ['doctor'] lɛ́ɛw maa) is more clearly the words of the narrator of the poem and the clarity is welcome here, even though the wording change does not directly affect the rhyme link problem. We know that the female magician leads the two young women to the home of Samingphray's disciple, referred to as mɔ̌ɔ, and then leaves, but after that the wording becomes confused about just who is going to see him.

There are two main problems in this passage. First is the rhyme link problem; maa (มา) 'come', spelled with no tone mark, is in the sɔ̀ŋ position and must rhyme with the only likely ráp word, khâa (ข้า) 'I', spelled with the second tone mark. Second is the semantic problem; the first person singular pronoun khâa has no likely referent. The old woman has departed, leaving only Run and Roy, who are acting in unison rather than as individuals, and for whom a singular pronoun is therefore not appropriate.

154

The solution to both problems lies in changing *khăa* 'I' to *khăa* (ขา), a third person dual pronoun, 'they two', written with no tone mark, which is the spelling found in six of the manuscript copies. It is then clear that the passage is narration and means something like, "She led them to the lane [where the disciple of Samingphray lived] and then left. The two of them then went in toward him." The rhyme is then between two A-column words, and the meaning is far clearer. Undoubtedly, part of the difficulty with this passage, and others like it, has developed because modern Central Thai does not use dual pronouns. Speakers of that dialect have probably assumed that *khăa* was an erroneous spelling of the only common word that was close to being semantically appropriate, the singular pronoun *khăa* 'I'.

3)   Stanza 73 - *wăk* 28 and *wăk* 29

    thàp   *thŭŋ* *tὲε* *tiin khăw*
    immediately reach only foot hill

    As soon as (they) reached the foot-
        hills,

    mɔ̌ɔ   *thâw lon*   *càak cháaŋ*
    doctor old   descend from elephant

    the magician dismounted the   ele-
    phant.

This passage describes a journey under- taken by the ladies Run and Roy to find the most powerful of magicians, Samingphray. They are led on the trip by the former disciple of Samingphray, mentioned above, who is referred to by two honorific titles, *mɔ̌ɔ thâw* (*thâw* 'old') and *mɔ̌ɔ pùu* (*pùu* 'paternal grand- father'). The purpose of the trip is to

155

enlist the assistance of Samingphray in the plan to cast a spell on Phra Law that will attract him to the royal sisters Phra Phuan and Phra Phaeng of the city of Song.

The trip takes the travelers through a strange forest filled with frightening creatures and then into a set of mountains where Samingphray lives. The magician who guides the travelers is amused by their fear and tells them not to worry, saying that the dangers are mere illusions, created by Samingphray himself. Once through the forest, we are told in *wák* 26, they waste no time in driving their elephants into the mountains; *kháw* (เขา) 'hill; mountain' is the word used.

The two *wák* given above are joined in the Ministry of Education text by a link between *kháw*, an A-column word, and *tháw* (เท่า), a B-column word. The word *tháw* is pronounced with the falling tone in modern Thai, and it is written with a low-category consonant and the first tone mark and is, thus, treated as a B-column word. However, evidence from comparative studies shows that the historically correct spelling would use a high-category consonant and the second tone mark (เถ้า). The Ministry of Education text uses the modern conventional spelling, which is historically aberrant. However, the Royal Library edition uses the historically accurate spelling as do thirteen of the manuscript copies. Even the use of the historically correct spelling does not solve the rhyme link problem, however, because the rhyme link between an A-column and a B-column word is replaced with one between an A-column word and a C-column word.

If we follow this line of reasoning, we may find an appropriate link in this case if we can show that the *sòŋ* word should also be one from the ancient C column, and that is indeed possible. The expression *tiin kháw* (*tiin* 'foot') is commonly used to mean 'foothills', and so the word *kháw* 'hill; mountain'

156

seems, at first glance, to be correct. However, *wǎk* 26, given below, makes this reading suspect.

> *khàp cháaŋ wîŋ khûn khǎw*
> drive elephant run ascend hill
>
> (They) ran the elephants up the
> mountain(s).

It would seem illogical to follow this *wǎk* so quickly with another stating that they dismounted the elephants as soon as they reached the foothills. If we assume, however, that *khǎw* in *wǎk* 28 should actually be the word *khâw* (เข้า) 'enter' we can provide both a semantically acceptable reading, and a C-column *ráp* word to rhyme with *thâw*, which also originated from the C column, despite the modern spelling.

The word *khâw* is a verb meaning 'to enter', but modern speech also uses the word as a verb modifier that, among other meanings, can serve to emphasize the suddenness or rapidity of an action.[12] An example of a modern sentence using the word in this way is given below.

> *phɔɔ hěn khâw kɔ̀ núkʔɔ̀ɔk*
> enough see enter pt. remember
>
> I remembered just as soon as I
> caught sight (of him).

Modern Thai makes extensive use of this verb, and many others as well, to create textual coherence.[13] It is not possible to say, at this point, just how extensively ancient Thai used verbs is this way, but there are passages in the poem that resemble the modern patterns. Also, three of the manu-

157

scripts that have this passage use the C-column spelling. It is thus at least plausible that the word *khǎw* was used in the manner illustrated in the example sentence given above. If we accept the possibility, then the reading of *wǎk* 28 becomes something like "Immediately on reaching the foot [of the mountain] the magician dismounted the elephant." The earlier *wǎk* used the word for mountain, providing *tiin* with an appropriate referent, and so this reading is semantically acceptable and also provides for an appropriate rhyme link between two words from the same ancient tone column, in this case the C column.

This section of the poem has an unusually large number of problem links. Along with those between *wǎk* 28 and 29, the links between *wǎk* 23 and 24, 26 and 27, and 29 and 30 are also problems. Solutions to the some of these problems are corrected in alternate readings available in published texts of the poem, and so they have not been discussed here, but it should be noted that the links 23/24, 26/27, and 28/29 all involve rhymes between words ending with the diphthong *aw*. All versions of the text, both the manuscript copies and the printed editions, are garbled here, and one published edition even omits *wǎk* 27 and 28 entirely.[14] The rhymes used in the original are, in all likelihood, partly to blame for the problem. If, as has been frequently suggested, ancient texts as we know them today are reconstructions done from memory by scholars of the early Bangkok period, it is easy to understand how the frequent repetition of the same vowel sound in the *wǎk* links could have led to confusion. Even if there was no need to reconstruct the texts from memory, simply the process of copying and recopying over the course of centuries would provide ample opportunity for confusion and unintentional alterations. In the case of the link between *wǎk* 29 and 30, the manuscript copies offer no appropriate solution, and in fact suggest that

158

at least some of this section may be an insertion made after the changes in the tone system of the spoken language. Unfortunately, our analysis of these passages will probably never be able to provide us with absolute certainty as to the date of such probable additions to the older version or versions of the text.

4)   Stanza 85 - *wâk* 1 and *wâk* 2

     phrá? ?əəy khŭa(?) *khâa   maa*
     title oh! you two servant come

     Oh Lord! We two(?) servants have
        come.

     càk taay châa taay mɔɔt
     pt. die slow die fade

     We almost died [of fright].

This brief stanza of only six *wâk* relates comments made by the ladies Run and Roy to Samingphray after he agrees to help them lure Phra Law away from his home to meet with the royal sisters. The ladies are profuse with their thanks but ask one last favor, that Samingphray grant them a trip home that is less frightening than the trip to meet with him had been. The wording is very garbled at this point, with footnoted differences in the Ministry of Education text for five of the six *wâk* of the stanza, and with unrecognized differences between that text, the Royal Library edition, and the *Handbook* text as well. Even a critical edition would not be able to resolve all of these difficulties since this confusion in the printed texts is matched by great variation in the manuscripts themselves. This discussion will cover one problem word as well as the problem rhyme link between *wâk* 1 and *wâk* 2.

First of all, the reading given for *wâk* 1

is probably incorrect. The word *khŭa* 'you two' is a second person dual pronoun and does not fit here; there are only three people in the scene, Samingphray and the two ladies. The previous stanza, also a brief one, is narration telling of the reaction that the two ladies have to Samingphray's decision to help them. The expression that opens the stanza, *phrá? ?əəy* 'Oh, Lord!', must be addressed to Samingphray, and so, therefore, are the rest of the words in the *wák*. Clearly, the first person dual pronoun *phŭa* 'we two' was intended instead of *khŭa*, and the point is supported by the wording of eleven of the manuscripts.

The second problem is the rhyme link between the words *maa* (ม) 'come', from the A column, and *cháa* (ช้า) 'slow', from the C column. The irrealis particle *càk* begins *wák* 2, and phrases with this particle followed by *taay* 'die' and some type of adverbial modification are common in modern Thai speech, and also, one would suspect, in older speech as well. Thus, the ladies tell of their mortal terror at the sights that had surrounded them as they approached the mountain dwelling of Samingphray. The word *cháa* 'slow' follows the word *taay* 'die' most appropriately; the word *mɔɔt* 'fade out (of fire)' is also appropriate following *taay*, giving a reading something like "(we thought we would) slowly die (of fright)." This reading, however, does not solve the rhyme link problem of a *sòŋ* syllable from the A column and a *ráp* syllable from the C column. There are no suitable alternatives for *maa* that would solve the problem, but one can argue that *cháa*, while semantically appropriate, was actually intended to be *chaa* (ชา) 'numb; inactive'. The reading would be something like "(we thought we would) be paralyzed and die (of fright)." The word *chaa* presents an acceptable semantic parallel with *mɔɔt* in that both imply a gradual lessening of activity, but the more important point is that the use of *chaa* provides a rhyme link between two words of the same column in the tone chart, in

160

this case the A column. Two of the manuscript copies do, in fact, use this word, which suggests that the reasoning suggested here is at least worth considering.

5)   Stanza 224 - *wák* 26 and *wák* 27

thápsuaŋ   sĕɛŋ   rûaŋrúŋ
breastplate light lustrous

The breastplate shown brilliantly.

phlɔɔy phét   phûŋ yanyoŋ
gem   diamond hurl beauty

The jewels radiated beauty.

This passage describes the radiant beauty of Phra Law's garments. The rhyme in question is between *rúŋ* and *phûŋ*. Both words have the same vowel and final, but different modern tones; *rúŋ* (รุ่ง) is written with the second tone mark, and *phûŋ* (พุ่ง) is written with the first tone mark, which suggests that they originated in the C and the B columns, respectively. In this case there is an alternate reading available, but it is really a modern invention and, rather than solving the problem, actually adds to the confusion. The Royal Library edition wording is the same as that given in the Ministry of Education text, and the wording seems to make perfect sense, despite the mix of the ancient tone columns in the link.

An alternate reading that seems to solve the problem is to be found in the *Handbook* text, but in fact this reading leads us in the wrong direction. The wording found in the Handbook text agrees with that of the Ministry of Education text, but spells *phûŋ* in a different way, one considered incorrect in modern Thai. The same modern initial, vowel, and final sounds, and the same modern tone are

161

represented in each of ther versions, but the Ministry of Education text uses a low-category letter (หฺง) in the syllable-initial position along the first tone mark, and the *Handbook* text uses a high-category letter (หฺง) and the second tone mark. A footnote to the Handbook text explains that the seemingly peculiar spelling is used because the poet "wanted a word with second tone mark" at that point, that is, the author considered the spelling to be a *thoo thôot* (Worawet 1974: 1,156). In this case, however, the reading using the second tone mark is spurious. The historically correct spelling for the word (Donaldson 1970: 301) is that used in the Ministry of Education text, and that spelling is also the one used in eleven of the extant manuscript copies.

In fact, the explanation lies not with the spelling of the word *phûɲ* but with confusion over the expression *rûaɲ rúɲ* (ร่วงรุ้ง) 'lustrous'. Modern Thai forms compounds from *rûaɲ* 'to drop, fall' and *rúɲ* 'rainbow', but *rúɲ* is from the C column and is, therefore, a problem. The word *rûɲ* (รุ่ง) 'dawn; bright' however, is found in eight manuscript copies. It is from the B column and also is semantically as acceptable as the word from the C column for use in poetic descriptions of the radiance of gems. The original meaning would have been something like "to cast (the light of)" either the rainbow or the dawn, depending on which of the words was chosen. The modern preference for *rúɲ* does not lessen the acceptability of the use of the other word here. One additional bit of evidence is the rhyme link between the seventh and eighth *wák* of the same stanza. That link is formed by *rûɲ* and *phûɲ*, both from the B column, and there is no ambiguity to confuse the wording, since the *wák* describe the coming dawn. If we accept *rûɲ* in the stanza link, both words are from the B column, and the meaning is not altered.

162

6)   Stanza 228 - *wǎk* 18 and *wǎk* 19

sûu   sùk   yɯɯn   bɔmí   phâay
fight enemy stand neg. lose

(When the horses) fight the enemy
     (they) stand and are not de-
     feated.

naay   khìi   khàp   khêm   khĕŋ
title ride drive vehement strong

The riders drive (them) boldly.

This passage describes events after Phra
Law has been charmed by the magic of Samingphray. Unable to resist that magic, Phra Law
decides to go and raises an army to accompany
him on his journey. Stanza 228 is a long and
elaborate description of the force that has
been gathered for the trip. The problem link
to be examined here is between the *sòŋ* word
phâay (พ่าย) 'lose', spelled with the first
tone mark, and the *ráp* word *naay* (นาย), a
title for males, spelled with no tone
mark.[15] Two of the manuscripts provide an
alternate wording that solves the cross-column
rhyme problem by replacing the word *phâay* with
chaay (ราย) 'to turn or alter course'.[16]
The reading for *wǎk* 18 would thus become "(The
horses) fight the enemy; (they) stand and are
not turned away." In this reading both the
sòŋ and the *ráp* words are from the A column.

7)   Stanza 228 - *wǎk* 27 and *wǎk* 28

hɛ̂ɛ   lăŋ làak   lŭa   lăay
procession rear various abundant many

Those in the rear were various and
     numerous;

hɛ̀ɛ   *fàay sǎay dàatdaa*
procession side left abundant

Those on the left side were
     abundant...

     This passage contains the description of
the procession that accompanies Phra Law on
his journey. The problem link is formed by
the *sòŋ* word *lǎay* 'many', spelled with no tone
mark, and the *ráp* word *fàay* 'side'; group',
spelled with the first tone mark. An alternate reading found in two of the manuscripts
provides a solution, however, with no change
in the meaning of the *wák* by replacing the
word *lǎay* (หลาย) with the word *lɛ̀ɛ* (แหล่),
'much; many'. The alternate reading provides
a *sòŋ* and *ráp* pattern between two B-column
words.

8)   Stanza 318 - *wák* 50 and *wák* 51

       kày   *tham khrâan*   *maanyaa*
       chicken make inactive trick

       The cock, as a trick, became still.

       hěn kày   *cháa thá kɔ̀ sǎaw*
       see chicken slow he pt. step

       Seeing the cock (moving) slowly, he
           walked forward.

     This passage describes the last bit of
magic that Samingphray uses to bring Phra Law
to the young women.   The magician sends a
spirit into the body of a wild cock and, by
magic, makes its beauty irresistibly fascinating to Phra Law, who unwittingly follows the
bird toward the city. The problem rhyme links
the second syllable of *maanyaa* (มารยา) 'trick',
spelled with no tone mark, and *cháa* (ช้า)
'slow', spelled with the second tone mark.

164

There is considerable variation in the manuscript copies, and two separate acceptable
readings can be found. In one of the readings, *wâk* 50 ends with the word *lâa* (ล้า) 'to
be slow; fatigued (as if from exertion)',
making for a C-column rhyme and giving a
reading of something like, "The cock acted
tired and slowed down." The change is in *wâk*
51 in three other manuscripts, which replace
the word *châa* with *chaa* (ชา) 'numb; inactive' giving the somewhat different but
equally acceptable wording "...seeing the cock
not moving, he walked forward." This reading
provides for both a *sòŋ* and *ráp* syllable from
the A column. It is interesting to note that
the various readings found in the texts all
involve the vowel *aa* and the significance of
this point will be discussed in the next
section.

The Nature of Rhyme in Ancient Thai

A factor that must have contributed to
the difficulty of dealing with the cross-
column rhyme problem, both in preparing the
published editions and in interpreting the
text, is the great variation found in the
manuscripts. In some cases the alternate
reading that makes for a rhyme within the
ancient tone categories is found in all, or
nearly all, of the manuscripts. In such cases
the problem indicates that the editors of the
printed edition in question either based their
work on only a single manuscript copy or
perhaps "corrected" what they felt to be an
imperfect wording. In other cases, the manuscripts are far from uniform, and the alternate may be found in only a few of the copies.
In such cases editors have selected one of the
available readings, often justifying that
selection on modern stylistic preferences. In
still other cases, the majority of the manuscripts agree on the suspect wording, and only
a few have an alternate reading that solves
the problem. Perhaps, in such cases, the

editors were unaware of the variant reading, or based their selection partly on the force of numbers. If we are to deal with the situation successfully we must first ask how these variations may have come about, and then decide how are we to assess the material that we have to work with. As this section will show, detailed consideration of the problem passages leads to important conclusions about the nature of rhyme in ancient Thai.

It is often said that most of the art and books of Ayutthaya were destroyed in the sack of the city by Burmese invaders in 1767. It became the task of the king of Thonburi and the early kings of Bangkok to rebuild the lost grandeur of the old city in the new capitals they built on the banks of the Chao Phraya River.[17] As part of this task, a great deal of effort was devoted to the arts. For example, successive new versions of the story of Rama, known in Thai as the "Ramakian," were composed, and perhaps there were also efforts at this time to recreate, from memory, the texts of the ancient classics.

Although the matter has not been exhaustively studied, all the extant manuscript copies of *Lilit Phra Law* in the National Library appear to date from the Bangkok period. It is possible that these texts now available to us are copies of versions that were written by memory, by individuals who recalled what they had heard performed or had read before the fall and destruction of the old city. If the texts are the product of such an effort, the results are strikingly good, and the problems that we find in them are most understandable.

Reconstructions done after the fall of Ayutthaya would have been done by people whose language had undergone the changes described in the discussion on linguistic background in chapter 3. The speech of those attempting the reconstruction would have been fundamentally different from the speech that gave rise to the *khlooŋ* and *râay* forms. Even if some copies of the poem survived the destruction of the old capital city and it was not necessary to reconstruct the poem from memory, just to produce new accurate copies of older manuscripts under such circumstances would have been difficult. Some of the spellings that we now know to be historically incorrect were already in vogue when the texts were being recreated or recopied, which means that the scribes would have to have been extremely faithful to the old texts and the seeming errors that they contained. It is easy to see how obscure or archaic words could have been replaced with more contemporary ones.[18]

Similarly, convoluted passages, or those with numerous rhymes consisting of the same common vowel or final consonant sound, could easily have become garbled. The confusion in stanza 73, with numerous rhymes between words ending with the diphthong *aw* and in stanza 318, for which the manuscripts use various words with the vowel *aa*, are good examples. It is instructive to note, in this regard, that the one feature involved in nearly all of the fifty-one problem readings in stanzas of *râay* is tone, which is what we would expect from reconstructions based on memory if they were prepared by speakers of a tone system in which rhyme played no role.

Given these circumstances, we are more than justified in our decision to search among the various manuscript copies for alternate readings and to consider carefully even those that appear in a limited number of copies. Also, comparative linguistic analysis can resolve with certainty at least some of the points of confusion, freeing us from the need of relying primarily on matters of style and taste, which change from age to age. Approaching matters in this way enables us to draw interesting conclusions about the nature of poetry, and in fact, about the nature of rhyme in the speech of the ancient poets.

If we consider carefully all of the
alternate readings found in the manuscripts,
and if we accept them as at least plausible
solutions to the problem of cross-column
rhymes, we have new totals for the various
rhyme link categories. There are 1,818 opportunities for rhyme links between *wâk* in *râay*
stanzas (exclusive of those *wâk* in which rhyme
links are required by *khlooŋ 2* ending patterns).[19] In chart 1 the rhymes are divided
according to the columns of the Proto-Tai tone
chart, and the new totals for each column
include the fifty-one problem links.

Chart 1: Rhyme Distribution by Tone Category

A	B	C
908 (50%)	208 (11%)	242 (13%)
Ds	Dl	Problems
231 (13%)	219 (12%)	8 (1%)

These totals show a clear preference for
rhyme links using words from the A column,
which constitute half of the rhyme links. The
rhyme links created by words from other columns divide nearly equally. The most striking
fact is that there are so few *wâk* that do not
rhyme within columns. There are only eight
cases out of 1,818 in which there is no available reading, or no reading that can be rea-
soned to easily in which there is not such a
rhyme link. Even if we consider only those
readings for which there is no uncertainty, by
far the majority of *wâk* are linked by rhymes
of the expected type. In the final analysis,
the rhyme links between *wâk* of *râay* follow a
regular pattern throughout the poem, and there
is little if any support for the contention
that the ancient poets were inconsistent in
their work.

In light of the overwhelming regularity of the pattern of rhyme described above, we must re-examine the "rule" about the rhyme system in use at the time of the composition of *Lilit Phra Law*. Textbook authors and scholars who have examined the text have noticed the frequency with which rhymes seem to include a match in tone mark and have described that pattern as a consciously invented "rule." Thus, it was assumed that syllables written with the first tone mark, for example, had to be found to create rhymes with other such syllables because that was one of the set of patterns that ancient poets devised and then combined to create *khlooŋ* and *râay*. In addition, that part of the pattern came to be seen as an orthographic one, a constraint based not on the sound of the syllables, but on the written representation of them.

The presence of a number of seeming violations of this rhyme pattern has also given credence to the idea that the attention to the tone mark in rhyme was no more than a convention, one that inexpert poets could ignore, if necessary. These apparent violations have no doubt contributed to the conclusion that the ancient poets, who it seemed could not even obey their own rules with complete regularity, were not as skillful as those of the present day.

In modern Thai speech rhyme is a somewhat ambiguous phenomenon, at least in comparison to what it must once have been. The pitch contours that distinguish the five modern tones certainly serve to differentiate words, but they are not sufficiently different to restrict rhyme across those tones. Thus, in modern poetic forms tone plays no role whatever. But, as the previous discussion shows, nearly all of the supposed violations in *Lilit Phra Law* of the "rule" requiring rhyme within tone categories can be shown to be corruptions of the text. The great numbers of rhymes

169

within tone categories found in the *râay* stanzas of the poem indicate that it was more than simply a "rule" that tone be part of the rhyme. It must, rather, have been a part of the phonetic features of the ancient tones that compelled such regularity. Words from different tone categories must have sounded basically different and, therefore, could not have rhymed.

This argument becomes all the more probable when we also consider the nature of the *khloon* stanza, with its patterns not only of rhyme, but also of tone placement. Combining rhyme and tone patterns to create a poetic stanza format could only have made good sense if the tones were audibly different to the degree that there was no ambiguity. That is, the ancient tones must have sounded distinctly different from each other -- qualitatively different, in a way not found in the modern contour-tone system that is based on pitch height -- in order to have become one of the building blocks of the poetic system.

Types of *râay* Found in *Lilit Phra Law*

This chapter has devoted a great deal of discussion to the structure of the *wâk* in *râay* and to rhyme as it is used within the stanza. There remains one additional point that is given attention in the textbooks but has yet to be discussed here, and that is the type of *râay* used in the poem. It is possible, and indeed necessary, to discuss this point separately because, as the textbooks state, the difference between *râay sùphâap* and *râay dân* is that stanzas of the former type end in a *khloon 2 sùphâap* pattern, and those of the latter type end in a pattern that is the same as the last two lines of a stanza of *khloon 4 dân*. It is said that *râay booraan* ends "abruptly," with no particular pattern of tone or rhyme (Uppakit 1968: 419). But all these types are said to be composed of *wâk* of five syllables each, and so the various types of *râay* are distinguishable only by the pattern found in the last few *wâk* of the stanza.

It is said in the textbooks that stanzas of *râay* in *Lilit Phra Law* are mainly of the *sùphâap* variety, but that *râay dân* and *râay booraan* are also used occasionally throughout the poem. The discussion of *khlooŋ 4* has demonstrated that there is little evidence to support the contention that *khlooŋ 4 dân* is used in the work at all, and the examination of the other *khlooŋ* forms below will show that there is also little there that can be called *dân* poetry. The details of tone placement in the *khlooŋ* patterns that close *râay* stanzas will be discussed at that point, so that all the stanzas of *khlooŋ 2* can be discussed together. For the present, however, a general statement can be made regarding the *khlooŋ* patterns that close the stanzas of *râay*. Of 113 stanzas of *râay* in *Lilit Phra Law*, 108 (96%) end in a pattern that is unmistakably *khlooŋ 2 sùphâap*, leaving only five problematic stanzas.

One of the five problematic stanzas, which is the first one of the poem, does not end in a pattern of *khlooŋ 2 sùphâap*, but neither does it end in a pattern of *khlooŋ 2 dân*. The stanza closes with elaborate praise of the city of Ayutthaya and ends with the following pattern in the last two *wâk*.

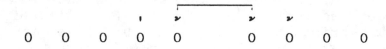

This pattern does not appear in the text-books, and so the stanza is neither *sùphâap* nor *dân* as they are described in those sources. Neither, however, does it end "abruptly" with no pattern, and so it also does not conform to the description of *râay*

booraan. This stanza, and the three stanzas of *khlooŋ 4* following it, precede the actual story of *Lilit Phra Law*, and all have tone or rhyme patterns that do not match the textbook descriptions.[20] At the same time these stanzas are not just haphazard arrangements. As with the *khlooŋ* stanzas that begin the poem, it seems more reasonable to assume that this stanza of *râay* is part of an otherwise unmarked prologue section that has been created for the text and set apart by the use of distinctly different forms. At any rate, the stanza in question is a special case and is not evidence of the mixing of forms or of the use of an unpatterned *râay booraan* form.

Thus, there remain only four stanzas out of a total of 113 *râay* stanzas that are anomalous and, therefore, difficult to categorize.[21] The ending pattern of each is not as regular as the ending patterns found in the vast majority of the *râay* stanzas, but they do not simply come to an end, as *râay booraan* stanzas are said to do. The manuscript copies of some of these stanzas vary greatly, and one, stanza 43, even has a standard *khlooŋ 2* ending in one of the manuscripts, but this single copy does not resolve the doubts. Even though no better readings are available, however, there are still only four stanzas out of 113 that do not fit the expected pattern.[22]

CONCLUSIONS: THE ANCIENT *râay* STANZA

In studying the *râay* passages of the poem, we must be aware of the fragility of the manuscripts that we have as our oldest sources for the text. There is great potential for loss or error in reconstructing stanzas of rhymed prose from memory, as may have been done during the early part of the Bangkok period. And even if such reconstruction did not actually have to be done, the potential for error in copying and recopying the manuscripts over the course of time is still

great. We must not rely on a single manuscript as the primary source of our information about the poem, and we certainly must
look beyond the printed editions in dealing
with what appear to be problem passages.

If we study the passages carefully,
consulting all the available sources of information, we see that most of the seeming problems in the *râay* passages can be clarified.
There hardly seems to be sufficient evidence
for saying that the ancient poets were less
careful than their modern counterparts or that
they mixed forms together at will. Rather,
what emerges, again, is a picture of a fully
developed and complex oral form that was used
to create work of great auditory richness and
beauty. The strong similarity between the
râay and *khlooŋ* forms is clear, as is the
intimate relationship between those forms and
the speech patterns from which they developed.

NOTES

1. A fourth variety of the form, know as *râay*
yaaw, is said to have an indefinite number of
wâk with an indefinite number of syllables per
wâk and no specific ending pattern. The form
is used in religious chanting and nothing of
this type appears in *Lilit Phra Law*.

2. As has been stated previously, the text of
the Ministry of Education is used here as the
reference text because it is the most readily
available one, and it is the only one that
numbers the stanzas consecutively. A critical
edition will no doubt alter slightly the
specific numbers arrived at in this study, but
the overall picture will remain unchanged.

3. The first stanza of the poem is by far the
most inconsistent in this regard. The wording
varies considerably in both printed editions

and in the manuscript copies, and one finds *wâk* of three, four, five, and six syllables. It is the only stanza in the poem that has *wâk* of fewer than five syllables, and like stanzas 2, 3, and 4, it is structurally and thematically different from those that form the rest of the poem. It would appear that these stanzas were composed separately from the rest of the poem, perhaps using standard phrasing from elsewhere, or were designed as an otherwise unmarked prologue that followed different compositional constraints.

4. Note that the normal modern pronunciation of this title is *phíyaa*, as for example, when it is used in speech to refer to two well-known Thai scholars, both now deceased: Phrayaa Uppakit Silapasarn and Phrayaa Anuman Rachathon. The spelling "phrayaa," used throughout the present study, reflects the current preferred spelling of the title.

5. For a full discussion of this complex pattern, see Patcharin Peyasantiwong (1986).

6. For a discussion of "weak syllables" and their representation in Thai writing, see Brown (1979: 29).

7. This point is also addressed in Bickner (1986).

8. The word is considered coarse and vulgar in modern, urban Thai, but this is evidently a recent development.

9. In modern pronunciation the word is pronounced with a short vowel.

10. See previous note.

11. Unfortunately, there seems to be a printing error in the two-volume edition of the *Handbook* text (1974) that complicates the problem. As it appears in that edition, the *wâk* ends with *khɔɔŋ* (คอง), which is not

174

listed as a word in any of the dictionaries consulted for this study. In the earlier one-volume edition of the *Handbook* (1961), however, the final word in the *wăk* is spelled out as *khlɔɔŋ* (คลอง). A comparison of other passages makes it clear that no changes were intended in the later edition, and so we must assume that *khɔɔŋ* is a misprint for which *khlɔɔŋ* was intended. This reference is to the one-volume 1961 edition of the *Handbook*; unless otherwise specified, all other references are to the two-volume edition of 1974.

12. See Noss (1964: 183ff), for a detailed treatment of verb modification in Thai.

13. A part of this coherence system as it is used in modern literature is discussed in detail in Bickner (1989).

14. Worawet, vol. 1, p. 54. This is clearly an inadvertent omission. The two *wăk* appear in all extant manuscript copies.

15. The *sòŋ* word *khěŋ* 'strong' is also part of a problem rhyme link, but the *Handbook* text suggests that the word intended was *khèŋ* 'compete', which is semantically acceptable and also solves the rhyme problem. One of the thirteen legible *samùt khɔ̀y* (#20) also uses this wording. See appendix 2.

16. The Dictionary of the Royal Institute (1982: 623) equates the word *phăay* 'move from position', spelled with no tone mark (พาย), and the word *phâay* spelled with the second tone mark (ผ้าย). This spelling does not appear in the manuscripts, but it could have been the original ending, lost or forgotten and then replaced by a more familiar word.

17. For a discussion of the vitality of artistic endeavors that concentrates on the reign of Rama III but also touches on the

earlier reigns of the period, see Vella (1957: 43-58).

18. According to Vella the decision by Rama III to break with tradition and not patronize performers and poets had the effect of dispersing and actually increasing the popularity of the secular arts. Members of the royalty and the nobility, free from the problem of potentially competing with the king, patronized their own troops (Vella 1957: 55). This spread of activity would have created a need for more copies of texts to be used in staging productions. This may help to explain why the extant manuscripts of *Lilit Phra Law*, although they retain what is clearly archaic language, all appear to have been made relatively recently.

19. The figure of 1,818 is taken from the wording of the Ministry of Education text. My studies of the manuscript copies in the National Library collection suggest that a critical edition of the poem would allow us to change a few of these totals slightly, but the differences would not alter the conclusions arrived at in this study, and in some cases would even serve to reinforce them.

20. See chapter 4 for more discussion of these stanzas, and also for a detailed treatment of tone placement in stanzas of *khlooŋ 4* in *Lilit Phra Law*.

21. The stanzas in question are numbers 43, 198, 230, and 637.

22. The patterns found in the other three anomalous stanzas as they appear in the Ministry of Education text are given below in diagram form. Unfortunately, there is a great deal of variation in the manuscript copies of the poem, and even a critical edition would not resolve the confusion entirely.

Stanza	Final Pattern										
198	0	0	0	0	0		0		0	0	0	0		0
230	0	0	0	0	0		0	
637	0	0	0	0	0		0	0	

Chapter 6

THE *khlooŋ 2* AND *khlooŋ 3* STANZAS
OF *LILIT PHRA LAW*

The *khlooŋ 2* pattern appears both inde-
pendently as individual stanzas of the poem,
and it also as the ending pattern for the many
stanzas of *râay* in the text. Both uses of the
pattern will be discussed in this chapter,
although certain details make it necessary to
cover them separately. We will also cover in
this chapter the small number of *khlooŋ 3*
stanzas that appear in the poem. They will
also be treated separately, but this will be
done primarily to conform to conventional expectations. As we shall see, there is really
no need to conceive of *khlooŋ 3* as a separate
form, and we could just as well group these
stanzas with stanzas of *râay*. Again, we will
use points from Phrayaa Uppakit's treatment as
the starting point for the discussion, although with the same reminder that there is
much of significance that needs to be added to
those points.

Independent Stanzas of *khlooŋ 2*

Discussion of the nature of the poetic
forms used in *Lilit Phra Law* centers mainly on
the *khlooŋ 4* stanzas, although general statements about the poem suggest that the alleged
mixing of *sùphâap* and *dân* varieties took place
in all of the *khlooŋ* forms, including the
independent *khlooŋ 2* stanzas as well as in the
khlooŋ 2 endings of stanzas of *râay*. The
khlooŋ 2 pattern is shorter and less complex
than that of the *khlooŋ 4* stanza, and so the
differences between the *sùphâap* and *dân* form
are more distinct. Nonetheless, there is
confusion regarding the forms as they appear
in the poem, and a close examination is in
order. For convenience, the diagrams of
khlooŋ 2 sùphâap (diagram 1) and *khlooŋ 2 dân*
(diagram 2) are here given together, below.

Diagram 1: *khlooŋ 2 sùphâap*

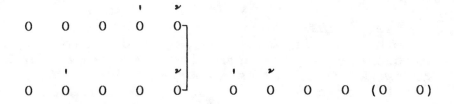

Diagram 2: *khlooŋ 2 dân*

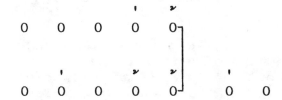

A detailed examination of the stanzas of the poem is useful both for what it reveals about the controversy over the forms and also for what it reveals about aspects of the poetry not mentioned in the textbooks. The results of the examination of *khlooŋ 2* stanzas will be presented in the same format as was used for the results of the examination of *khlooŋ 4* stanzas. The four points on which the *sùphâap* and *dân* varieties are generally said to differ are: the number of syllables per stanza; the use of *kham sɔ̌y*; the tone placement pattern; and the rhyme placement pattern. These four points will be taken up in that order.

1) Length of the final *wâk* of the stanza
    According to the textbooks *khlooŋ 2 sùphâap* and *khlooŋ 2 dân* differ in syllable count in only one respect. The final *wâk* of the *sùphâap* variety is said to require four syllables, whereas stanzas of the *dân* variety may have only two syllables in this position. All 243 of the *khlooŋ 2* stanzas of *Lilit Phra Law* end with a four-syllable *wâk* and thus, by

179

this measure at least, are from the *sùphâap* variety.

2) Use of *kham sɔ̌y*

The use of *kham sɔ̌y*, according to the textbooks, is not permitted in stanzas of *khlooŋ 2 dân*, but stanzas of the *sùphâap* variety may add them following the final *wák* of the stanza. Of the 243 verses of *khlooŋ 2* in *Lilit Phra Law*, eighty-two (38%) do end in *kham sɔ̌y*. At least according to the modern formulation of the rules concerning the use of additional syllables, then, the poets were working with the *sùphâap* variety of forms.

3) Tone placement

As with *khlooŋ 4*, a major difference between the varieties of *khlooŋ 2* is in the placement throughout the stanza of syllables from a specific ancient tone category. Tone placement in *khlooŋ 2 sùphâap* stanzas differs from that of the corresponding *dân* variety in the same way that it differs in the *khlooŋ 4* forms. In the *sùphâap* variety, the penultimate *wák* requires one syllable spelled with the first tone mark (that is, a B-column word) and one spelled with the second tone mark (C column) as shown in the diagram. The *dân* form adds to this the requirement that the fourth syllable of the *wák* should also be one spelled with the second tone mark. The result is a sequence of two syllables with the second tone mark, known as *thoo khûu* 'paired second tone' or, in linguistic terms, two consecutive syllables derived from the ancient C tone. The final *wák* of the *sùphâap* stanza requires one syllable spelled with the first tone mark followed immediately by one spelled with the second tone mark. The final *wák* of the *dân* stanza, however, requires that the first of two syllables be spelled with the first tone mark and that the second be spelled with no tone mark.

There are no independent stanzas of *khlooŋ 2* in *Lilit Phra Law* that deviate significantly from the idealized *sùphâap* pattern. The only point on which the stanzas resemble the textbook description of the *dân* form is in the use of the so-called *thoo khûu* 'paired second tone' in the penultimate *wák*. As with *khlooŋ 4*, use of this pattern in *khlooŋ 2* is supposed to be characteristic of *dân* poetry and therefore not appropriate for use with *sùphâap* stanzas. However, seventy-seven (32%) of the 243 *khlooŋ 2* stanzas that appear in the Ministry of Education text of the poem have the *thoo khûu* pattern, which is roughly equivalent to the percent of *khlooŋ 4* stanzas that have the pattern. In every other respect they match the idealized *sùphâap* pattern.

The supposed mixing of *sùphâap* and *dân* forms is taken to be evidence either of uncertainty on the part of the poets or of a state of flux in the forms as the supposedly less elaborate *dân* form developed toward a more fully worked out *sùphâap* form. The presence of the *thoo khûu* alone, however, is not sufficient evidence to support either suggestion from the point of view of tone placement. In all respects other than the *thoo khûu* the stanzas are completely realized examples of *khlooŋ sùphâap* as it was known centuries later. If the forms were in a state of transition from *khlooŋ dân* to *khlooŋ sùphâap* at the time that *Lilit Phra Law* was composed, then the *thoo khûu* is the only aspect of the tone pattern that shows any evidence of it.

The independent *khlooŋ 2* stanzas, like those of *khlooŋ 4*, are very carefully worked out, with complex patterns that modern writers have not recognized. A cursory examination of the Ministry of Education edition of *Lilit Phra Law* may seem to suggest that the poets, as is said often in modern textbooks and articles, were not very careful with the "required" tone placements. But a closer look shows that, as with *khlooŋ 4*, some parts of the idealized *khlooŋ 2* pattern are adhered to more carefully than others, suggesting again that the modern, highly visual conception of the stanza format differs significantly from what must have been the highly auditory conception of the ancient poets. The second chart in appendix 1 shows the types of syllables used in the Ministry of Education edition in those *khlooŋ 2* positions that are said to require a specific tone mark. Clearly, there are a number of places in which the textbook pattern is not followed as completely in the *khlooŋ 2* stanzas as it is in the *khlooŋ 4* stanzas, but the variation is also not simply haphazard.

According to the textbooks, the pattern of the first *wák* of the *khlooŋ 2* stanza is the same as that of the first *wák* of the *khlooŋ 4* stanza. In this modern formulation of the ideal stanza, the last two syllables of the *wák* should be written with the first and the second tone marks, respectively. If we again rephrase this description and state it in terms of the ancient sound pattern of Thai, we find that a B-column word should be followed by a C-column word. In *khlooŋ 2*, unlike *khlooŋ 4*, this tone sequence may not be reversed. In fact, the rhyme pattern of these shorter stanzas makes this impossible.

In many *khlooŋ 2* stanzas, however, there is great variety in the type of syllable that appears as the fourth syllable of the first *wák*. Of the 243 *khlooŋ 2* stanzas, 126 (52%) have syllables spelled with the expected first tone mark (B-column syllables). Other stanzas have what has been described as an acceptable substitute for the B-column word. A total of forty-three (18%) stanzas have a long-vowel, closed syllable (D-long), and thirty-five (14%) others have a short-vowel, closed syllable (D-short) instead of one with the first tone mark. A syllable with a nasal final appears in this position in fifteen (6%) of the stanzas, but there are no cases of this type of substitution in the first *wák* of the stanzas of *khlooŋ 4*. In thirteen (5%) of the stanzas a syllable spelled with the second tone mark appears in this position, and in eleven (5%) of the stanzas the syllable is not spelled with either tone mark, nor is it one that is a recognized substitute for a B-column syllable. This position shows greater variation from the textbook pattern than any other position in which a *khlooŋ* form is said to require a syllable with the first tone mark immediately preceding a syllable requiring the second tone mark. The last position in the first *wâk*, on the other hand, is very regular and has the prescribed second tone mark in all but one highly doubtful case.[1]

In *wâk* two of the stanza there is also considerable variation in the position said to require a syllable written with the first tone mark. In ninety-six (40%) of the 243 *khlooŋ 2* stanzas the syllable in this position is spelled with the expected first tone mark (B-column syllable). In a total of 113 stanzas, however, a closed syllable (D-column syllable) substitutes for one spelled with the first tone mark; in fifty-six (23%) of the stanzas the vowel is long and in sixty-seven (23%) stanzas the vowel is short. In nineteen (8%) stanzas a syllable with a nasal final appears in this position and in five (2%) stanzas the syllable is neither one with the first tone mark nor one recognized as an appropriate substitute. In ten (4%) of the stanzas the syllable appearing in this position has the second tone mark instead of the expected first tone mark. The final position of the *wâk* is said to require a syllable with the second tone mark, and in all but the single highly doubtful case mentioned in the previous paragraph, this is the case.

In the third *wâk* the syllables with the first tone mark (B column) and second tone mark (C column) follow each other in sequence as the first two syllables of the *wâk*, and here there is considerable regularity in both positions. In 159 (65%) of the stanzas the first syllable is from the B column. In seventy (29%) stanzas a long-vowel, closed syllable (D-long) appears in this position, and in fourteen (6%) stanzas the syllable is closed, but with a short vowel (D-short).[2]

The second position of the final *wǎk* calls for a syllable with the second tone mark. Only two stanzas, numbers 40 and 304, do not follow the pattern, but there are alternate readings for both that provide the expected C-column syllable. Both anomalous readings should probably be disregarded as copying errors.[3] All other stanzas have a syllable with the expected second tone mark.

Clearly there is greater variation in the independent *khlooŋ 2* stanzas than in those of *khlooŋ 4*. However, the pattern of less variation at structural boundaries than elsewhere in the stanza that appears in *khlooŋ 4* is found in stanzas of the shorter form, as well. Again, the pattern seems to suggest that the ancient forms were oral in nature and not the visual forms that they have become in the modern conception.

4) Rhyme placement
Rhyme placement is identical in *khlooŋ 2 sùphâap* and *khlooŋ 2 dân*, so there is no dis-agreement on this point as to the variety of the form used in *Lilit Phra Law*. The only required rhyme is between the last syllable of the first *wǎk* and the last syllable of the second *wǎk* of the stanza. All of the *khlooŋ 2* stanzas of the poem (except for the highly suspect reading of stanza 16, and the obvious copying error of stanza 243) have this rhyme pattern exactly as expected.[4]

"Extra" Syllables in the Final *wǎk* of *khlooŋ 2*

There is an additional observation made by Phrayaa Uppakit in his description of *khlooŋ 2* that should be mentioned at this point. The observation concerns the structure of the final *wák* of the stanza and a modification made to it, supposedly in compositions involving the use of more than one verse form. Phrayaa Uppakit says that if stanzas of *khlooŋ 2* (or *khlooŋ 3*, which will be discussed below) are used with *ráay booraan*, which ends with a five-syllable *wák*, then the last *wák* of the *khlooŋ 2* stanza, which normally has only four syllables, may also have five syllables. He says, in effect, that in such cases the requirements for placement of syllables with specific tone marks will be shifted by one syllable each, that instead of appearing in their normal positions as the first and second of the *wák*, those syllables with required tone marks will appear in the second and third positions. An example quoted in Phrayaa Uppakit's text is reproduced below. It is stanza 212, according to the numbering system used in the Ministry of Education text. The length of the glosses requires that the three *wák* of the stanza be presented on separate lines, unlike the normal printed format.

> *thaaŋ klay yiaw sàt ráay*
> way far might animal fierce
>
> *phĭi khanooŋ lɔ̆ɔn khlăay*
> ghost wild scare like
>
> *tham lêe hây hĕn tua*
> make ruse give see body
>
> The way is long and fierce animals
> and wild spirits may scare you, appearing
> before you by [magic] tricks.

In order to demonstrate that this is an intentional change and not an error, Phrayaa Uppakit cites a pair of stanzas, numbers 212 and 213 in the Ministry of Education text, which do, indeed, have the described five syllables in the final *wák* of the stanza, and eleven of thirteen legible *samùt khɔy* copies have this wording. However, stanzas 208 through 211 are also *khlooŋ 2*, and they have only four syllables each in the stanza-final *wǎk* in both the printed editions and all but one or two of the dozen or so manuscript copies that have each of the stanzas. In addition, the passage of *râay* that precedes all of these *khlooŋ 2* verses, stanza 207, is not *râay booraan*, but *râay sùphâap*, ending in the normal *khlooŋ 2* format. Clearly this is a significant point, but close examination suggests that a better explanation for the pattern can be offered.

There are actually fifty-six stanzas of *khlooŋ 2* in which the final *wǎk*, as it appears in both the published texts and many of the manuscript copies, has five rather than four syllables.[5] Many of the extra syllables are not independent lexical items and, as has been explained previously, are the sort of syllables commonly reduced in normal speech and presumably also in ancient performance styles. But there are thirty-one cases scattered throughout the poem in which the extra syllable is an independent lexical item, not normally reduced in speech. In each case, moreover, the pattern is the same; the extra syllable is the first one in the *wǎk*, and it is followed by four more syllables of which the first is a B-column syllable and the second is a C-column syllable.

As Phrayaa Uppakit points out, the presence of the five-syllable *wǎk* is clearly intentional and not simply the result of a scribe's error, or the like. Also, however, and contrary to the explanation offered by Phrayaa Uppakit, it is clear that the use of this pattern is not connected with the pattern used in the preceding stanza. Rather, the presence of this "extra" syllable in so many stanzas suggests that we must rethink a basic assumption about the forms.

186

In all of the descriptions of the various *khlooŋ* and *râay* patterns, the rhyme and tone placements are noted as falling on such and such a syllable of a given *wăk*, counting from the beginning of that *wăk*. For the final *wăk* of the stanza, we are accustomed to saying that the first syllable must be one with the first tone mark (B column) and the second syllable must be one with the second tone mark (C column). It now seems best to say that the ancient pattern required a B-column syllable positioned four syllables from the last required syllable, and a C-column syllable three syllables from the last required one. This conception is the only one that allows for these "extra" syllables and still provides for the integrity of the stanza. It seems that the ancient *wăk* structure allowed for a preceding *kham sƏy*, without disturbing the syllable count. Such a conception suggests, again, that the ancient poets were working with auditory forms in which such "extra" syllables would not have been the problem that they are for modern visual conceptions of the forms. I will return to this important point for further elaboration in the treatment of tone placement in the *khlooŋ 2* patterns that end stanzas of *râay* in *Lilit Phra Law*. That discussion follows in the next section.

The *khlooŋ 2* Pattern in *râay* Stanzas

Having discussed the independent stanzas of *khlooŋ 2*, I now turn to the *khlooŋ 2* patterns that end stanzas of *râay*. This further discussion will both add to the picture of the *khlooŋ* verse form and also address the controversy over what type of *râay* is actually used in the poem, since it is here that the difference between types of *râay* appears. By definition, it is the ending pattern of the stanza of *râay* that determines the category in which that stanza belongs. There are 113 stanzas of *râay* in *Lilit Phra Law*, and 108 of them end in a pattern that is clearly *khlooŋ 2*. The

187

discussion of the ending patterns for these 108 stanzas will address the same points covered for the independent *khlooŋ 2* stanzas. The remaining five stanzas of *râay* end in irregular patterns that cannot be readily categorized as any type of *khlooŋ*; they are discussed separately in chapter 5, which is devoted to *râay*.

1) Length of the final *wák* of the stanza
      Of the 113 stanzas of *râay* in the poem, 108 end in the pattern of *khlooŋ 2*. In each of these cases the final *wák* has the four-syllable ending pattern expected in the *sù-phâap* variety rather than the two-syllable ending pattern expected in the *dân* variety. Thus, according to the textbook descriptions, the *râay* of **Lilit Phra Law** is nearly all of the variety known as *sùphâap*, and the *dân* variety does not appear in the text at all.

2) Use of *kham sɔ̌y*
      Of the 108 stanzas of *râay* that end in a *khlooŋ 2* pattern, fifty-three (49%) have *kham sɔ̌y* following the last required syllable. Stanzas of *khlooŋ 2 dân* are said not to allow such extra syllables, and so in this respect the stanzas of *râay* in **Lilit Phra Law** fit the description of the *sùphâap* variety.

3) Tone placement
      Although the textbooks often give a different impression, tone placement found in the *khlooŋ 2* ending patterns of the stanzas of *râay* is clearly that of the *sùphâap*, and not the *dân* variety. The third chart in appendix 1 gives the types of syllables used in each position said to require a specific tone mark in these *khlooŋ 2* patterns. The chart shows that there is approximately the same degree of regularity in the type of syllable used in each position as there is in the independent stanzas of *khlooŋ 2*.

      In the first *wák* of the pattern, forty-five stanzas (42%) have a syllable spelled

188

with the first tone mark (B column) as the second to the last syllable. Fifteen of these stanzas (14%) have long-vowel, closed syllables (D-long) in this position, and an equal number have short-vowel, closed syllables (D-short). In ten (10%) stanzas the syllable in this position ends with a nasal final.[6] In seven (6%) stanzas the syllable is not one from the B column and is not one normally considered an acceptable substitute, and in sixteen (15%) cases the syllable is spelled with the second tone mark instead of the first. There are several alternate readings in the manuscript copies, some of which would lower the totals of missing first tone marks, or of second tone marks found in positions where the first mark was expected, but the pattern would not be changed greatly even if all the alternates were found to be the most faithful reflection of the ancient wording. In contrast to the variation in the fourth syllable position, the final position of the *wắk* has the expected C-column syllable in all 108 of the stanzas.[7]

In the second *wắk* of the pattern the second syllable is one spelled with the first tone mark in forty-six (43%) of the 108 stanzas. In seventeen (16%) of the stanzas the syllable is closed, with a long vowel (D-long), and in twenty-seven (25%) stanzas it is closed but with a short vowel (D-short). A syllable with a nasal final appears in seven (6%) of the stanzas. In five (5%) of the stanzas the syllable in this position is not spelled with the first tone mark or with a recognized substitute, and in six (6%) stanzas the second tone is used. Again, the regularity of the final syllable position of the *wắk* contrasts with the earlier position. In all 108 of the stanzas the final position is filled with the expected C-column syllable.

The first syllable of the final *wắk* of the pattern is one spelled with the first tone mark (B column) in seventy-five (69%) of the stanzas. In a total of twenty-one (19%) of the stanzas a long-vowel, closed syllable (D-long) appears in this position, and in seven (7%) more stanzas a short-vowel, closed syllable (D-short) appears here. In only one stanza is a syllable with a nasal final used in this position. In four (4%) stanzas a syllable spelled with the second tone mark appears here, but in three of those stanzas the reading is confused and doubtful at best.[8] The second syllable of the *wâk* is written with the second tone mark in 107 of the 108 stanzas, and the single exception is a doubtful case.[9]

4) Rhyme placement
    Comments made regarding the rhyme placement in independent stanzas of *khloong 2* apply equally well to those patterns when used to end stanzas of *râay*. Since rhyme placement is identical in *khloong 2 sùphâap* and *khloong 2 dân* there is no disagreement on this point as to the variety of the form used in *Lilit Phra Law*. All of the *khloong 2* patterns that close *râay* stanzas are linked to the prior *wâk* in the expected manner.

"Extra" Syllables in the Final *wâk* of *râay*

    It is the final *wâk* of the *khloong 2* patterns that close stanzas of *râay* that is the likely source of much of the confusion about the form as it appears in the poem. As with the independent stanzas of *khloong 2*, a number of these patterns have a *wâk* with five syllables rather than the prescribed four; this is the case in twenty-eight (27%) of the stanzas, and one even has six syllables.[10] These syllables appear to be a violation of the normal pattern since they push the B-column and C-column syllables out of their expected positions at the beginning of the *wâk*. But we can find a solution to the problem if we again interpret the stanza from an auditory rather than a visual perspective.

If the structural boundaries are the most significant points in the stanza -- and the increased regularity of tone placement at structural boundaries is evidence that we ought to accept this interpretation -- then we should think of the final *wâk* as being a structure made up of four syllables, in which the final one should be from the A column, the fourth from the end of the pattern should be from the B column, and the third from the end should be from the C column. This pattern would form an unambiguous audible signal that the stanza was at an end, and extra syllables, or *kham sɔ̌y*, either before or after that pattern, would not be a cause of confusion. Indeed, they would only be a problem if one were to conceive of the relationship between the structural elements of the poetic forms in visual rather than auditory terms. The position of primary importance in auditory terms was probably the final point in each of the structural divisions. Modern authors, on the other hand, have conceived of the forms in primarily visual terms and have assumed incorrectly that the beginning point of each structural division was the most important. This interpretation is supported by the pattern of tone placement in the final *wâk* of the stanzas in question, for it is here that we see the greatest degree of regularity, suggesting that the auditory pattern signaling the end of the stanza was the one that should be maintained most carefully.

The only feature of the *khloоŋ 2* pattern at the end of the stanzas of *râay* that resembles the textbook description of *khloоŋ dân* is the pattern known as the *thoo khûu*. The *thoo khûu* appears in a total of thirty-nine (36%) of the 108 *râay* stanzas that end in a *khloоŋ* pattern, nearly equal to the frequency with which it appears in independent *khloоŋ 2* stanzas and *khloоŋ 4* stanzas. But this is the only feature that appears in these stanzas that is identified by the textbook authors as being characteristic of *dân* forms. In all other respects the poetry clearly belongs to the *sùphâap* variety. Rather than citing this single point as support for the idea that *Lilit Phra Law* was composed at a time of transition in which *dân* forms were developing into *sùphâap* forms, it seems better to refine the textbook descriptions of the characteristics of the forms.

CONCLUSIONS: THE ANCIENT *khlooŋ 2* STANZA

A detailed examination of *khlooŋ 2* stanzas in *Lilit Phra Law*, both those that appear as separate stanzas and those that serve as the concluding elements of stanzas of *râay*, leads again to the conclusion that the poem is an example of fully developed and skillfully crafted *sùphâap* poetry. There is more deviation from the expected tone placement pattern in these passages than there is in stanzas of *khlooŋ 4*, but this deviation leads us to important conclusions about the differences between ancient and more recent poetry. In all of the *khlooŋ 2* stanzas the treatment of positions said to require a B-column syllable is more consistent in the second *wâk* than in the first, and still more consistent in the third than in the second. The later *wâk* have fewer instances of unexpectedly absent tone marks and fewer substitutions than the earlier ones, and the final *wâk* shows a clear preference for words with the tone mark than for substitutes. In each case the positions described as requiring the second tone mark are very regularly filled with such syllables, although a number of garbled stanzas and the presence of some *kham sɔy* in the final *wâk* can give the opposite impression.

The variation is similar to that found in the tone placement patterns of *khlooŋ 4*, in which, as we have seen, the even numbered *wâk* show less variation in the type of syllable filling the B-tone position that do the odd numbered *wâk*. In both cases there seems to be

192

greater regularity in tone placement at structural boundaries, with the *wák* 'hemistich', the *bàat* 'line', and the *bòt* 'stanza' boundaries calling for increasing degrees of regularity. As with other features of the pattern that are not captured by the textbook formulations of the "rules" of the forms, this pattern of increased regularity at structural boundaries only makes good sense if we conceive of the forms as strictly auditory phenomena, in which the position of primacy was that at the end of each part of the structure. The pattern becomes meaningful if we suppose that it was designed to signal the approach of the end of each part of the structure, with the *wák*, *bàat*, and *bòt* boundaries having respectively greater importance. The pattern then becomes very similar to the patterns that form the units of ancient Thai music.

The *khlooŋ 3* Stanza

There are ten stanzas of poetry labeled *khlooŋ 3* in the Ministry of Education text of **Lilit Phra Law**. As later discussion will show, there is actually little practical benefit to be derived from treating these stanzas separately, especially since there are so few of them, but conventional analysis always does so, and I will follow that practice here.

With only one exception, number 87 of the Ministry of Education text, the stanzas match the textbook descriptions of *khlooŋ 3 sùphâap*. The structure of *khlooŋ 3 sùphâap* is shown in diagram 3, and the discussion is divided into the same four sections used previously in comparing poetry of the *sùphâap* and *dân* varieties: the number of syllables per stanza; the use of *kham sɔ̆y*; the tone placement pattern; and the rhyme placement pattern.

Diagram 3: *khlooŋ 3 sùphâap*

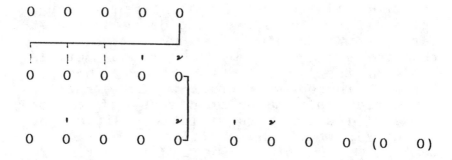

1) Length of the final *wâk* of the stanza

The stanzas of *khlooŋ 3* all have the number of syllables stipulated in the textbook descriptions of *khlooŋ 3 sùphâap*. As with *khlooŋ 2* the *sùphâap* and *dân* varieties of *khlooŋ 3* are said to differ in the final *wâk*, which is described as having four syllables in the *sùphâap* form but only two in the *dân* form. All of the stanzas of *khlooŋ 3* in **Lilit Phra Law** have a final *wâk* of four syllables.

2) Use of *kham sɔ̌y*

One of the stanzas of *khlooŋ 3* uses *kham sɔ̌y*, which, according to the textbooks, are permitted only in stanzas of *khlooŋ sùphâap*. By this measure, then, the poem fits the description of the *sùphâap* form.

3) Tone placement

The pattern of tone placement in stanzas of *khlooŋ 3* resembles that found in stanzas of *khlooŋ 2*. That is, there is variety in the type of syllable used to fill the positions that require the first tone mark. Less variation is found in the second *wâk* than in the first, and the third *wâk* has even less.

The positions requiring a syllable spelled with the second tone mark have syllables spelled with the first tone mark in two cases, but both are from a single garbled stanza (#87), which in the printed editions follows the pattern given in diagram 4.

194

Diagram 4: Tone Placement in Stanza 87

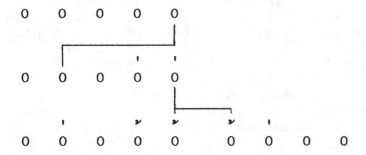

If this were the actual reading it would be a striking departure from the norm, but it is most likely not an accurate reproduction of the original wording. The stanza is suspect first because the wording is particularly difficult to interpret, to the degree that one suspects that something has been omitted or copied incorrectly, and second because of the aberrant tone and rhyme patterns. Given below is the reading as it appears in the Ministry of Education text.

sɔ̌ɔŋ naaŋ mɨa   hěn wan
two   lady return see day

coŋ   than ʔɔ̌ɔk pàak   pàa
imp. equal exit mouth forest

pay wâa lǎan kɛ̂ɛw thâa   thâa thân thuun sǎan
go say niece gem wait   wait he? say   news

> "(You) two ladies go back, so you will reach the edge of the forest while it is still day. Go tell the royal sisters to wait. Wait for him(?). Tell them this message."

This reading places *pàa* (ป่า) 'forest', a

word spelled with the first tone mark, in a position said to require the second tone mark. It also reverses the expected pattern of the final *wák* with *thâa* (ถ้) 'wait', spelled with the second tone mark, followed by the pronoun *thân* (ท่าน)[11], spelled with the first tone mark. In fact, none of the *samùt khɔ̀y* copies have this switch in the pattern. All ten of the copies that have this *wák* reverse the word order of the published texts to give the expected tone sequence. The use of this pronoun casts further doubt on the reliability of the reading since the speaker, Samingphray, elsewhere refers to himself with the personal pronoun *kuu* 'I'.

An alternate reading that appears in three of the *samùt khɔ̀y* copies is semantically acceptable and also matches the tone placement requirements. This reading is given below.

sɔ̌ɔŋ naaŋ mɯa   hěn wan
two   lady return see day

cùŋ than ʔɔ̀ɔk pàak pàa
pt. equal exit mouth forest

rêŋ   pay wâa lǎan kêɛw
hurry go say niece gem

kuu ca chûay coŋ lɛ́ɛw   yàa rɔ́ɔn cay   lǎan
I   pt. help pt. pt.   neg. hot heart niece

> "(You) two ladies go back so you
> will reach the edge of the forest
> while it is still day. Hurry to
> tell the royal sisters that I will
> help them, and not to worry."

While this reading solves a number of problems it does create another problem of a different type. If this is a faithful reproduction of the ancient wording then the stanza is not one of *khlooŋ 3*, which by definition has only four *wák*, but a stanza of *râay*. Curiously, this is the reading given in the

Handbook, and it is labeled as *khlooŋ 3*, even though it has five *wák* and is, therefore, according to all the textbook descriptions, ought to be labeled as *ráay*.

Several aberrant tone placements in *khlooŋ 3* stanzas are resolved by alternate readings in the printed editions, readings that are supported by the manuscript copies. Thus, the pattern found in *khlooŋ 2* stanzas is also present here. That is, the position said to require a B-tone syllable shows much less variation in the last *wák* than in the first two *wák*, and the placement of C-tone syllables is always regular.

4) Rhyme placement
As with the *khlooŋ 2* forms, rhyme place-ment is identical in *khlooŋ 3 sùpháap* and *khlooŋ 3 dân*, so there is no disagreement on this point as to the variety of the form used in *Lilit Phra Law*. The required rhyme between the last syllable of the first *wák* and the last syllable of the second *wák* of the stanza appears as expected in each example.

The *khlooŋ 2* and *3* Stanzas as Auditory Phenomena

The stanzas of *khlooŋ 2* and *khlooŋ 3* found in *Lilit Phra Law* do not seem to follow the textbook rules nearly as closely as do the stanzas of *khlooŋ 4*, and this is probably part of the dissatisfaction that modern writers have expressed with the work of the ancient poets. But an examination of each point shows that the poets have not simply disregarded the "rules." It shows, rather, that some parts of the pattern are more uniform than others, and that the modern formulations of the "rules" for the forms are probably very different from the conceptions of the forms that guided the ancient poets.

There is great variety in the type of

syllable found in those positions said to require the first tone mark, the ancient B tone, but this should not be taken as evidence of ineptitude on the part of the ancient poets. Many of the readings are doubtful, and if a critical edition of the poem can be undertaken, it will regularize the pattern considerably. The variety will still remain, however, and it is clear that it was intended, or at least allowed by the ancient poets. Instead of seeing this as weakness, however, we must look at the great similarity between the B and D columns of the ancient tone chart and consider the probability that words that come from these sources were phonetically much more similar in ancient speech than they are today. What seems to us today as a striking difference must have been far less so in ancient speech and did not interfere with the need to distinguish elements of the poetic form. In any case, the variety is distinctly less in the final *wâk* than in the first two *wâk* of the stanza, which is reminiscent of the pattern found in *khlooŋ 4*, in which variation decreases near major structural boundaries.

On the other hand, placement of syllables with the second tone mark, those with the ancient C tone, is very regular in these stanzas throughout the poem. Those few exceptions that do exist are extremely doubtful readings and can probably be disregarded as corruptions introduced during centuries of copying and recopying.

In addition, the required rhyme link between the syllables with the second tone mark is present in all but three of the 361 stanzas in question as they appear in the Ministry of Education text (ten *khlooŋ 3* stanzas, 243 *khlooŋ 2* stanzas, and 108 *khlooŋ 2* patterns at the end of stanzas of *râay*). Satisfactory alternate readings are to be found in the manuscript copies and are reproduced in the Ministry of Education text footnotes for these three stanzas. The alternate readings suggest that the apparent flaws are corruptions introduced into the text by copyists and editors.

These points are made more significant if, as with the *khlooŋ 4* stanza, we conceive of the *khlooŋ 2* stanza (and by implication the *khlooŋ 3* stanza, as well) as a strictly auditory rather than orthographic structure. Diagram 5 is a representation of the *khlooŋ 2* stanza, which, like the diagram of the *khlooŋ 4* stanza discussed previously, includes letters to indicate the ancient tone positions and punctuation to indicate the likely recitation style.[12]

Diagram 5: The *khlooŋ 2* Recitation Style

```
0   0,  0   B   C;⌉
                 |
0   B,  0   0   C;⌋  B   C,  0   A(; 0  0).
```

Of course, we have no written evidence that ancient performers used this style, but a pattern of this type can be applied to nearly all Thai poetry. It is highly likely, therefore, that something like this was intended by the poets.

If we assume that the poem was meant to be performed aloud then we must view the stanza as a structure formed from several components, among them syllable count, tone placement, rhyme, and performance style. We can see that the textbook formulations are followed most carefully at transition points. Ending consecutive *wâk* with rhyming syllables with the C tone would have signaled performers and audience alike that the *khlooŋ 2* pattern was being used, and that the following *wâk* would have the four-syllable pattern that forms the end of the stanza. Even the presence of an extra syllable or syllables, either

199

at the beginning or end of the third *wâk*,
would not have been a problem; the C-tone
rhyme of the first two *wâk* is an absolutely
unambiguous signal that the pattern is *khlooŋ*
2, and that only one more *wâk* will follow.

Within that final *wâk* the significant
relationship is between the individual syllables from specific tone categories. Thus, the
B-column syllable is not necessarily the first
one in the third *wâk*, but the fourth one from
the A-column syllable that ends the pattern of
the *wâk*, and the C-tone syllable is not necessarily the second one of the *wâk*, but the
third from the final required A-column syllable. Having heard the rhyme formed by the C-
column syllables in the previous two *wâk*, the
audience would listen for a sequence of a B-
column word followed by a C-column word, and
they would then know that only two more syllables would appear in the pattern, perhaps to
be followed by *kham sƆy*. And the expected
slowing of the pace culminating in a lengthening of the A-column word and a distinct pause
in recitation would show again that the *khlooŋ*
2 pattern was being brought to an end.

This description of various features of
poetry in terms of the end points of poetic
units is similar to the description of part of
the structure of traditional Thai music given
by David Morton, who says,

> These patterns are made much
> clearer and become more organized
> and systematic if the patterns are
> notated in Javanese style in which
> the rhythmic pulse leads up to the
> emphasis on the final beat of the
> phrase (1964: 90).

This description fits the *khlooŋ* patterns
well and explains why tone placements that
mark structural boundaries seem to be more
regular than those that do not. The similari-

ty between music and ancient poetry is an area that deserves a great deal of attention.

CONCLUSIONS: THE RELATIONSHIP BETWEEN
khlooŋ AND *râay*

A point that has yet to be explored in the scholarly writing on Thai poetry is the relationship between *khlooŋ 2*, *khlooŋ 3*, and *râay*, on the one hand, and *khlooŋ 4*, on the other. All textbooks treat the forms as though they were very different entities, in all probability separating them more than is necessary. As the different readings for stanza 87 illustrate, the first three forms mentioned above are similar enough to be confused. In fact, *râay* and *khlooŋ 3* differ only in length; there is no conceptual or structural difference to require that separate names be invented for the forms, or that they be covered separately in studies of the forms. And these two forms differ from *khlooŋ 2* in only one respect: any *wâk* that precede the third from the last of the stanza are joined to that *wâk*, and in turn are joined to each other, by a rhyme link between the last syllable of the preceding *wâk* and the first, second or third of the following *wâk*. Interestingly, the positioning of this rhyme link is exactly the same as the rhyme link that joins some stanzas together, and the only difference is that stanza-link rhymes are almost always formed with syllables from the A column of the Proto-Tai tone chart, but rhymes that link *wâk* together use other syllable types approximately half of the time.

We can take this point one step further, and compare these forms with the structure of *khlooŋ 4*. In fact, the *khlooŋ 2* pattern, whether it stands as an independent stanza or serves to complete a stanza of *khlooŋ 3* or *râay*, is identical to the first, seventh, and eighth *wâk* of the *khlooŋ 4* stanza. These *wâk* are crucial in each of the forms. In the *khlooŋ 4* stanza two extra five-syllable *wák* are introduced between the two five-syllable *wák* required of the *khlooŋ 2* pattern. In the *râay* stanza (and the conceptually identical, although shorter *khlooŋ 3* stanza) the additional five-syllable *wák* are added prior to rather than between the five-syllable *wák* required of the *khlooŋ 2* pattern. This great structural similarity suggests that we ought to abandon speculation over whether the *khlooŋ* and *râay* forms were borrowed from another language. Unlike the Thai forms known as *chǎn*, which are clearly borrowed from Indic sources and depend in part on the nature of the syllable in Indic languages for their structure, *khlooŋ* and *râay* forms clearly depend on the structure and rhythms of Thai for their origin. Although they are always treated separately in the text books, they are simply different variations on the same poetic phenomenon: a five-syllable unit broken into two phrases of different length and joined to other such units by rhyme link patterns of varying complexity.

This basic conceptual unit of five syllables also explains the final *wák* in each stanza type. The bulk of each stanza is made up of five-syllable units, embellished in different ways depending on the stanza type. The presence of a four-syllable unit, whether or not it is preceded or followed by *kham sɔ̂y*, is an unambiguous signal that the stanza is at an end. In light of all of this it seems more than appropriate to say that *khlooŋ* and *râay* are different variations on the same theme, and that they must have sprung from the same source, the normal speech patterns of the time.

NOTES

1. The stanza in question is number 16, in which closed syllables, *mâat* (มาด) and *râat* (ราช), appear as the final syllables of the first and second *wák* of the stanza. Those *samùt khɔ̀y* that have the stanza agree on this wording, but several of the manuscripts omit stanzas 16 through 22. Thus, the entire sequence may be a modern addition. At any rate, the presence of a single exception to the normal pattern calls into question the integrity of the extant texts, not the skill of the ancient poets. See also note 4.

In addition, stanza 243 as it appears in the Ministry of Education text contains a clear error in this position, one that suggests that the two C-column words *nɔ́ɔŋ* (น้อง) and *phíaŋ* (เพียง) are meant to rhyme. The fourteen *samùt khɔ̀y* that contain this stanza, however, all have the word *líaŋ* (เลี้ยง) as the first part of the rhyme, which solves the problem. The Royal Library edition, the supposed source for the Ministry of Education text, also has the word *líaŋ* at this point, leaving one to wonder where the erroneous wording came from.

2. One stanza, number 40, violates the expected pattern. The Ministry of Education text reads *maa sùu rooŋ thaan*, which replaces the expected sequence with an A-column word followed by a B-column word. An examination of the sixteen *samùt khɔ̀y* that are legible at this point, however, shows that only one of them (#10) has the Ministry text reading. The other fifteen copies have either *sùu thɔ́ɔŋ rooŋ thaan* (a total of four copies), or *sùu thɔ́ɔŋ rooŋ thɔɔŋ* (a total of eleven copies), either of which provides a reading that is both semantically acceptable and also follows the expected tone pattern (see Worawet 1974: v.1, p.31). The problem evidently stems in part from the presence of an extra syllable

maa at the beginning of the *wâk* in thirteen of the sixteen *samùt khɔ̌y*.

3. Stanza 304 reads *yùu tem baathaa*, which satisfies the need for an initial syllable with the first tone mark, but places a word with no tone mark in the second position. However, the alternate given in the Ministry of Education text footnote reads *yùu tây baathaa*, which makes better sense and also fits the pattern. This is the wording found in ten of the twelve manuscripts that have this stanza. The Ministry of Education text main reading does not appear in any of the manuscripts, and one is again left wondering where the erroneous wording came from. See note number 2 regarding stanza 40.

4. Stanza 16 has the words *mâat* and *râat* as the final syllables of the first and second *wâk*, in that order. The words both have the long vowel *aa* and stop final *t*, and so they rhyme, but this is the only stanza in the poem in which B-column syllables are used as substitutes for syllables with the second tone mark. This curious pattern is more likely the result of an erroneous reconstruction or a modern insertion into the text than a faithful rendition of the original. See also note number 1.

5. The stanzas of *khloog 2* that have extra syllables in the final *wâk* are identified by number below. The extra syllables are also given following the stanza number. In some cases the extra syllable is the first of a disyllabic word, but in many others it is a separate lexical item.

Stanza/Syllable		Stanza/Syllable		Stanza/Syllable	
12	*thûan*	249	*sa*	483	*chəən*
15	*lɔɔ*	253	*mǔan*	515	*sa*
16	*prà*	281	*phráʔ*	517	*sa*
19	*phráʔ*	284	*ka*	521	*ka*

204

39	*lɔɔ*	287	*thǎŋ*	532	*ʔòt*
47	*tham*	309	*dûay*	541	*ca*
64	*yiaw*	323	*phráʔ*	542	*thǎŋ*
70	*phǔa*	374	*sɔɔ*	549	*thǐ*
74	*nam*	392	*kàp*	552	*sa*
77	*pay*	429	*maa*	580	*thǐ*
79	*phráʔ*	433	*phǔa*	583	*phráʔ*
81	*ʔa*	445	*maa*	610	*sɔ̌ɔŋ*
95	*maa*	449	*sùk*	614	*kɛ̀ɛ*
120	*prà*	452	*phráʔ*	616	*chəən*
143	*phráʔ*	453	*sɔ̌ɔŋ*	618	*phráʔ*
173	*thǐ*	462	*phráʔ*	619	*kɛ̀ɛ*
212	*tham*	463	*yók*	622	*kɛ̀ɛ*
213	*dùt*	464	*khayòt*	646	*thǐ*
214	*phráʔ*	479	*thǐ*		

6. Stanza number 54 as it appears in the Royal Library edition differs from the Ministry of Education text reading. The second-last syllable of the *wák* in both the Royal Library edition (1926: 15) and the *Handbook* text (1974: v.1, p.40) is *sɔ̌ɔŋ*, not *mɔ̌ɔ* as it appears in the Ministry text. Of eighteen legible *samùt khɔ̌y* copies, sixteen agree with the Ministry of Education text, and only two agree with the two editions cited here.

7. The single exception must be disregarded as erroneous. The wording found in the Ministry text for stanza 72 requires that the final syllable of *cɔɔrakhlâay*, spelled with the first tone mark (จระคล่าย), rhyme with *khláay*, spelled with the second tone mark (คล้าย). However, fourteen of the manuscript copies use the expression *cɔɔraklâay* (จระกล้าย), which provides the expected tone (see also Worawet 1974: v.1, p.52).

8. In stanza 89 the order of the first tone followed by second tone is reversed; since this is the only case in the poem in which reversal occurs in the final *wák* of a stanza of *khlooŋ* it must be considered questionable. Stanza 389 uses the expression *bɔrâaŋ*, and in this stanza the second syllable is spelled with the second tone mark, but elsewhere in

the poem it is written with the first tone mark; and the various manuscripts do show great variation at this point. The word that appears at this point in stanza 656 is written in three different ways in three different sources: the Ministry of Education text, the *Handbook* (1974: v.2, p.173), and the Royal Library edition (p.164); and according to the Royal Academy Dictionary (p.887) the words used in the phrase are commonly spelled in different ways.

9. See the portion of note number 8 devoted to stanza 89.

10. The stanzas of *râay* that have extra syllables in the final *wâk* of the *khlooŋ 2* ending pattern are identified by number below. The extra syllables are also given following the stanza number.

Stanza	Syllable	Stanza	Syllable
8	*lân*	379	*sɔ̌ɔŋ*
20	*phráʔ*	381	*sɔ̌ɔŋ*
34	*sɔ̌ɔŋ*	385	*pay yʉan*
54	*sɔ̌ɔŋ*	386	*thǐ*
66	*maa*	389	*bɔ̀*
78	*phráʔ*	430	*nâa*
84	*maa*	465	*maa*
91	*wâa*	482	*hàp*
93	*rɔɔy*	576	*kàp*
139	*phûu*	590	*kàp*
206	*mʉ̌an*	607	*ʔôo*
286	*thʉ̌ŋ*	611	*câaw*
358	*maa*	620	*hâam*
364	*sɔ̌ɔŋ*		

11. Although always pronounced with a short vowel in modern speech, the word is written with the long vowel symbol.

12. This material is based in part on a description of recitation styles found in Nuphuk (1939: 184ff).

Chapter 7

THE *lílít* STYLE OF *LILIT PHRA LAW*

The word *lílít* is a technical term that refers to a specific compositional style. In the modern formulation, a poem done in the *lílít* style includes a combination of stanzas of *khlooŋ* and stanzas of *râay*, with each stanza linked to the next by rhyme. The rhyme link as described in the textbook treatments of *lílít* joins the last syllable of a given stanza with a syllable in the next, and Phrayaa Uppakit notes a "preference" for syllables written with no tone mark (that is, A-column words) in this rhyme link (1968: 428). No explanation is given in the literature as to why it is these stanza types that are combined, nor is there any attempt to explore the motivation either for the presence of the rhyme link, or for the supposed preference for A-column words.

In studying the ancient *lílít* works, one wonders how the poets hit upon this combination of verse types for their work. In the discussion of *khlooŋ* and *râay* as they appear in *Lilit Phra Law* I have identified patterns in those forms that have not been previously noted. These patterns suggest that instead of being treated as separate entities, the forms should really be seen as different manifestations of the same poetic phenomenon, that is, a five-syllable unit, broken into two phrases of unequal length, and embellished in different ways. The forms must have developed out of the flow of everyday speech, with tone and rhyme placement constraints combined to form a strongly auditory pattern easily accessible to any speaker of the language. There are also other previously unrecognized patterns that appear when one looks at the work as a whole, and that explain, I believe, a great deal about what the *lílít* style was to the ancient poet and audience. Unfortunately, these patterns seem to have escaped the notice both

of more recent poets who inherited and continued to use the style after the ancient poets
left the scene, and also of modern scholars
who have studied and written about both *Lilit
Phra Law* and other *lilit* compositions. This
chapter will discuss both those patterns and
also the implications of the presence of the
patterns for our appreciation of the *lilit*
form.

There is no disagreement in the literature over the fact that *Lilit Phra Law* is an
example of *lilit* poetry, although frequently
one does find comments to the effect that the
authors of *Lilit Phra Law* were not very strict
in following the "rule" requiring a rhyme link
between all stanzas of verse in a work of
lilit. Nor, it is said, were they careful in
following the stipulation that the words forming the stanza link should both be written
without a tone mark. An examination of stanzas of the poem is most instructive in this
regard.

There are 660 stanzas in the poem as we
know it today, and there are, therefore, 659
opportunities for a given stanza to rhyme with
the following one.[1] A total of 255 (39%) of
the stanzas in the poem clearly do not rhyme
with the following stanza, and another several
dozen stanzas seem to rhyme, but in patterns
that do not follow the textbook "rules."
There is more than enough apparent inconsis-
tency to trouble the modern student of Thai
poetry, who is accustomed to a different
degree of uniformity in stanza-link rhymes.
On the other hand, with nearly 40% of the
stanzas clearly not rhymed at all it does not
seem reasonable to resolve the issue simply by
saying that those who composed *Lilit Phra Law*
were careless about the point. A closer look
at the text is in order.

If all the stanzas are examined by type
for the presence or absence of rhyme links an
interesting picture emerges. The four charts

below show the pattern of stanza-link rhymes
for each of the types of verse found in the
poem. They show the type of verse in which
the *sòŋ* 'send' syllable is located as well as
the type of verse in which the *ráp* 'receive'
syllable is located.

**Chart 1. Stanza-Link Rhymes Originating
in stanzas of *khlooŋ 4* (293)**

Type of Stanza in Recipient Position	Presence or Absence of Link	
	Link	No Link
khlooŋ 4	31 (13%)	207 (87%)
khlooŋ 2	23 (92%)	2 (8%)
khlooŋ 3	2 (100%)	0 (--)
ráay	22 (79%)	6 (21%)
Total	78 (27%)	215 (73%)

**Chart 2. Stanza-Link Rhymes Originating
in stanzas of *khlooŋ 2* (243)**

Type of Stanza in Recipient Position	Presence or Absence of Link	
	Link	No Link
khlooŋ 4	13 (59%)	9 (41%)
khlooŋ 2	170 (97%)	6 (3%)
khlooŋ 3	5 (100%)	0 (--)
ráay	39 (97%)	1 (3%)
Total	227 (93%)	16 (7%)

209

Chart 3. Stanza-Link Rhymes Originating in *khlooŋ 3* (10)

Type of Stanza in Recipient Position	Presence or Absence of Link	
	Link	No Link
khlooŋ 4	1 (50%)	1 (50%)
khlooŋ 2	6 (100%)	0 (--)
khlooŋ 3	2 (100%)	0 (--)
râay	-	-
Total	9 (90%)	1 (10%)

Chart 4. Stanza-Link Rhymes Originating in *râay* (113)

Type of Stanza in Recipient Position	Presence or Absence of Link	
	Link	No Link
khlooŋ 4	19 (59%)	13 (41%)
khlooŋ 2	33 (92%)	3 (8%)
khlooŋ 3	3 (100%)	0 (--)
râay	38 (90%)	4 (10%)
Total	93 (90%)	20 (10%)

As has been explained in previous sections, the vast majority of the seemingly aberrant passages that occur within stanzas can be corrected, often by simply referring to alternate readings found in the various manuscript copies. The few remaining problems are negligible in number and can safely be disregarded as corruptions of the ancient wording.

210

The same proves to be true for stanza-link rhymes.

Several factors were taken into consideration in deciding whether or not a pair of stanzas should be considered linked by rhyme. The vowel and final of the *sòŋ* syllable and any possible *ráp* syllables were considered first. If, as analysis of the *thôot* concept demonstrates, the poets who composed the poem did not actually resort to imperfect rhymes in links formed within stanzas of any type, then it seems most unreasonable to assume that they would do so only in creating rhyme links across stanza boundaries. Thus, any mismatch in tone category or in vowel length was rejected as a potential rhyme link.

Any occurrence of the same word in both the *sòŋ* and *ráp* position was also rejected as a rhyme link. Support for this position lies in the many rhymes formed within both *khlooŋ* and *râay* passages without repetition of a rhyming word. In the *sòŋ-ráp-rɔɔŋ* pattern of *khlooŋ 4* it is particularly evident that the poets avoided any repetition without an intervening word participating in the rhyme pattern. In the final analysis fewer than a half dozen possible links were eliminated on this point. Even if these cases were to be accepted as rhyme links the number is so small that the overall pattern would not be changed.

Another point considered was the location of the *ráp* syllable within the *wâk*. If a possible *ráp* syllable were the fourth or fifth stressed syllable of the first *wâk* of the stanza, the two stanzas were considered not linked. Support for this position lies in the more than 1,800 rhyme links in stanzas of *râay*, in which the *ráp* syllable is uniformly one of the first three stressed syllables of the *wâk* in which it appears. There is no reason to suppose that the ancient poets would alter this very regular pattern found within stanzas when forming links between stanzas.

211

This is particularly so for stanzas of *khlooŋ*
2 or *khlooŋ 4*, because a *ráp* syllable appearing after the third position in the first *wâk*
of such a stanza would involve a mismatch in
the tones of the syllables involved.

The major point considered in assessing
stanza link rhymes was tone. Phrayaa Uppakit
points out that the presence or absence of
rhyme links seems inconsistent, and he notes
that in many places there seems to be a rhyme
link, but one that is not carried out according to the expected pattern (1968: 428). In
all probability he was referring to cases in
which the *sòŋ* syllable is spelled with no tone
mark, but the syllable that seems to be in the
ráp position is written with either the first
or the second tone mark. The evidence gathered in this study suggests that such cases,
rather than being seen as imperfect links,
should not be considered rhyme links at all.

Comparative linguistic studies show that
the ancient language had only three tones on
live syllables, and we must assume that words
written with different tone marks were fundamentally different. This suggestion is
supported by the great regularity in the more
than 1,800 rhyme links between *wâk* of *râay*.
All but a very few of the links are formed
within the ancient tone categories, and the
few exceptions are highly suspect readings.
This great regularity suggests a fundamental
difference between the tone categories rather
than simply a conventional separation for
poetic purposes. We must assume that in the
ancient three-tone system, unlike the modern
five-tone system, words written with different
tone marks (that is, words that originated
from different columns in the ancient tone
chart) did not share the same phonetic features and, therefore, could not have rhymed.
Rather than considering these cases as examples of imperfection or error, it is best not
to count them as rhyme links at all.

An example of a doubtful link is that between stanzas 56 and 57, two stanzas of *khlooŋ 4*. The syllable in the *sòŋ* position is *dii* (ดี), written with no tone mark, and the only word with that vowel in position to be the *ráp* syllable is *phîi* (พี่), which is written with the first tone mark, and is the first syllable of the following stanza. These syllables come from different proto-tone categories and, rather than being seen as a weak or imperfect link, must be rejected as a possible link. In other cases an alternate reading or a reinterpretation of the main reading given in the published editions provides an acceptable link.

Of the number of possible links, only forty-four, or slightly more than 6% of the total, are for one reason or another doubtful links. They are listed in appendix 3. In those cases for which a published text provides a reading with an acceptable link, the source of the reading is given along with the number of manuscripts in which it appears.

The overall pattern is quite different from that which one would expect after reading some of the textbook commentaries dealing with **Lilit Phra Law**. The 293 stanzas of *khlooŋ 4* rhyme with following stanzas in only seventy-eight (27%) cases, but there is a clear connection between the presence or absence of a rhyme link and the nature of the verse in the stanza following the stanza of *khlooŋ 4*. There are 238 cases in which a stanza of *khlooŋ 4* follows another stanza of *khlooŋ 4*, and in only thirty-one (13%) of these cases is there a rhyme link. If the following stanza is *khlooŋ 2*, *khlooŋ 3*, or *râay*, however, the stanzas are very likely to be linked by rhyme. A total of twenty-three (92%) of the twenty-five stanzas of *khlooŋ 2* that follow a stanza of *khlooŋ 4*, for example, are linked to that stanza by rhyme. Of the twenty-eight *râay* stanzas following *khlooŋ 4* stanzas, twenty-two (82%) are linked to that stanza by rhyme.

As the charts demonstrate, there are clear patterns for *khlooŋ 2*, *khlooŋ 3*, and *râay* as well. Stanzas of those types of verse are linked to following stanzas of *khlooŋ 4* slightly more than half of the time. When they are followed by other stanzas of *khlooŋ 2*, *khlooŋ 3*, or *râay*, however, the likelihood that a rhyme link will exist is 90% or more.

The overall differences, then, are between *khlooŋ 4*, on the one hand, and *khlooŋ 2*, *khlooŋ 3*, and *râay* on the other. Stanzas of *khlooŋ 4* are linked by rhyme with other stanzas, either preceding or following, far less often that are stanzas of *khlooŋ 2*, *khlooŋ 3*, or *râay*. Moreover, the pattern that emerges is not one of carelessness or inattention to rules. Inconsistencies that do exist in the text as we know it today are most likely the result of changes, both intentional and unintentional, that have been made in the text over the centuries of copying and recopying, and in the editing of the text for printing.

CONCLUSIONS: THE ANCIENT *lílít* COMPOSITION

There is a likely explanation for this clearly different treatment that the ancient poets gave to stanzas of *khlooŋ 4*, on the one hand, and *khlooŋ 2*, *khlooŋ 3*, and *râay*, on the other. In fact, this difference may have been what defined the original conception of *lílít* poetry.

If *Lilit Phra Law* was composed to be performed aloud, or if the text as we know it today is simply a written record of a once popular version of a commonly told tale, then it was probably intended for performance combining instrumental music, singing and dance, or perhaps puppets. Thai traditional music and poetry, like that of much of the rest of Southeast Asia, is cyclical in format. Just as the *khlooŋ 4* pattern may be repeated as many times as is needed to tell the part of

214

the story involved, so may musical patterns be repeated without limits. Moreover, in many modern performance styles throughout the region the artists work within the outline of a given story that offers multiple opportunities for variation, and they are not bound by a fixed version of the text. Thus, the individual performer works within the framework of the main plot and is free to digress or develop subplots, depending on personal choice. In this way timely reference can be made to conditions or situations of current local interest, and this is often the part of the performance that audiences appreciate most because of the high degree of skill required in this sort of extemporaneous composition.

It is quite likely that this was the case in performances of *Lilit Phra Law* prior to the time that changes in speech left the story more accessible as a written than oral text. This sort of open structure in which performers could introduce material of local or current interest and later return again to pick up the main story line would, in fact, help to explain certain points in the story in which potential plot lines are not pursued. For example, after completing his work of charming Phra Law, the magician Samingphray simply disappears from the story, without further mention. Also, as Phra Law moves closer to his destination he leaves groups of his soldiers behind, presumably to await his return, but nothing further is said of these individuals. If the poem had come into being first as a written text such details would most likely not have been left unresolved. If, on the other hand, the story as we have it today is a record of the conventional parts of the typical performance, with the extemporaneous parts left to the artistry of the individual performer, then such unresolved points would have been expected as the points at which the story could, if desired, be pursued in new directions.

A performance of this type would require not only that the plot of the story provide for easy expansion, but that the music intended to accompany it be equally flexible. It would have been necessary to incorporate auditory signals in music to alert the performers when a change in pattern or tempo was coming. Although we do not know what music might have been used with *Lilit Phra Law* it is reasonable to assume that it was cyclical in nature, and it is quite possible that the rhyme links in the oldest *lílít* works were the sung or spoken counterpart of a musical signaling pattern, or perhaps were considered a part of that pattern.

As has been said, the *khlooŋ 2*, *khlooŋ 3*, and *râay* forms are actually far more similar to each other than is indicated by the text-book descriptions, and structurally they all differ from *khlooŋ 4* in the same way. It may be that in performance they also shared a common tempo or musical style that differed significantly from the tempo or style associated with *khlooŋ 4*, and that this accounts for the difference in rhyme links.

But this does not explain why more recent works of *lílít* have a different pattern of stanza-link rhymes, at least according to the textbook descriptions. The more modern compositions, unlike the pattern of *Lilit Phra Law* described above, are said to join every stanza with the following one by a rhyme link. There is an explanation for this difference that does not conflict with our hypothesis about the original role of the stanza-link rhymes, and it has to do with the impact of the tone splits on the development of Thai poetry.

Once the tone splits had taken place, and the original three-tone system had become the system of five contour tones that we know today, the phenomenon of rhyme must have become very ambiguous compared to what it had been previously. Part of the problem must

216

have been that the nature of what we now refer to as "tone" was changed in fundamental ways. The common substitution of words ending in a stop consonant sound for B-tone words, for example, suggests that words of these two types must have shared common phonetic features, but it could not have been anything like the contours of the modern tone system. The change in the nature of tone must have simultaneously destroyed some ancient rhymes and created other new ones. Words that had once shared the same ancient tone, and whatever phonetic features that consisted of, and could therefore rhyme, came to be pronounced with two different contours. That is, they now sounded different. (See, for example, the modern mid tone and the modern rising tone, which developed only in words from the A column of the ancient tone system.) On the other hand, words that once had different ancient tones, and could not therefore have rhymed, came to be pronounced with identical contours. That is, they now sounded the same. (See, for example, the one modern falling-tone contour that developed in some words from the ancient B column and also in some words from the ancient C column.)

At this point, it must have become conceptually impossible to maintain a rhyme structure that included tone. This, in turn, would have changed fundamentally the nature of the *lílít* composition. The usefulness of rhyme as a part of, or as a vocal counterpart to a musical signal would have been destroyed, and once the original motivation behind the system had disappeared, it would have been forgotten. For later generations the modern reflection of the old system became exploited strictly for euphony and not utility, and rhyme proliferated to the degree that it became expected as a link for every stanza of *lílít* poetry.[2]

NOTES

1. There are discrepancies in the manuscripts that cause some doubt here. For example, most of the manuscript copies combine stanzas 229 and 230, as they appear in the Ministry of Education text, into a single lengthy passage of *râay*, thus eliminating one potential stanza-link rhyme. The question of the age of the first four stanzas and the last two stanzas of the poem remains, as well. Despite such problems, however, the overall pattern described in this section is clear.

2. This basic change in the nature of rhyme also helps to explain why rhyme is used so differently in the forms of poetry known as *klɔɔn*, which developed from the modern five-tone system. As rhyme and tone became disassociated from one another the number of potential rhymes must have proliferated, giving rise to expectations of more frequent rhymes, and increased use of multi-position rhymes. This point is worthy of additional study.

Chapter 8

SUMMARY AND CONCLUSIONS

An examination of the text of *Lilit Phra Law* shows that a number of common assumptions about the poem are not, in fact, correct. Nearly all of those who write about the poem praise it for its beauty, but they also say that the ancient authors either were not strict in following the forms, or were not as well educated as modern authors and therefore did not, or could not, produce poetry that was uniform in quality. Modern commentators, with the attention to visual concerns that characterizes our age, have read the extant manuscript copies of *Lilit Phra Law* and have assumed that the ancient and modern conceptions of poetry match in every detail. In fact, while the manuscripts are a priceless treasure from an age now gone by, they are only a partial record of what ancient performance must have been like. To the eye, they seem deceptively easy to interpret, and modern commentators have not seen the need for looking more deeply. The result has been a great deal of confusion and unnecessary criticism of the poets of long ago. Four specific points are generally raised in this context.

The Concept of the *thôot* Words

The most commonly repeated point is the concept of the *thôot* words, the supposed purposeful misspellings designed to place a syllable with a particular tone mark in the position dictated by the poetic form. Linguistic evidence shows that this point is backwards. The poets did, in fact, know what they were doing. It is only in modern times that speakers of the language have, for one reason or another, come to spell a number of words in ways that do not accurately reflect the historical developments, in ways that are not historically "correct."

219

While the concept of *thôot* words does seem, on the surface at least, to be a reasonable explanation for different spellings for the modern falling tone, it is actually groundless and must be completely abandoned. Quite the opposite has taken place, however. The concept has been applied to a wide variety of seemingly anomalous forms found in the poem. It appears that the ready availability of a facile explanation for these problem forms has hidden the need for further analysis.

The Nature of the Poetic Forms of *Lilit Phra Law*

A second commonly repeated criticism of the poem is that the authors did not consistently follow the rules regarding tone placement in *khloop* and *râay*. This is sometimes interpreted as evidence of a lack of education or expertise on the part of the poets, and sometimes as evidence that the poem was written at a time of transition during which *khloop dân* was developing into *khloop sùphâap*. Those who raise this point also often say that the poets mixed different varieties of *khloop* and *râay*. Thus, there are said to be stanzas of both *khloop sùphâap* and *khloop dân* and also stanzas of *râay sùphâap*, *râay dân*, and *râay booraan* mixed together in the poem.

An examination of the text itself shows that these criticisms are not well founded. All of the stanzas of *khloop* are well-formed examples of the *sùphâap* variety. The first stanza of *râay* and the first three stanzas of *khloop 4* that appear in the poem are part of what appears to be an unmarked prologue, and they do differ from the other stanzas of the poem, but not sufficiently to be called stanzas of *dân* poetry. All of the rest of the *khloop* stanzas are clearly examples of the *sùphâap* variety. Stanzas of *râay* that seem to violate the constraints of the *sùphâap* variety are few in number, and for some there are

alternate readings available that are actually
sùphâap in form. Only four out of the total
of 113 stanzas of *râay* are clearly anomalous,
and since the number is so small it seems more
reasonable to suspect the accuracy of the
extant manuscripts than to suggest that the
poets were careless or inept, or that they
resorted to the use of a somehow easier form
in these stanzas.

Regarding tone placements, an examination
of those syllables that appear in positions
said to require syllables of a specific type
shows a pattern not noted in any of the textbooks. That is, tone placements that mark
boundaries between poetic units are more
regular than those that do not. The patterns
of variation, especially in positions said to
require syllables with the first tone mark,
suggest that the tone placement originally had
both a structural as well as euphonic purpose.
That is, tone placement served to differentiate each section of the stanza on structural
grounds, and provided a set of auditory signals by which the performers and the audience
alike might mark progress through the stanza.

The Use of Rhyme Links in *Lilit Phra Law*

A third point that is raised, although
less frequently than the first two, is the
presence of rhyme links, mainly between the
wâk of *râay* stanzas, formed in seeming violation of the "rule" that rhymed syllables
should have the same tone mark. A careful
analysis of the rhymes indicates that this
criticism is also not well founded. Alternate
sources and reinterpretations provide solutions for most of the problem rhyme links.
Some of the problems are the result of simple
copying errors, and some are the result of
modern misconceptions about the ancient forms
of speech. The problems that remain are so
few in number -- only eight out of 1,818 rhyme
links between *wâk* of *râay* -- that one is again

inclined to doubt the accuracy of the manuscripts rather than the ability of the poets.

The availability of solutions in the *samùt khɔ̌y* texts for many of the problem rhyme links has been overlooked, it seems, due to a misunderstanding of the nature of rhyme in the language of the ancient poets. Prior to the changes in the tone system, known as the tone splits, syllables that were written with different tone marks must have sounded fundamentally different from each other. There were no cases of ambiguity such as there are in the modern language in which a single tone contour can be represented by different sets of written symbols, or in which a single tone mark can represent two different tone contours, depending on the symbol used to represent the initial consonant sound of the syllable. We are led to conclude that it was not actually a poetic "rule" that rhymes should be made by syllables with the same tone mark, but was a fact of the language. Syllables that came from different tone categories, and therefore had different tone marks in the written system, did not and could not rhyme. Those who did not know this did not realize that they should seek further for an explanation for seemingly anomalous passages.

The Nature of the *lílìt* Style

A fourth point on which the authors of *Lilit Phra Law* are criticized is the supposed lack of attention to the stanza link rhymes said to be required in the compositional style known as *lílìt*. An examination of the poem shows that the presence or absence of a rhyme link is not haphazard but follows a pattern. Stanzas of *khlooŋ 2*, *khlooŋ 3*, and *râay* are far more likely to be joined to following stanzas by a rhyme link than are stanzas of *khlooŋ 4*. In all probability, the rhyme link between stanzas once had structural significance, participating in or mirroring changes

in music and tempo associated with changes
between the two broad categories of verse:
khlooŋ 2, *khlooŋ 3*, and *râay*, on the one hand,
and *khlooŋ 4* on the other. Following the tone
splits rhyme must have become an ambiguous
phenomenon, and thus the original motivation
for the stanza-linking pattern was lost. The
lílít form itself must have then changed as
later generations exploited the new rhyme
pattern strictly for euphony, to the point
that the original form and purpose of the
stanza-linking rhymes have been overlooked in
modern times.

The Ancient Forms and Their Modern Counterparts

A close examination of the criticisms of
Lilit Phra Law, and of certain aspects of the
poem revealed in a detailed study of the text,
each of which has been dealt with in detail in
the concluding sections of the preceding chapters, shows that modern commentators have not
fully understood the nature of the poem and
have based much of their thinking on misconceptions. The poem is a much more consistent
and polished example of poetic art than it is
commonly thought to be, and the ancient poets
were every bit as expert in the manipulation
of language as are those of the present day.
Modern attitudes toward language and education, and the emphasis on visual rather than
auditory aspects of language in our modern
print-oriented world, have combined with
ignorance of the history of the development of
the language to hide these facts from modern
commentators.

Composing verse in *khlooŋ* and *râay* today
is a most complex task, demanding not only
that the poet have a fine ear for his or her
language, but also that he or she be extremely
well schooled in the intricacies of the Thai
writing system. Modern commentators have
assumed that this has always been the case,
but linguistic evidence argues in the opposite

direction. Although today they have become the province of highly-trained scholars, the *khlooŋ* and *râay* forms must originally have sprung up from the rhythms of ordinary speech, accessible to anyone familiar with the ancient three-tone system that gave them life. One must assume that a listener did not have to be literate in order to understand and appreciate *khlooŋ* and *râay* poetry. In fact, it is also necessary to go a step further and assume that one did not have to be literate in order to compose verse in these forms, very much like the modern "illiterate rhymester" that Prince Bidyalankarana spoke of in 1926 (1926: 102), who can readily deal with the modern *klɔɔn* forms that take their life from the five-tone system in use today.

This is not to say that those who composed *Lilit Phra Law* were necessarily not literate. It is a fact, however, that literacy must have been irrelevant to poetic composition, even to the highly skilled artist or artists who are responsible for the creation of *Lilit Phra Law*, as we know it today. It is clear that the *khlooŋ* and *râay* forms and the *lilit* style of composition were essentially auditory phenomena, and that both creating and appreciating work in these forms were independent of literacy. Unlike the situation in more recent centuries, the language of the court and that of the common people could not have differed greatly. The poem must have been composed in language not much, if at all, removed from that of the common people. The forms used in it could not have been created by highly-trained scholars for the appreciation of an exclusive and highly-educated audience of the elite, but must have developed out of the common speech of the day.

Much modern thinking and writing about Thai poetic art is overly concerned with writing. Even in the creation of poetry, orthographic correctness has taken a position of major importance. This could not have been the case at the time that the oldest surviving works were composed, a fact that has escaped most modern scholars.

It has been said that "the Thai do not theorize about their own music" (Morton 1964: 221), and the same can be said about Thai studies of poetry. The approach is very conservative, and in the best cases very observant. Because of the nature of historical events, however, a conservative approach will ultimately be unsuccessful. The ancient and modern forms of Thai speech are fundamentally different, and the ancient and modern forms of Thai poetic art are equally so. Any attempts to study ancient poetry without taking into account those differences will be unable to resolve the many points that concern us today. Only when this fact is widely realized and fully accepted will those who study Thai poetry be able to place both ancient and modern works in proper perspective, and come to appreciate fully the true richness and depth of the poetic heritage of the Tai language family.

VARIATION IN TONE PLACEMENT IN *khlooŋ*

Chart 1. *khlooŋ 4*

wǎk #	One				Three	
	#	%	#	%	#	%
mǎy ʔèek	115	39%	41	14%	160	54%
may thoo	61	21%	233	79%	0	0
long vowel + C	104	35%	14	5%	76	26%
short Vowel + C	14	5%	6	2%	49	17%
nasal	0	0	0	0	9	3%
X	0	0	0	0	0	0
Total	294		294		294	

Chart 1. *khlooŋ 4* (continued)

wák #	Four			
	#	%	#	%
máy ʔèek	195	66%	0	0
may thoo	0	0	294	100%
long vowel + C	75	26%	0	0
short Vowel + C	24	8%	0	0
nasal	0	0	0	0
X	0	0	0	0
Total	294		294	

Chart 1. *khlooŋ 4* (continued)

wák #	Five		Six	
	#	%	#	%
máy ʔèek	154	52%	189	64%
may thoo	0	0	0	0
long vowel + C	52	18%	101	34%
short Vowel + C	71	24%	4	2%
nasal	16	5%	0	0
X	1	.3%	0	0
Total	294		294	

Chart 1. *khlooŋ 4* (continued)

wǎk #	Seven			
	#	%	#	%
máy ʔèek	163	55%	0	0
may thoo	0	0	294	100%
long vowel + C	61	21%	0	0
short Vowel + C	60	21%	0	0
nasal	10	3%	0	0
X	0	0	0	0
Total	294		294	

Chart 1. *khlooŋ 4* (continued)

wǎk #	Eight			
	#	%	#	%
máy ʔèek	209	71%	0	0
may thoo	0	0	294	100%
long vowel + C	76	26%	0	0
short Vowel + C	9	3%	0	0
nasal	0	0	0	0
X	0	0	0	0
Total	294		294	

Chart 2. *khlooŋ 2*

wǎk #	One			
	#	%	#	%
máy ʔèek	126	52%	0	0
may thoo	13	5%	242	99%
long vowel + C	43	18%	1	.4%
short Vowel + C	35	14%	0	0
nasal	15	6%	0	0
X	11	5%	0	0
Total	243		243	

Chart 2. *khlooŋ 2* (continued)

wǎk #	Two			
	#	%	#	%
máy ʔèek	96	40%	0	0
may thoo	10	4%	242	99%
long vowel + C	56	23%	1	.4%
short Vowel + C	57	23%	0	0
nasal	19	8%	0	0
X	5	2%	0	0
Total	243		243	

Chart 2. *khlooŋ 2* (continued)

wǎk #	Three			
	#	%	#	%
mǎy ʔèek	159	65%	0	0
may thoo	0	0	243	100%
long vowel + C	70	29%	0	0
short Vowel + C	14	6%	0	0
nasal	0	0	0	0
X	0	0	0	0
Total	243		243	

Chart 3. *khlooŋ 2* in *rǎay*

wǎk #	One			
	#	%	#	%
mǎy ʔèek	45	42%	0	0
may thoo	16	15%	108	100%
long vowel + C	15	14%	0	0
short Vowel + C	15	14%	0	0
nasal	10	9%	0	0
X	7	6%	0	0
Total	108		108	

Chart 3. *khlooŋ 2* in *râay* (continued)

wák #	Two			
	#	%	#	%
máy ʔèek	46	42%	0	0
may thoo	6	6%	108	100%
long vowel + C	17	16%	0	0
short Vowel + C	27	25%	0	0
nasal	7	6%	0	0
X	5	5%	0	0
Total	108		108	

Chart 3. *khlooŋ 2* in *râay* (continued)

wák #	Three			
	#	%	#	%
máy ʔèek	75	69%	1	1%
may thoo	4	4%	107	99%
long vowel + C	21	19%	0	0
short Vowel + C	7	7%	0	0
nasal	1	1%	0	0
X	0	0%	0	0
Total	108		108	

Chart 4. *khlooŋ 3*

wǎk #	Two			
	#	%	#	%
máy ʔèek	2	20%	1	10%
may thoo	1	10%	107	90%
long vowel + C	3	30%	0	0
short Vowel + C	0	0	0	0
nasal	2	20%	0	0
X	2	20%	0	0
Total	10		10	

Chart 4. *khlooŋ 3* (continued)

wǎk #	Three			
	#	%	#	%
máy ʔèek	5	20%	0	0
may thoo	0	10%	10	100%
long vowel + C	2	30%	0	0
short Vowel + C	3	0	0	0
nasal	0	20%	0	0
X	0	20%	0	0
Total	10		10	

Chart 4. *khlooŋ 3* (continued)

wǎk #	Four			
	#	%	#	%
máy ʔèek	8	80%	1	10%
may thoo	2	20%	9	90%
long vowel + C	0	0	0	0
short Vowel + C	0	0	0	0
nasal	0	0	0	0
X	0	0	0	0
Total	10		10	

Appendix 2

PROBLEM *wǎk* LINKS WITHIN *rǎay* STANZAS

The first list below gives twenty of the total of fifty-one problem *wǎk* links from the passages of *rǎay* used in *Lilit Phra Law*. The stanza number is given first, then the position of the *wǎk* in question within the stanza. The words that are supposed to form the link follow, along with the letters A, B, or C to specify the column of the Proto-Tai tone chart indicated by the spelling given in the Ministry of Education text main reading. Given next is the alternate wording that solves the problem of rhymes across the ancient tone columns, and then letters to indicate the Proto-Tai column involved in the alternate link. A published source that the interested reader may consult for the complete alternate reading is also given: the designation "H" refers to the Phra Worawet Phisit's *Handbook* text; "CK" refers to the Chanthit Krasaesin text; "RL" refers to the Royal Library edition; and "MT" refers to readings found in the footnotes of the Ministry of Education text. Given last is the number of manuscript copies (indicated by "sk" for the Thai term *samǔt khǝ̌y*) that have the alternate reading.

The second list gives an additional twenty-three of the problem links. It follows the same format as list 1 but gives alternate readings that can be found only in the manuscript copies. It should be pointed out again that just as there is variation among the printed editions, so is there variation in the manuscript copies, and for some problem passages more than one alternate reading exists, although in only a very few cases are the different readings equally plausible alternatives. A critical edition that addresses each of the variations in detail may one day help us to clarify these points. In the meanwhile, however, this list will serve to show that many of the problem readings in the printed editions clearly do not reflect the ancient wording, or are at least highly suspect.

The third list gives information about the eight problem links for which no alternate reading is available either in the printed editions or in the manuscript copies, and for which no ready solution can be proposed. In all likelihood the text as we have it today has been corrupted beyond repair at these points, and we shall never be able to resolve these problems completely. Nonetheless, the number of problem readings is very small, too small to justify the popular criticisms of the poem and the artists who created it.

List 1. **Alternate Readings Available in Printed Editions and in Manuscript Copies**

Stanza & *wák*	Problem Wording		Alternate Wording		
29/ 2-3	*chŭa- khŭa*	B-A	*chŭa- phŭa*	B-B	H + 12sk
49/ 4-5	*khlɔ́ɔŋ- nɔɔŋ*	B-A	*khlɔɔŋ- nɔɔŋ*	A-A	H + 6sk
73/ 10-11	*nám- kralâm*	C-B	*nám- klâm*	C-C	H + 9sk
73/ 26-27	*khăw- khrâw*	A-B	*khăw- ʔaw*	A-A	MT+ 15sk
88/ 4-5	*khăw- tâw*	A-C	*khăw- thaw*	A-A	H + 2sk
131/ 6-7	*tâw- pâw*	C-B	*tâw- câw*	C-C	CK+ 1sk
144/ 27-28	*cháaŋ- kwaaŋ*	C-A	*săaŋ- kwaaŋ*	A-A	MT+ 16sk
144/ 47-48	*sùu- phuu*	B-A	*hăən- chəən*	A-A	MT+ 14SK

Stanza & *wâk*	Problem Wording		Alternate Wording		
155/ 4-5	*sɔ̌ɔn-yɔ́ɔn*	A-B	*sɔ̌ɔn-yɔ́ɔn*	A-A	H + 5sk
198/ 31-32	*mɯaŋ-rɯ̂aŋ*	A-B	*mɯaŋ-rɯaŋ*	A-A	MT+ 12sk
224/ 10-11	*ráw-wâw*	C-C	*râw-wâw*	B-B	H + 4sk
228/ 19-20	*khɛ̂ŋ-nɛ̀ŋ*	A-B	*khɛ̌ɛŋ-nɛ̀ŋ*	B-B	H + 1sk
229/ 25-26	*dii-sìi*	A-B	*thîi-sìi*	B-B	H + 12sk
262/ 6-7	*fay-phày*	A-B	*fay-phay*	A-A	MT+ 1sk
365/ 2-3	*nɔ́ɔŋ-X*	B-X	*naaŋ-klaaŋ*	A-A	RL+ 13sk
388/ 2-3	*thâa-daa*	B-A	*laa-daa*	A-A	MT+ 11sk
423/ 4-5	*kháa-thâa*[1]	C-B	*kháa-thâa*	C-C	H + 7sk
576/ 6-7	*kɛ̂ɛ-ŋɛ̂ɛ*	C-B	*kɛ̀ɛ-ŋɛ̂ɛ*	B-B	H + 7sk
590/ 9-10	*caa-nâa*	A-B	*caa-naa*	A-A	H + 4sk
599/ 121-2	*khâw-thâw*	C-B	*khâw-tháw*	C-C	MT+ 10sk

List 2. Alternate Readings Found Only in Manuscript Copies

Stanza & *wăk*	Problem Wording		Alternate Wording		
8/ 18-19	*thɛɛŋ- yéɛŋ*	A-C	*thɛɛŋ- yɛɛŋ*	A-A	8sk
53/ 6-7	*maa- khăa*	A-C	*maa- khăa*	A-A	6sk
71/ 5-6	*-lîw- thíw*	B-A	*-liw- thíw*	A-A	6sk
73/ 23-24	*câw- raw*	C-A	*câw- ráw*	C-C	2sk
73/ 28-29	*khăw- thâw*	A-B	*khăw- thâw*	C-C	3sk
73/ 29-30	*cháaŋ- naaŋ*	C-A	*klây- wáy*	C-C	3sk
83/ 13-14	*thaa- X*	A-X	*kuu- duu*	A-A	17sk
85/ 1-2	*maa- cháa*	A-C	*maa- chaa*	A-A	2sk
89/ 8-9	*phɛɛn- ?êɛn*	A-B	*phɛɛn- ?ɛɛn*	A-A	6sk
131/ 2-3	*kàw- câw*	B-C	*kàw- câw*	A-A	1sk
131/ 10-11	*khɐɐn- fɐɐn* (Vowel length)	C-C	*khɐɐn- fɐɐn*	A-A	4sk
147/ 1-2	*dɛɛn- khéɛn*	A-C	*dɛɛn- khɛɛn*	A-A	3sk
198/ 27-28	*cháy- cay*	C-A	*cháy- hây*	C-C	6sk
224/ 26-27	*rûŋ- phûŋ*	C-B	*rûŋ- phûŋ*	B-B	8sk

237

Stanza & wák	Problem Wording		Alternate Wording		
228/ 18-19	phâay- naay	B-A	chaay- naay	A-A	2sk
228/ 27-28	lăay- fàay	A-B	lɛ̀ɛ- hɛ̀ɛ	B-B	2sk
229/ 22-23	khwăa- nâa	A-C	máa- nâa	C-C	3sk
251/ 6-7	khaa- phàa	A-B	sɛ̆ɛŋ- dɛɛŋ	A-A	2sk
278/ 15-16	sŭa- phùa	C-B	phâa- cháa	C-C	2sk
318/ 50-51	-yaa- cháa	A-C	láa- cháa	C-C	2sk
			-yaa- chaa	A-A	3sk
599/ 21-22	yày- dây	B-C	yày -sày	B-B	2sk
599/ 39-40	fan- bàn	A-B	fan- ban	A-A	3sk
599/ 95-96	sɔ́ɔn- ʔɔ̆ɔn	C-B	sɔ̀ɔn- ʔɔ̆ɔn	B-B	2sk

List 3. Remaining Problem Links (Total of 8)

Stanza & *wák*	Wording	Columns
6/ 1-2	*yày- sây*	B-C
52/ 5-6	*yày- khray*	B-A
89/ 2-2	*wàw- tâw*	B-C
150/ 16-17	*pùu- phûu*	B-C
198/ 50-51	? - ?	?
230/ 2-3	*phan- chán*	A-C
230/ 14-15	*lăay- sáay*	A-C
576/ 10-11	*khrâaŋ- bâaŋ*	B-C

239

Appendix 3

DOUBTFUL STANZA-LINK RHYMES

The three lists below indicate those cases in which a potential stanza link violates the expected pattern, either because of a cross-column rhyme, a difference in vowel length between the two syllables that seem to form the link, or the position of the *ráp* syllable. The stanza number is given first, and then the words that are supposed to form the link, along with the letters A, B, or C to specify the column of the Proto-Tai tone chart indicated by the spelling given in the Ministry of Education text main reading. Given next is the alternate wording that solves the problem, if one is available, and then letters to indicate the Proto-Tai column involved in the alternate link. A published source that the interested reader may consult for the complete alternate reading is also given, wherever one is available: the designation "H" refers to the Phra Worawet Phisit's *Handbook* text; "CK" refers to the Chanthit Krasaesin text; "RL" refers to the Royal Library edition; and "MT" refers to readings found in the footnotes of the Ministry of Education text. The designation "X" indicates that no rhyme is to be found at that point in the various sources. Given last is the number of manuscript copies (indicated by "sk" for the Thai term *samùt khɔ̀y*) that have the alternate reading.

List 1. *khlooŋ 4*

a) *khlooŋ 4* Followed by *khlooŋ 4*

Stan-zas	Suspect Wording		Alternate Wording		
55-56	*dii -X*	A-X	*dii- sĭi*	A-A	MT+ 16sk
56-57	*dii- phîi*	A-B	X	X	X
59-60	*ʔan- khrán*	A-C	X	X	X
123-124	*yaa- yàa*	A-B	X	X	X
125-126	*khlaŋ- khlaŋ*	same	X	X	X
182-183	*pay- hây*	A-C	X	X	X
187-188	*tham- phrâm*	A-B	X	X	X
195-196	*cay- wáy*	A-C	X	X	X
200-201	*kruŋ- fŭuŋ*	*u- uu*	X	X	X
201-202	*phay- dây*	A-C	X	X	X
219-220	*-lǎəm- phəəm*	A-B	X	X	X
222-223	*khruan- thûan*	A-C	X	X	X
246-247	*day- ráy*	A-C	X	X	X
247-248	*cay- cay*	same	X	X	X

Stan-zas	Suspect Wording		Alternate Wording		
272-273	ʔaasăa-nâa	A–C	X	X	X
288-289	thăŋ-thăŋ	same	X	X	X
339-240	riam-X	A–X	maa--kaa	A–A	MT+13sk
414-415	bua-bua	same	X	X	X
435-436	maa-maa	same	X	X	X
513-514	-dii-níi	A–C	X	X	X
563-564	sɔ̌ɔŋ-nɔ́ɔŋ	A–C	X	X	X

b) *khlooŋ 4* Followed by *khlooŋ 3*

Stan-zas	Suspect Wording		Alternate Wording		
165-166	khwaam-khwaam	same	thaam-khwaam	A–A	MT + 12sk

c) *khlooŋ 4* Followed by *rãay*

Stan-zas	Suspect Wording		Alternate Wording		
146–147	*kan-kan*	same	*kan-can*	A–A	3sk
291–292	*thăŋ-cáŋ*	A–B	*thăŋ-cáŋ*	A–A	$3sk^2$
410–411	*phlaaŋ-naaŋ*	A–A (5th syl)	*phlaaŋ-naaŋ*	A–A	H + 4sk

List 2. *khlooŋ 2*

a) *khlooŋ 2* Followed by *khlooŋ 4*

Stan- zas	Suspect Wording		Alternate Wording		
377- 378	*făn- făn*	same	*făn- thuun*	X	10sk

b) *khlooŋ 2* Followed by *khlooŋ 2*

Stan- zas	Suspect Wording		Alternate Wording		
74- 75	*maa- wâa*	A-B	X	X	X
325- 326	*sŭu- rúu*	A-C	X	X	X
398- 399	*raw- X*	A-X	*raa- maa*	A-A	H + 11sk
531- 532	*ʔaw- pralăw*	A-C	*ʔaw- -pralaw*	A-A	2sk
553- 554	*tʉan- lâan*	A-B	*tʉan- cʉan*3	A-A	7sk
633- 634	*mii- thɔɔ- ranii*	C-A	*mii- thɔɔ- ranii*	A-A	H + 11sk
647- 648	*kam- khwâm*	A-C	*kan- khwăn*	A-A	14sk

List 3. *rāay*

a) *rāay* Followed by *khlooŋ 4*

Stan-zas	Suspect Wording		Alternate Wording		
35-36	*thiam-X*	A-X	*rʉaŋ-mʉaŋ*	A-A	MT+16sk
355-356	*bun-thuun*	*u-uu*	*bun-khŭn*	A-A	H +13sk

b) *rāay* Followed by *khlooŋ 2*

Stan-zas	Suspect Wording		Alternate Wording		
283-284	*ʔoŋ-doŋ*	Posi-tion	X	X	X
389-390	*cay-cay*	same	*cay-nay*	A-A	3sk

c) *rāay* Followed by *rāay*

Stan-zas	Suspect Wording		Alternate Wording		
6-7	*cay-thăy*	A-C	X	X	X
9-10	*lŭaŋ-sŭaŋ*	Posi-tion	X	X	X
52-53	*thăŋ-cùŋ*	A-B	*thăŋ-cʉŋ*	A-A	MT+6sk
206-207	*yaŋ-sàŋ*	A-B	X	X	X

245

Stanzas	Suspect Wording		Alternate Wording		
235-236	*-maa-khâa*	A-C	*-maa-khăa*[4]	A-A	1sk
349-350	*-thraa-khâa*	A-C	*-thraa-khăa*[5]	A-A	2sk
423-424	*-mɔɔn-nǎ-khɔɔn*	Position	X	X	X

NOTES

1. The historically correct spelling uses a high-category initial and the second tone mark, indicating an origin in the C column of the tone chart. Both this ancient spelling and the current one, which uses a low-category initial and the first tone mark, indicate the modern falling tone.

2. The word *cɑɲ*, which functions like an English preposition, is sometimes spelled in modern printed texts with the first tone mark, and sometimes without a tone mark. There is similar variation in the manuscript copies of the poem.

3. The wording found in the Ministry of Education text does not appear in any of the manuscript copies and so must be considered spurious.

4. In both stanza 236 and stanza 350 the spelling given indicates that the *ráp* syllable is the word *khâa* 'slave', and the reading is acceptable with that interpretation. However, in both cases the individuals referred to are the two companions of Phra Law, Kaew and Khwan. It is more in keeping with the tone of the narrative to assume that the two men are

referred to not as *khāa* 'slave', but as *khăa*,
the dual pronoun meaning 'they two'. The fact
that modern Thai does not use dual pronouns
could be the source of some of the confusion
about the text not only for modern printers
and editors, but also for the many scribes who
must have been responsible for copying the
manuscripts in previous centuries. In several
of the garbled passages in the poem this
problem seems to be responsible for most, if
not all of the confusion.

5. See note number 2 for a clarification of
this problem.

REFERENCES

Backus, Charles
1981   *The Nan-chao Kingdom and T'ang China's Southwestern Frontier.* Cambridge: Cambridge University Press.

Bickner, Robert J.
1981   "A Linguistic Analysis of a Thai Literary Classic." Ph.D. dissertation, University of Michigan.

1986   "Changing Perspectives on Language and the Poetic Arts in Thailand." *CROSSROADS* 3(1): 104-117.

1989   "Directional Modification in Thai Fiction: The Use of 'Come' and 'Go' in Text Building." In *Pacific Linguistics*, A(77); *Papers in South-East Asian Linguistics no. 11; Asian Syntax*, edited by David Bradley, 15-79. Canberra: The Australian National University.

Bidyalankarana, Prince
1926   "The Pastime of Rhyme-Making and Singing in Rural Siam." *Journal of the Siam Society* 20(2): 101-127.

Brown, J. Marvin
1965   *From Ancient Thai to Modern Dialects.* Bangkok: Social Science Association Press of Thailand.

1967   *AUA Language Center Thai Course.* Bangkok: American University Alumni Association Language Center.

1975   "The Great Tone Split: Did It Work in Two Opposite Ways?" In *Studies in Tai Linguistics in Honor of William J. Gedney*, edited by Jimmy G. Harris and James R. Chamberlain, 33-48.

Bangkok: Central Institute of English Language.

1976   "Dead Consonants or Dead Tones?" In
            *Thai Linguistics in Honor of Fang-
            Kuei Li*, edited by Thomas W.
            Gething, Jimmy G. Harris, and Pranee
            Kullavanijaya, 28-38. Bangkok:
            Chulalongkorn University Press.

1979   *AUA Language Center Thai Course
            Reading and Writing Text*. Bangkok:
            American University Alumni Associa-
            tion Language Center.

Chanthit Krasaesin
1954   *Prachum wannákhadii thay pháak 2:
            phrá? lɔɔ lílít* [Thai Literature
            Collection Part 2: *Lilit Phra Law*].
            Bangkok: Thai Watana Panich.

Compton, Carol J.P.
1977   "Linguistic and Cultural Aspects of
            Lam: The Song of the Lao Mohlam."
            Ph.D. dissertation, University of
            Michigan.

Cooke, Joseph R.
1980   "The Thai Khlong Poem: Description
            and Examples." *Journal of the Ameri-
            can Oriental Society* 100(4): 421-
            437.

Crystal, David.
1980   *A First Dictionary of Linguistics
            and Phonetics*. Boulder, Colorado:
            Westview Press.

Dhani Nivat, Prince
1969   "The Date and Authorship of the
            Romance of Phra Lô." *Collected Arti-
            cles by H. H. Prince Dhani Nivat
            Kromamun Bidayalabh Bridhyakorn*,
            141-143. Bangkok: The Siam Society.

Dhanit Yupho
1952   *Classical Siamese Theater.* Bangkok:
        Hatha Dhip Company.

1963   *The Khon and Lakon: Dance Dramas
        Presented by the Department of Fine
        Arts.* Bangkok: The Department of
        Fine Arts.

Donaldson, Jean and Dieu Chinh Nhim
1970   *Tai-Vietnamese-English Dictionary.*
        Saigon: Bo Giao-Duc Xuat Ban.

Em-on Chitasophon
1986   *Wannákhadii wícaan sɔ̌ɔŋ chəəŋ* [Two
        Techniques of Literary Criticism].
        Bangkok: Sukanya Press.

1982   *Wannákam lílít* [Lilit Literature].
        Chiang Mai, Thailand: The Office of
        Chiang Mai University Library.

Fine Arts Department (Thailand)
1971   *Lílít phráʔ lɔɔ* [*Lilit Phra Law*],
        14th printing. Bangkok.

1971   *Cindaamanii, 1-2* ["Jindamani, 1-2"],
        6th printing. Bangkok: Bannakhan
        Publishers (by permission of the
        Fine Arts Department).

Gedney, William J.
1964   "A Comparative Sketch of White,
        Black, and Red Tai." In *The Social
        Science Review*, Special Edition, 1-
        47. Bangkok: Chulalongkorn Universi-
        ty Press.

1972   "Checklist for Determining Tones in
        Tai Dialects." In *Studies in Lin-
        guistics in Honor of George L.
        Trager* (Janua Linguarum, Ser. Maior,
        52), edited by M. Estelle Smith,
        423-437. The Hague: Mouton.

1985   "Patrons and Practitioners: Chakri Monarchs and Literature." *CROSS-ROADS* 2(2): 1-22.

1988   "Siamese Verse Forms in Historical Perspective." In *Selected Papers on Comparative Tai Studies*, by William J. Gedney, and edited by Robert J. Bickner, John Hartmann, Thomas John Hudak, and Patcharin Peyasantiwong, 489-544. Michigan Papers on South and Southeast Asia, no. 29. Ann Arbor: Center for South and Southeast Asian Studies, University of Michigan.

Haas, Mary R.
1964   *Thai-English Students Dictionary*. Stanford: Stanford University Press.

Hudak, Thomas John
1986   "Meta-Rhymes In Classical Thai Poetry." *Journal of the Siam Society* 74: 38-61.

Jones, R. B.
1970   *Introduction to Thai Literature*. Ithaca: Cornell University Southeast Asia Program.

Li, Fang-kuei
1977   *A Handbook of Comparative Tai*. Honolulu: The University Press of Hawaii.

McFarland, George B.
1944   *Thai-English Dictionary*. Stanford: Stanford University Press.

Ministry of Education (Thailand)
1975   *Naŋsɯ̌ɯ ʔàan kawii níphon rɵ̂aŋ lílít phráʔ lɔɔ* [Reading Text of the Poetic Composition *Lilit Phra Law*], 21st printing. Bangkok: Khurusapha.

1984 *Naŋsŭɯ ʔàan kawii níphon rɒ̂aŋ lílít phrá ʔ lɔɔ* [Reading Text of the Poetic Composition *Lilit Phra Law*], 25th printing. Bangkok: Khurusapha.

Mosel, James N.
1961 *Trends and Structure in Contemporary Thai Poetry*. Southeast Asia Program Data Paper no. 43, Ithaca: Southeast Asia Program, Cornell University.

Morton, David
1964 "The Traditional Instrumental Music of Thailand." Ph.D. dissertation, University of California at Los Angeles.

Noss, Richard B.
1964 *Thai Reference Grammar*. Washington, D.C.: Foreign Service Institute.

Nuphuk Chaychana
1939 *Banthŭk làk phaasăa thay* [Notes on the Principles of the Thai Language]. Bangkok.

Patcharin Peyasantiwong
1986 "Stress in Thai." In *Papers from a Conference on Thai Studies in Honor of William J. Gedney*, edited by Robert J. Bickner, Thomas J. Hudak, and Patcharin Peyasantiwong, 211–230. Michigan Papers on South and Southeast Asia, no. 25. Ann Arbor: Center for South and Southeast Asian Studies, University of Michigan.

Pluang Na Nagara
1974 *Prawàt wannákhadii thay sămràp náksɯ̀ksăa* [History of Thai Literature for Students], 8th printing. Bangkok: Thai Watana Panich.

Prem Chaya (H. H. Prince Prem Purachatra)
1946 *Magic Lotus: A Romantic Fantasy*. Bangkok: Chatra Books.

Royal Institute (Thailand)
1974   *Phôtcanaanúkrom   chabàp   râatcha-
        bandìtsathăan* [Dictionary of the
        Royal Institute], 14th printing.
        Bangkok: Center for Infantry Af-
        fairs.

1984   *Phôtcanaanúkrom   chabàp   râatcha-
        bandìtsathăan phɔɔ sɔ̆ɔ 2525* [Dic-
        tionary of the Royal Institute, A.D.
        1982], 2nd printing. Bangkok: Aksorn
        Charoen That.

Schweisguth, P.
1951   *Etude sur la littërature siamoise.*
        Paris: Imprimerie Nationale.

Seni Pramoj, M. R.
1968   *Interpretative Translations of Thai
        Poets.* Bangkok: Thai Watana Panich.

Sumonnachat Sawatdikun, M. R.
1945   *"Sɔ̀ɔp sŭan kaan tɛ̀ŋ lílít phrá? lɔɔ"*
        [Investigation of the Composition of
        Lilit Phra Law], *Waarásăan samaakhom
        khón wíchaa prathêet thay* [Proceed-
        ings of the Society for the Study of
        Thailand] 3, 1-54.

Thawisak Pinthong, et al.
1980   *Wannakam kèp tòk.* Bangkok: Odeon
        Store Publishers.

Uppakit Silapasarn, Phrayaa
1968   *Làk phaasăa thay* [Principles of Thai
        Language]. Bangkok: Thai Watana
        Panich.

Vella, Walter F.
1957   *Siam Under Rama III 1824-1851.*
        Locust Valley, N.Y.: J. J. Augustin
        (for the Association for Asian Stud-
        ies).

Wachirayan Royal Library
   1926   *Lílít phrá? lɔɔ* [*Lilit Phra Law*].
            Bangkok: Sophon Phiphatthanakorn.

Wibha Senanan Kongkananda
   1982   *Phra Lo: A Portrait of the Hero as a
            Tragic Lover* (A Paper Presented to
            UNESCO,   Paris).   Nakhon Pathom,
            Thailand: Faculty of Arts, Silapakon
            University.

   n.d.   "Phra Lo: A Portrait of the Hero as
            a Tragic Lover" (A condensation of
            the original).   In *A Study of Thai
            Heroes From Thai Classical Litera-
            ture*, 37-61. Bangkok: Office of the
            National Culture Commission.

Worawet Phisit, Phra
   1961   *Khûu mɨɨ lílít phrá? lɔɔ*, [Handbook
            for *Lilit Phra Law*]. Bangkok: Chula-
            longkorn University.

   1974   *Khûu mɨɨ lílít phrá? lɔɔ*, [Handbook
            for *Lilit Phra Law*] (2 volumes).
            Bangkok: Khurusapha.

MONOGRAPH SERIES

Occasional Paper Series

#15—Michael Aung-Thwin. *Irrigation in the Heartland of Burma: Foundations of the Pre-Colonial Burmese State.* 1990. 76pp. Maps and chart. $8.00

#14—Susan D. Russell, editor. *Ritual, Power, and Economy: Upland-Lowland Contrasts in Mainland Southeast Asia.* 1989. 143pp. $10.00

#13—E. Paul Durrenberger. *Lisu Religion.* 1989. 44pp. Figures. $7.00

#12—Raymond Lee, editor. *Ethnicity and Ethnic Relations in Malaysia.* 1986. 178pp. Bibliography. $15.00

#11—John A. Lent and Kent Mulliner, editors. *Malaysian Studies: Archaeology, Historiography, Geography, and Bibliography.* 1985. 235pp. Bibliographies. $14.00

#10—Lawrence F. Ashmun. *Resettlement of Indochinese Refugees in the United States: A Selective and Annotated Bibliography.* 1983. 207pp. Indices (DAI; ERIC; RMC; subject). $14.00

#9—Penny Van Esterik, editor. *Women of Southeast Asia.* 1982. 279pp. Tables, figures, appendix, bibliography, index. **(Out of Print)**

#8—Donn V. Hart, editor. *Philippine Studies: Political Science, Economics, and Linguistics.* 1981. 285pp. Bibliographies, index. $14.00

#7—John A. Lent, editor. *Malaysian Studies: Present Knowledge and Research Trends.* 1979. 466pp. Charts, tables, bibliographies. **(Out of Print)**

#6—Donn V. Hart, editor. *Philippine Studies: History, Sociology, Mass Media and Bibliography.* 1978. 402pp. Charts, graphs, bibliographies, index. **(Out of Print)**

#5—Donn V. Hart. *Thailand: An Annotated Bibliography of Bibliographies.* 1977. 96pp. Index. **(Out of Print)**

#4—Donn V. Hart. *An Annotated Bibliography of Philippine Bibliographies, 1965-1974.* 1974. 158pp. Index. $7.50

#3—Gerald S Marynov. *The Condition of Southeast Asian Studies in the United States: 1972.* In cooperation with the Southeast Asian

Regional Council, The Association of Asian Studies. 1974. 68pp. Tables, bibliography. **(Out of Print)**

#2—Ronald L. Krannich, Herbert J. Rubin, Pratya Vesarach, and Chakrapand Wongburanavart. *Urbanization in Thailand.* Center for Governmental Studies, Northern Illinois University. 1974. 116pp. Bibliographies. **(Out of Print)**

#1—David W. Dellinger, editor. *Language, Literature, and Society: Working Papers from the 1973 Conference of American Council of Teachers of Uncommonly-Taught Asian Languages.* 1974. 85pp. Tables, charts. **(Out of Print)**

Special Report Series

#24—Robert Wessing. *The Soul of Ambiguity: The Tiger in Southeast Asia.* 1986. 148pp. Bibliography. $9.50

#23—Phil Scanlon, Jr. *Southeast Asia: A Cultural Study through Celebration.* 1985. 185pp. Photographs, index. $14.00

#22—David Hicks. *A Maternal Religion: The Role of Women in Tetum Myth and Ritual.* 1984. 146pp. Index, photographs. **(Out of Print)**

#21—Theodora Helene Bofman. *The Poetics of the Ramakian.* 1984. 258pp. Appendices, bibliography. $15.00

#20—Dwight Y. King. *Interest Groups and Political Linkage in Indonesia, 1800-1965.* 1982. 187pp. Bibliography, index. $12.50

#19—Robert J. Morais. *Social Relations in a Philippine Town.* 1981. 151pp. Tables, photographs, bibliography, index. $11.00

#18—Carol J. Compton. *Courting Poetry in Laos: A Textual and Linguistic Analysis.* 1979. 257pp. Photographs, charts, appendices, bibliography. **(Out of Print)**

#17—John B. Haseman. *The Thai Resistance Movement During the Second World War.* 1978. 192pp. Maps, charts, tables, bibliography, index. **(Out of Print)**

#16—George Vinal Smith. *The Dutch in Seventeenth Century Thailand.* 1977. 203pp. Maps, charts, tables, glossary, appendices, bibliography, index. **(Out of Print)**

#15—Michael M. Calavan. *Decisions Against Nature: An Anthropological Study of Agriculture in Northern Thailand.* 1977. 210pp. Maps, illustrations, charts, tables, bibliography, index. **(Out of Print)**

#14—John A. Lent, editor. *Cultural Pluralism in Malaysia: Polity, Military, Mass Media, Education, Religion and Social Class.* 1977. 114pp. Charts, tables, bibliography, index. **(Out of Print)**

#13—Douglas E. Foley. *Philippine Rural Education: An Anthropological Perspective.* 1976. 114pp. Table, bibliography, index. **(Out of Print)**

#12—G. N. Appell, editor. *Studies in Borneo Societies: Social Process and Anthropological Explanation.* 1976. 158pp. Maps, bibliography, index. **(Out of Print)**

#11—Howard M. Leichter. *Political Regime and Public Policy in the Philippines: A Comparison of Bacolod and Iloilo Cities.* 1975. 163pp. Bibliography, maps, charts, table, index. $4.00

#10—Fredrick Wernstedt, Wilhelm Solheim II, Lee Sechrest, George Guthrie, and Leonard Casper. *Philippine Studies: Geography, Archaeology, Psychology, and Literature: Present Knowledge and Research Trends.* 1974. 113pp. Annotated bibliography, index. **(Out of Print)**

#9—Harry Aveling. *A Thematic History of Indonesian Poetry: 1920-1974.* 1974. 90pp. Selected bibliography. **(Out of Print)**

#8—Herbert J. Rubin. *The Dynamics of Development in Rural Thailand.* 1974. 159pp. Maps, charts, tables. **(Out of Print)**

#7—Carl H. Landé with the assistance of Shirley Advincula, Augusto Ferreros, and James Frane. *Southern Tagalog Voting, 1946-1963: Political Behavior in a Philippine Region.* 1973. 159pp. Bibliography, index, maps. $4.00

#6—Richard L. Stone. *Philippine Urbanization: The Politics of Public and Private Property in Greater Manila.* 1973. 149pp. Bibliography, appendices. **(Out of Print)**

#5—David H. de Queljoe. *A Preliminary Study of Some Phonetic Features of Pentani, with Glossaries.* 1971. 114pp. Glossary. **(Out of Print)**

#4—Clark D. Neher. *Rural Thai Government: The Politics of the Budgetary Process.* 1970. 60pp. **(Out of Print)**

#3—Chan Ansuchote. *The 1969 General Elections in Thailand.* 1970. 44pp. **(Out of Print)**

#2—David H. de Queljoe. *A Preliminary Study of Malay/Indonesian Orthography.* 1969. 91pp. Bibliography. **(Out of Print)**

#1—J. A. Niels Mulder. *Monks, Merit, and Motivation: Buddhism and National Development in Thailand.* Second (revised and enlarged) edition. 1973. 58pp. (*Monks, Merit, and Motivation: An Exploratory Study of the Social Functions of Buddhism in Thailand in Processes of Guided Social Change.* 1961. 43pp.) **(Out of Print)**

Other Center Publications:

Donn V. Hart, compiler. *Theses and Dissertations on Southeast Asia Presented at Northern Illinois University, 1960-1980: An Annotated Bibliography.* Bibliographical Publication No. 6, 1980. 33pp. $4.00

Richard M. Cooler. *British Romantic Views of the First Anglo-Burmese War, 1824-1826.* 1977. 41pp. $4.00

The Twenty-fifth Anniversary of the Center for Southeast Asian Studies, Northern Illinois University, DeKalb, Illinois. 1988. 40pp. $2.00

For information and order forms, contact the

Publications Program
Center for Southeast Asian Studies
140 Carroll Ave.
Northern Illinois University
DeKalb, IL 60115 USA

Crossroads

An Interdisciplinary Journal of Southeast Asian Studies

Volume 1, #1	Philippine Studies—Topical Issue **(Out of Print)**
Volume 1, #2	General Issue **(Out of Print)**
Volume 1, #3	Southeast Asian Studies and International Business **(Out of Print)**
Volume 2, #1	General Issue **(Out of Print)**
Volume 2, #2	Two Hundred Years of the Chakri Dynasty **(Out of Print)**
Volume 2, #3	General Issue
Volume 3, #1	Seven Hundred Years of Thai Writing
Volume 3, #2-3	General Issue
Volume 4, #1	Special Burma Issue **(Late 1991 reprint)**
Volume 4, #2	Special Thai Issue (Part One)
Volume 5, #1	Special Thai Issue (Part Two)
Volume 5, #2	General Issue
Volume 6, #1	Modern Malay Music

Subscriptions are available at $12 per year for two issues delivered at book rate. All individual and back issues are $8. For air mail delivery, add $8 per subscription year. Send subscription orders to: *CROSSROADS*, Center for Southeast Asian Studies, 140 Carroll Ave., Northern Illinois University, DeKalb, IL 60115. Checks should be made payable to the "Center for Southeast Asian Studies."